Almost the Perfect Murder

The killing of Elaine O'Hara,
the extraordinary Garda investigation
and the trial that stunned the nation

The only complete inside account

PAUL WILLIAMS

LIBRARIES NI
WITHDRAWN FROM STOCK

PENGUIN
IRELAND

PENGUIN IRELAND

UK | USA | Canada | Ireland | Australia
India | New Zealand | South Africa

Penguin Ireland is part of the Penguin Random House group of companies
whose addresses can be found at global.penguinrandomhouse.com.

First published 2015
001

Copyright © Paul Williams, 2015

The moral right of the author has been asserted

Set in 13.5/16 pt Garamond MT Std
Typeset by Jouve (UK), Milton Keynes
Printed in Great Britain by Clays Ltd, St Ives plc

A CIP catalogue record for this book is available from the British Library

ISBN : 978–1–844–88362–2

LIBRARIES NI
WITHDRAWN FROM STOCK

www.greenpenguin.co.uk

Penguin Random House is committed to a sustainable future for our business, our readers and our planet. This book is made from Forest Stewardship Council® certified paper.

To the memory of the innocent victims of
evil people everywhere

Contents

1. A Missing Person

The anguish was written on the man's face when he walked through the front doors of Stepaside Garda Station. Frank O'Hara was facing every parent's worst nightmare: one of his children was missing and he feared the worst. He had been unable to reach his daughter Elaine for nearly two days and no one had seen or heard from her. It was out of character – Elaine spoke to him on the phone at least once a day – and he was deeply concerned. It was Friday morning, 24 August 2012. He had last seen her on Wednesday afternoon, when she had called in to him after being discharged from hospital. They had visited Shanganagh Cemetery and placed some fresh plants on her mother's grave. He told the officers his daughter had seemed in good spirits.

The previous morning – Thursday – Elaine O'Hara had been due to start working as a volunteer at the Tall Ships Festival in Dublin city centre. It was a significant event in his daughter's life and she had been looking forward to it for months. She had attended a training day for volunteers and wouldn't have missed it for the world. At the newsagent's where she worked part-time, Elaine had booked time off for the duration of the two-day festival. She had also arranged to get a lift into town from her father's partner, Sheila Hawkins, early on Thursday morning. Elaine suffered from a chronic lack of confidence and her appointment as a team leader at the festival was a major achievement. This was an important undertaking for her. Her family and doctors saw her enthusiasm for the Tall Ships event as hugely encouraging.

Sheila's apartment was directly opposite Elaine's, and late on Wednesday night she noticed that there was no sign of life inside. It seemed odd, but she told herself that Elaine had probably gone to bed early for the big day ahead. At 10.34 p.m. she sent Elaine a short text saying: 'See you 7.15 a.m.' There was no response.

When Elaine failed to turn up for her lift, Sheila drove over to the apartment. She rang the bell but got no answer. She tried Elaine's phone, got no answer to it either and left a voice message. Sheila called Frank O'Hara at 8.30 a.m. to tell him what had happened. Elaine's sister, Ann, had phoned her twice on Wednesday evening, to say she was glad she was out of hospital, but got no reply.

A few hours later Frank called round to Elaine's apartment, letting himself in with a key she had given him for emergencies. The apartment was empty and her iPhone, which was her permanent appendage, was plugged into the charger. He assumed that she had overslept and then rushed out in a panic, forgetting her phone. By 11.30 p.m. Frank still hadn't heard from his daughter, so he sent her a text: 'Are you alive?' Sheila Hawkins noticed that there was still no sign of life in the apartment and that Elaine's car was not in the underground car park. She thought Elaine must be working late at the festival in Dublin.

First thing the following morning Sheila Hawkins checked the apartment again. When there was still no sign of Elaine or her car, the niggling feeling she'd had since Wednesday night turned into apprehension. She called Frank O'Hara for the second morning in a row. He visited the apartment again and found nothing had moved since the previous day. The phone was still charging. He now noticed that Elaine's handbag had been left behind. It was obvious that she had not returned overnight.

Frank O'Hara phoned St Edmundsbury Hospital, the mental health facility Elaine had left two days earlier, and spoke to her doctor, Matt Murphy. He confirmed she hadn't returned. Frank's worry turned to dread after speaking to the organizers at the Tall Ships Festival. They told him Elaine hadn't turned up, which had surprised them because she had been so enthusiastic about her role as a team leader. They had also phoned Elaine but got no reply. Frank became distressed and called his other grown-up children to help him search. He couldn't quell the sense of foreboding that his daughter might have taken her own life. So he went to the local Garda station to report her missing.

Elaine's father and siblings had good reason to suspect the worst. Since childhood her life had been blighted by a variety of mental health issues. Born on St Patrick's Day in 1976, Elaine was the first child of Frank and Eileen O'Hara. Frank was a banker and Eileen a teacher. The couple lived in relative comfort in middle-class Killiney in South Dublin. In 1978 their second daughter, Ann, was born, followed by Frank junior in 1982 and John, the youngest, two years later. In 1986, when Elaine was ten, the family moved to Oakdene in Killiney. She attended St John's National School in Ballybrack, where her mother worked, and Our Lady of Good Counsel National School in Killiney when the family moved. She later went to St Joseph of Cluny Secondary School in

Killiney. When Elaine was fifteen her parents discovered that she had been the victim of bullying at school, and around the same time a close friend was killed in a road accident. Together these events became the triggers for underlying psychiatric problems which had been festering since about the age of twelve. After that she slid into a downward spiral of chronic depression and anxiety. To compound matters she suffered from asthma and diabetes and began smoking heavily. Dyslexia, which affected her writing and verbal abilities, added to her sense of insecurity and low self-esteem. Life had dealt Elaine O'Hara a raw deal.

Elaine's complex psychiatric issues manifested themselves when she started to self-harm by cutting herself. When Elaine was sixteen, Ann found her in the upstairs bathroom after she had cut her wrists. Her family were profoundly shocked by her suicide attempt, because there had been no warning that her problems had become so acute. In August 1992, Frank and Eileen O'Hara brought her to the high-profile psychiatrist Professor Anthony Clare. He agreed to take Elaine on as a patient and she was admitted for treatment to St Edmundsbury Hospital in Lucan, west Dublin. Professor Clare and his team were initially uncertain about Elaine's diagnosis and thought she had an emerging psychotic illness. She informed Professor Clare that she had had fantasies of being restrained or imprisoned from the age of twelve but wouldn't elaborate.

After her initial hospitalization, Elaine spent the rest of her adolescence heavily medicated on a cocktail of antidepressants and tranquillizers and did not have a normal teenage experience of life. Between periods spent in St Edmundsbury both as an inpatient and as an outpatient, Elaine changed schools and completed her Leaving Certificate at the Institute of Education on Leeson Street in central Dublin. She loved children and wanted to be a teacher, but she lacked the academic qualifications to achieve her ambition. Nevertheless, after school she completed a childcare course at Sallynoggin VEC and got a job working in a crèche.

Between February and May 2000 Elaine spent three months as an inpatient at St Edmundsbury. Her medical records noted that she was 'sad and angry', had low self-esteem and was finding it 'difficult to control her impulses'. Her diagnosis on that occasion was one of 'recurrent depressive disorder with a strong possibility of emotionally unstable personality disorder'.

The following year Elaine got a job as a childcare assistant in her first primary school, St John's in Ballybrack, where her mother still worked. But her efforts to escape the dark cloud of depression suffered a setback when her mother died in March 2002 at the age of fifty-two. Eileen O'Hara had been a rock of support to her daughter, and her death left Elaine deeply distressed. The following year she spent May to July as an inpatient at St Edmundsbury. Her medical notes on that occasion record that she had been expressing suicidal ideation and 'finding it difficult to think straight'. She had been cutting herself to inflict physical pain as a distraction from the emotional turmoil that besieged her mind. In therapy sessions her feelings of worthlessness and an obsessional fantasy about being restrained or imprisoned were recurring themes. Professor Clare was perplexed by his patient because it was unclear what she meant when speaking of these fantasies. She talked of a play in her head, but he was uncertain about how to interpret that in psychiatric terms. She spoke both of self-harming and of having harm inflicted on her by others in a consensual situation. During her years of treatment, Professor Clare noted Elaine's disturbed sexuality and how she once remarked: 'I'd rather be a boy . . . I don't like being a girl.' Elaine's poor self-esteem was reflected in her appearance: she was overweight and didn't care what she wore. Later in 2003 she enrolled in a night course to train as a Montessori teacher in St Nicholas Montessori College in Dun Laoghaire. She also worked part-time at Ken's Newsagents in Blackrock Shopping Centre.

Elaine moved out of the family home in early 2005 and rented a bedsit off Newtownpark Avenue in Blackrock. On St Patrick's Day, Frank O'Hara and the family organized a party to celebrate her twenty-ninth birthday. She was prone to bouts of frustration and anger that sometimes led to arguments, and that was what happened on this occasion. She became upset and stormed out. Her family were familiar with her mood swings, and immediately afterwards Ann and her husband went to check on her in her bedsit. By the time they arrived, she had taken an overdose and they called an ambulance. When she had recovered physically, Elaine was again admitted to St Edmundsbury for two months.

One evening in 2006 she was on the phone to her father. As she was about to hang up, she sounded strange and remarked: 'It doesn't matter now anyhow, because I have taken something.' Frank O'Hara rushed to her bedsit and found his daughter collapsed on the floor in a semi-conscious state. He drove her to St Vincent's Hospital, where she fell into a coma for almost twenty-four hours. Not long after that incident, on 22 April, she was admitted once again to St Edmundsbury. She told doctors: 'I am not well, I'm going insane, I'm becoming angry with small things. I have had this all my life; it is just coming to the surface now. I wish they would let me die.' Her hospital notes record thoughts of deliberate self-harm, fleeting suicidal thoughts and a 'possible death wish'. She said: 'I wasn't born for life, no one likes me, I am a bad person.' Social withdrawal was also noted, indicating a lack of social contact with others. Elaine was discharged in June but had herself readmitted on 21 July for another three weeks. The reason given was that: 'She believes people are watching her and talking about her and is preoccupied with some intrusive thoughts which she describes as a play in her head, in which she is being persecuted. She became agitated when asked to expand on this. She lives a very lonely life with no friends and finds it very difficult to trust people.'

In November 2006, in a letter sent to another consultant who was treating Elaine for diabetes, Professor Clare expressed his determination to get to the root of her disturbed behaviour and described her 'sexuality being certainly disturbed, masculinized even'. He added: 'It is not going to be diabetes, I'm afraid, or even a straightforward depressive illness that determines the fate of Elaine.'

Elaine suffered another setback when Anthony Clare died in 2007, which greatly upset her. Elaine's care then passed to Dr Matt Murphy. He began a process of gradually reducing her dependency on medication and took a more focused psychological approach through cognitive behavioural therapy. The therapist with whom she was working at St Edmundsbury, Stuart Colquhoun, noted that Elaine tended to avoid interacting with people and had a skewed view of how other people viewed her. When others were nice to her, she interpreted it as either not genuine or undeserved by her.

Despite her difficulties she remained close to her family, but never let them into her private life. She was particularly close to her father, always sought his reassurance and would ask regularly if he loved her. Frank O'Hara tried to convince his firstborn child that she was special and that she didn't realize the abundant talents she possessed. But Elaine's ongoing difficulties were a constant source of strain and worry for the family. She often had rows with them when she was angry or agitated. Blurting out something shocking in the heat of the moment was how she would bring arguments to an abrupt end. In the midst of an argument with her father in early 2008, Elaine suddenly announced that she liked to be tied up and hurt for sexual gratification. She told him that she was seeing a married man from Foxrock who worked as an architect and they would meet for bondage sessions. 'He ties me up and masturbates over me . . . we haven't had sex,' Elaine said. Then she claimed that she had asked the man to kill her but he had refused. The extraordinary disclosure stunned Frank O'Hara. He could not listen to any more and left the room. Later, as he pondered the outburst, he could not be sure if she had meant what she said or it was simply a ruse to end the discussion. Elaine was prone to embellishing her stories and could be flippant. In April she told her therapist about the incident and described her father as being left 'speechless'.

Over the last few years before her disappearance Elaine's condition had stabilized somewhat and she had attended St Edmundsbury for outpatient therapy sessions. Her family and doctors felt that she was making progress. In July 2011,

Elaine told her therapist that she had miscarried a few months earlier. She said she had been five weeks pregnant. That November she phoned her sister, Ann, to say that she had suffered a miscarriage in May. She wouldn't elaborate and would only say that she had become pregnant after a one-night stand. She confided in Sheila Hawkins too, revealing that she had become pregnant after having sex for the first time. Ms Hawkins was a psychologist and believed that although Elaine was inclined to embellish her stories, they were based in truth.

As summer 2012 approached, Elaine O'Hara began experiencing the familiar emotions that would trigger her descent to the depths of despair. She had constant money problems. In 2010 she had purchased a one-bedroom apartment using the county council's affordable housing scheme, but she had fallen behind in her mortgage payments for four months. She had accumulated debts of €4,000. Elaine had already borrowed €6,000 from her father, but her modest income as a childcare assistant and part-time shop assistant meant she had no hope of ever paying it back. She was also anxious about her upcoming exams for her Montessori teaching course. Then in July her apartment was flooded because the bath had not been installed correctly.

On 13 July, Elaine got a noose and considered hanging herself. Instead she had the presence of mind to phone St Edmundsbury. She told staff there that if she wasn't admitted she was likely to take her own life. Arrangements were made for her admission the following morning. St Edmundsbury had become a constant in her life: a place of refuge, where she went to feel safe. Later that evening, Elaine told her father that she was returning to hospital. He was surprised because he felt she had been doing well. 'You don't know what I've tried to do,' she replied.

While her admission was a setback, the fact that Elaine had recognized her own moods and sought help was interpreted as a positive development. She presented with 'very low mood, increased anxiety and irritability', the notes on her admission recorded. She showed signs of 'antihedonism' – the inability to enjoy anything – and generally found it very difficult to cope. She was 'constantly thinking about a noose and hanging'. 'Mood swings are bad and I feel I am about to burst,' she said. 'My chest is heavy and mixed up, as is my head. I am frustrated; I am so angry and fed up. I am fighting a losing battle.' The triggers for her relapse were blamed on the impending exams, money worries and the flood in her apartment. Other push factors from her tangled web of issues included a sense of loneliness and isolation, dark fantasies and her unstable sexuality.

Elaine remained in hospital between 14 July and 22 August. During this time, after her condition had settled down, she could sign out at the weekends to work in the newsagent's. Her risk of suicide was classified as medium. Going out at the weekends was intended to help her readjust to the environment outside the hospital. Although her moods continued to fluctuate, Elaine began to improve slowly. Around 11 a.m. on Wednesday 22 August she was discharged by Dr Murphy, who found her to be in an upbeat mood and looking forward to the Tall Ships Festival. He was optimistic that she would continue to make progress.

Around lunchtime, Elaine called in at her local pharmacy with a prescription for a month's supply of eleven different medicines for cholesterol, diabetes, asthma, a stomach ailment, a bowel problem, depression, anxiety and insomnia. The bill came to €132. Elaine had no money and assured the pharmacist, Soha Yazbeck, that she would settle the bill when she got paid, as had often happened in the past. When the pharmacist agreed, Elaine held her hand and thanked her before leaving.

At around 1.30 p.m. she went to see her father at the family home. Frank O'Hara was minding his two-year-old grandchild, who was also Elaine's godchild. She was in good spirits and brought her niece a present of a toy watch and bracelet. Elaine phoned Ken's Newsagents to say that she would not be available to work for the next two days because she would be at the Tall Ships Festival. After lunch Frank suggested that the three of them visit Eileen's grave in Shanganagh Cemetery. On the way they called in at Woodies in Sallynoggin and bought some plants to put on the grave. In the car Elaine was so preoccupied with texting that her father suggested she put her phone down for a while. They placed the plants on the grave and paid their respects. Elaine became emotional and kissed her mother's headstone. They returned to her father's house, where they had ice cream, and Elaine took her niece for a walk. At 4 p.m. she told her father that she wanted to get some rest to be ready for her early start the next morning. He recalled that she was both excited and apprehensive about her job at the Tall Ships. Frank O'Hara and his grandchild waved as she drove off. He was happy for his daughter and reflected that he had not seen her in such good form for a long time.

Now, two days later, Frank O'Hara was in Stepaside Garda Station giving the officer on duty a description of his firstborn child. She was five feet four inches in height, of stocky build with mousy brown, shoulder-length hair and wore glasses. He was joined by his other daughter, Ann. Meanwhile, Ann's husband, Mark Charles, drove out to Shanganagh Cemetery because Elaine had visited her mother's grave there on the Wednesday. He spotted her blue Fiat Punto parked along the side of the avenue that led to the cemetery car park. Elaine's brother John arrived at the cemetery and called the Automobile Association to open the car. Inside he found his sister's driving licence, two packets of cigarettes and a lighter, a satnav, and a charger for a different type of phone from the one she owned. Gardaí from Stepaside and Shankill stations were dispatched to search the area. Frank O'Hara travelled to the cemetery, accompanied by his partner and daughter. The discovery had deepened the nagging fear that Elaine might have taken her own life.

Shanganagh Cemetery sits on seventy acres and is situated off the old Shankill to Bray road. It is encircled from the south by Woodbrook Golf Club and from the north by Shanganagh Park. Beyond the park grounds to the east, it is bordered by a stretch of rocky strand and the Irish Sea. A path connects Shanganagh Park to the cemetery grounds, where Elaine's car was located. A train track cuts the park in two sections that are connected by a footbridge in the furthest north-easterly corner. On the other side of the footbridge a path winds around the edge of the park to a barrier. Beyond it a small lane leads down to the strand.

As showers swept in from the sea, the O'Haras joined the Gardaí in a search of the area. The summer had been one of the wettest on record. The inclement weather forced the

Garda helicopter to turn back after being dispatched to assist in the search with its specialist heat-seeking cameras, and the search was called off as the light began to fade.

Her father and siblings were distraught. Members of the family returned with detectives to Elaine's apartment in Stepaside to search for any clues that might help them find her. The search turned up more than they had anticipated. Detective Garda Ultan Sherlock found two heavy metal chains in a bedside locker. An assortment of chains, padlocks, a PVC dress, lubricant, a rope and a gas mask were also littered around the apartment. Elaine's fresh prescription of drugs remained unopened. Sheila Hawkins told Gardaí that the previous day she had discovered a black latex bodysuit in a wicker basket when she went there with Elaine's father. She had decided not to tell him at the time because he was already deeply distressed.

John O'Hara found printouts of hunting knives and Google maps of Killakee and Cruagh Wood in the foothills of the Dublin Mountains in Rathfarnham. Another printout featured Vartry Reservoir near the village of Roundwood in County Wicklow. Written in a notebook was the name of a website, www.fetlife.com. He looked it up on his phone and discovered it was a fetish lifestyle site for those interested in BDSM (an overlapping abbreviation of bondage and discipline, domination and submission, and sadism and masochism). John later logged on to the Fetlife website and created a username to see if he could garner any information about his sister. He used search parameters such as gender and appearance and found a username and profile, Chained Brunette, that he concluded might be Elaine's. He showed this to the police. The discovery shocked and disturbed him. He had been completely unaware of what his sister did in her private life.

The following morning, Gardaí launched an extensive search of the cemetery and park area at Shanganagh with the assistance of the Civil Defence and friends of the O'Hara family. A coastguard helicopter combed the shore and a section of the sea beyond. The search continued for two days with negative results. Over the course of the week following Elaine's disappearance, detectives conducted more thorough searches of her apartment. They seized the fetish paraphernalia and a large number of documents. The documents included one with the bizarre title 'The Gorean Lifestyle: A Woman's Right is Slave'. Elaine's iPhone, two laptops, and a second iPhone with a broken screen were also taken and sent to the Garda Computer Crime Investigation Unit (CCIU) for further analysis.

The apartment block's CCTV footage was downloaded and examined. Gardaí went back to 4 p.m. on Wednesday to establish if Elaine had returned there after visiting her father. She could be seen entering her apartment alone at 4.29 p.m. She left at 5.02 p.m. but returned a few seconds later. She left again at 5.05 p.m. wearing a bright blue zip-up top, navy tracksuit bottoms and white runners. She walked to her car and drove out of the car park. Her next-door neighbour confirmed he saw Elaine in the underground car park as he arrived from work. He honked the horn to acknowledge her but she didn't respond. Gardaí viewed other CCTV footage from the general area. The Belarmine complex where she lived is situated off the Enniskerry Road beside Stepaside Village in the foothills of the Dublin Mountains. At 5.12 p.m. cameras at Sandyford Community Centre, a little over a kilometre from Elaine's apartment at Belarmine Plaza, picked up her car before she turned right on to Hillcrest Road at Lamb's Cross. After that the trail went cold.

Something bothered the detectives who viewed the CCTV tape from the apartment complex. A mobile phone was clearly visible in her hand. Yet her iPhone had been in the apartment. Her family and work colleagues told Gardaí that Elaine carried her precious iPhone everywhere and they had never seen her with a different phone. The investigators made an urgent request to the CCIU to download the data from the seized phones and laptops.

As the investigation continued, Gardaí distributed leaflets containing Elaine's picture and appealing for information. A week after her disappearance, detectives and uniformed officers visited Shanganagh Park on the evenings of 29 and 30 August. It had been decided to canvass members of the public between 5 p.m. and 7 p.m. in the hope that people who regularly used the park at that time might remember seeing her. It proved a fruitful initiative. Music teacher Conor Guilfoyle had just finished his regular jog in the park when a Garda approached him to ask if he had seen Elaine. He confirmed that he had been there on the previous Wednesday but didn't recall meeting the smiling woman in the picture. Then, as the Garda walked away, Mr Guilfoyle called him back; he had just recollected seeing the woman in the picture.

On Wednesday 22 August, Mr Guilfoyle started his run at 6.11 p.m. It normally took him just over half an hour to complete. He recalled that it had been showery all day and there weren't many people in the park. Five minutes into his run he saw a woman putting on a blue jacket who appeared to be lost. She asked him: 'Is there a railway bridge near here?' He pointed her in the direction of the footbridge across the rail track. The woman did not acknowledge his assistance and seemed to be distracted and in a world of her own. He continued on his way and did his usual loop of the park, which took him over the footbridge and around the outer fields before returning to his starting point. As he jogged across the footbridge he saw the same woman coming towards him. He made eye contact with her and was about to say something about her finding the bridge, but she blanked him. She disappeared across to the other side in the direction of the seafront. What made the brief encounter stick in his mind was that the woman was so distant and uninterested in any social niceties. He was the last person to see Elaine O'Hara alive.

Detectives began taking statements from anyone who had been in contact with Elaine prior to her disappearance. Her family and work colleagues told the detectives that they did not know of any boyfriends in Elaine's life. Because of the fetish gear they had found in her apartment, detectives were particularly interested in whether there was any connection between her disappearance and her involvement in the fetish scene. Frank O'Hara recounted her extraordinary outburst four years earlier when she had spoken about her interest in bondage and involvement with a married man from Foxrock. But given his daughter's propensity for storytelling he doubted if it was true.

Gardaí also interviewed the staff who treated Elaine in St Edmundsbury. Dr Murphy confirmed that she had been entertaining suicidal thoughts when she asked to be admitted in July and he felt that she had improved by the time she left.

Stuart Colquhoun, who had been working with Elaine for almost five years, told detectives he had last met her on Tuesday 21 August, the day before she left the hospital. He said that for the first time she seemed to be in 'an almost happy', positive mood and was very excited about the Tall Ships Festival. Elaine invited him to come down to have a look and offered to show him around. He had been working on her socialization skills, trying to encourage her to engage more with people and not be alone. This was why volunteering for the Tall Ships had been such a significant step forward. In the past she had admitted to self-harming and had shown him marks and cuts to her arms and stomach. He told the detectives about a conversation he had had with Elaine in April 2008 when she first mentioned her interest in BDSM, and the outburst – where she talked about her BDSM affair – that had so shocked her father. Apart from that incident, she kept this part of her life private from her family. Elaine said she liked the fetish scene and that it was a way for her to meet people. She explained that through one of the BDSM websites she had become involved with a man who was married and had one child. He would come around to cut her and sometimes used a small knife to stab her. She had asked the man to kill her but he had refused. The therapist said Elaine had ended her association with the married man and that he hadn't noticed any injuries on her for the past two years. Then in July 2011 she had mentioned that she was back with this man.

In the meantime the investigation team received a batch of downloaded text messages and computer data from the devices seized in Elaine's apartment. The raft of text messages had arrived as a jumbled-up muddle of scattered letters, numerals and computer symbols. Many of them appeared to relate to S&M practices and referred to stabbing and blood-letting by a master she called 'sir'. It appeared the messages had ceased a number of months before Elaine disappeared. In another text message to a colleague at the shop, Elaine had spoken of losing all interest in life and of feeling like a burden and worthless.

Gardaí also traced eight men Elaine had met through fetish websites whose mobile numbers were stored in her phone. All of the men interviewed agreed they used various fetish websites but only two of them had actually met Elaine. Both men had had sex with her at different times but contact was broken off after that. One of the men told Gardaí that he found he and Elaine were incompatible because she had been into 'substantially more extreme practices' than he. Detectives checked the backgrounds and alibis for the men and found no reason to suspect any of them of being involved in the disappearance. Apart from the bizarre text messages, which were considered to be fantasies, there was no hint of foul play.

The Garda investigation into the disappearance of Elaine O'Hara involved 130 individual lines of enquiry. But every angle the Gardaí followed led them back to one conclusion: that she had taken her own life. It was an assumption shared by those who knew her best. When the available evidence was collated and analysed it seemed to be an open and shut case. Elaine O'Hara was the quintessential suicide victim. Her family, colleagues and medical records painted a picture of a deeply troubled woman who had tried to commit suicide on three occasions and had been hospitalized fourteen times, sometimes for months at a time.

Elaine disappeared on the same day that she had left hospital after weeks of therapy for suicidal ideation; her risk of suicide was classified as medium. Her history of self-harm and the nature of her involvement in BDSM reinforced the image of a woman with no sense of self-worth. She had major financial problems and was stressed out about her exams. When she went to Shanganagh Park, Elaine left behind the three essentials that she carried with her everywhere: a phone, inhaler and cigarettes. It was as if she had no further use for them and had no intention of coming back. The last sighting was of her walking alone across a footbridge in the direction of the sea. She appeared distant and preoccupied, just as one might imagine someone behaving who was intent on ending it all. The story Elaine told about the married man from Foxrock who tied her up and stabbed her could have been a fantasy. Her family and colleagues had admitted that she tended to exaggerate and 'tell stories'.

And so, as the weeks and months slipped by, Elaine O'Hara dropped down the priority list. A few months later Stepaside Garda Station closed as part of the government's programme of cutbacks. In the process the Elaine O'Hara case files were boxed and sent to Dundrum Garda Station. There simply weren't the resources available to conduct any further investigations and exhaust every possible line of enquiry into the disappearance. If Elaine had given herself to the sea, then her body would more than likely be washed up on a shoreline somewhere.

Shortly after her disappearance, human body parts were spotted on a beach not far from Shankill. At first it was thought that they might belong to Elaine, but DNA analysis established that the remains were those of a woman who had jumped into the water in the Dublin docks some time before. It somehow reinforced the belief that Elaine had done the same. So the tormented woman who believed that she didn't matter to anyone began to fade from public memory – just another name on the Garda missing persons list. Frank O'Hara and his family mourned in silence, and when the first anniversary of Elaine's disappearance came around only they remembered. But that was about to change. And it all began with a curious dog called Millie.

2. A Body in the Woods

Magali Vergnet became a dog trainer out of necessity more than choice. She had moved from Paris to Ireland in 2002 to work as a clinical laboratory technician. In 2009, after the economic crash hit Ireland, she lost her job. A lifelong animal lover, she then trained with the Dublin Society for the Prevention of Cruelty to Animals and set up a business, Wonder Walkies, training and walking dogs. In July 2013 she got permission from Frank Doyle to walk her dogs on fifty acres of dense forestry and gorse moorland he owned at Cruagh Wood in Killakee, in the foothills of the Dublin Mountains.

Every day Ms Vergnet walked up to seven dogs, including her own dog, Millie, through the forest. The land was accessed from the old Military Road that starts at Rathfarnham on the outskirts of the city, climbs up through the Dublin Mountains and continues deep into County Wicklow. She would unlock the gate at the entrance to Frank Doyle's land and drive her jeep 300 yards along a winding track to a clearing the size of a small football field that was used as a harvesting platform. She walked the dogs on a track that looped through the forest, a dense plantation of Sitka spruce.

On 21 August 2013 she was loading the dogs into the jeep when Millie disappeared into the wood behind a stack of four-inch concrete blocks. Millie was a small inquisitive dog, a cross between a cocker and a King Charles spaniel. When

Magali Vergnet called her, she returned carrying a long bone. Ms Vergnet placed it on the pile of blocks. Over the next few weeks Millie regularly disappeared at the same spot, often returning with bones. Ms Vergnet assumed they were from dead animals and placed them with the first one on the pile of blocks.

Two weeks later and over thirty kilometres from Cruagh Wood, on the other side of the mountains, anglers Brian O'Shaughnessy and Paddy Egan were standing on Sally's Bridge at Vartry Reservoir when they spotted a bag in the shallow water below. It was a black and red rucksack and they thought it might belong to another angler who fished the lake. They considered trying to pull it out but abandoned the idea because they didn't have the right equipment.

Five days later, on the evening of Tuesday 10 September, Billy Fegan, another local angler, was patrolling the shoreline of the reservoir on the lookout for illegal fishing when he also stopped on Sally's Bridge. It was 7.40 p.m. and the sun was beginning to drop down in the sky. He was joined by his brother James, the local angling gamekeeper, and a friend, Mark Quinn. They were discussing how the water had fallen to the lowest level they had seen for many years. Vartry consists of an upper and lower reservoir, the first of which was dammed in the mid 1800s and the other in the 1920s, to supply drinking water to Dublin. While the previous year had been the wettest since records began in the 1860s, the summer of 2013 had seen the hottest, driest weather in eighteen years. Normally the water under the bridge would have been over twenty feet deep but in September 2013 it had fallen to around eighteen inches.

Out of curiosity Billy Fegan leaned over to look at the water levels under the bridge. He noticed a piece of yellow rope floating on the surface. A shiny object then caught his eye; he thought it looked like a nose ring for a bull. Mark Quinn fetched a twenty-foot tension strap from his van and lowered the hook at the end into the water. After a number of attempts he snagged the rope and fished it out. When the three friends examined the items caught up in the rope they found a set of handcuffs and leg shackles, a black blindfold, a bondage collar, and a strap with a buckle fastener that had a large black ball about halfway along its length. They lowered the hook a few more times and pulled up a vest, a blue top and a tea towel. The men wondered what they were and thought it might be gear that had been dumped following a stag party. They put the things on a wall and went their separate ways.

That night Billy Fegan couldn't get the items out of his mind. He had a niggling feeling that they pointed to something more serious than lads getting up to high jinks at a stag party. The next day he returned to the same spot, put the objects into a bag and brought them to Roundwood Garda Station. He gave the bag to the officer on duty, Garda James O'Donoghue. The young Garda could easily have thrown the sodden paraphernalia in a corner and forgotten about it. Instead he hung the clothing up to dry and placed everything else in evidence bags.

As it had Billy Fegan, the collection of fetish items mystified him. He had the same niggling feeling as Mr Fegan and decided the find merited further investigation. The following day, 12 September, he phoned the angler for directions and went to the spot at the centre of the bridge where the items were found. He could see nothing because winds blowing across the shallow reservoir had churned up the silt on the bottom, turning the water dark and murky. He decided to return when the weather was calm.

Around 3.30 p.m. on Friday 13 September, Magali Vergnet was following her daily routine. She had finished the loop of the forest with the dogs and was in the process of loading them into the jeep to go home. Just as she had done the previous three weeks, Millie had disappeared into the forest behind the pile of blocks. But this time she didn't return when called. Ms Vergnet heard her scratching deep among the trees and decided to go in and fetch her. Millie's noises brought her along a muddy animal track through dense conifer. She pushed aside the prickly branches that were enmeshed across the path. Her boots sank into the boggy ground, which was flooded in places. The path meandered left and then right until it opened on to a small clearing between the trees. Bones were scattered around the uneven carpet of heather and grass. She saw a ribcage and vertebrae and thought they belonged to a big animal, possibly a deer. The grass was flattened and covered in a white greasy substance that she assumed was the spot where the animal had come to die, well hidden from human eyes.

She could hear Millie gnawing on a bone further away in the undergrowth but still couldn't see her. She struggled to make her way through the trees that surrounded her. On the ground she noticed a pair of blue tracksuit bottoms. She pushed it with her boot and realized a shoe was trapped inside one of the legs. An uneasy sensation washed over her and suddenly she felt like the trees were crowding in on her, making her feel claustrophobic. She no longer wanted to be there.

Ms Vergnet pushed another five metres through the wall of branches, turning left and then right, before finally spotting Millie. The dog was chewing on bones that were too big for her to carry back to the clearing. Ms Vergnet thought they looked like leg bones. The tracksuit and now the bones aroused an overwhelming suspicion that she had come upon human remains. She scooped Millie up into her arms and scrambled through the trees and undergrowth to the safety of her jeep.

When she got home she phoned Frank Doyle to tell him about the puzzling discovery. Later on Mr Doyle and a friend, Mick Tierney, accompanied her back to the spot where she had found Millie. At first the men also thought that the bones belonged to an animal. There was a large amount of hair matted among the white substance on the ground. They took it to be fur. Then as the three scanned the ground beneath the trees their eyes rested simultaneously on a lower jawbone with several teeth still intact. There was no way it belonged to an animal; it was obviously human.

All three were frozen to the spot. Magali Vergnet became upset and withdrew to the sanctuary of the track. Frank Doyle tried to call the police but there was no mobile coverage so far up in the hills. They went to his home and phoned Tallaght Garda Station at 7.05 p.m., explaining that they had found what looked like human remains.

A patrol car arrived at Frank Doyle's house around 7.20 p.m. Ms Vergnet and Doyle brought the officers back to the spot in the forest. The Gardaí agreed that the scattered remains looked human and called for back-up. Close to the pile of bricks the dog trainer pointed out a rusty knife blade on the ground. Detectives arrived quickly after and the area where the body parts were found was sealed off as a crime scene. By 8 p.m. a full-scale investigation had been launched. That night an incident room was set up in Tallaght Garda Station under the command of Detective Superintendent Brian Sutton. Sutton was head of all crime investigations in the Southern Division of the Dublin Metropolitan Region (DMR), which covers Rathfarnham and Tallaght.

A cursory examination of the fully decomposed and skeletonized remains indicated that the body had been lying in the same area for some time. Scavenging animals had scattered the bones over an area that covered several square yards of the forest floor. The isolated location where the remains had been found suggested that this was most likely a murder. Investigating such discoveries was nothing new for the officers in the Garda 'M' district of Rathfarnham and Tallaght, the edge of which reached into the foothills of the Dublin Mountains. The environs of Killakee, in the shadow of the sinister Hellfire Club on top of Montpelier Hill, is a short drive out of the city for killers who are either too lazy, in too much of a hurry, or too panicked, to dig a grave. Through the decades several decomposed bodies had been found scattered among the trees, heathers and gorse. Gangsters and terrorists had been dumping the bodies of their rivals in the windswept hills overlooking the city for as long as anyone could remember. Love rivals and unfaithful spouses – victims of crimes of passion – were also disposed of in the mountains, only to reappear years later for the police to unravel the truth of their violent ends. The bodies of two women, believed to have been murdered by jealous lovers, had been located in this area in the 1980s and '90s.

The immediate priority of this investigation would be to establish the gender of the skeletal remains and identify who it was. The next step would be to ascertain the cause of death and figure out how long the body had been there. The first stage in proceedings was to gather every scrap of evidence where the body was found. This required a meticulous fingertip search that would have to be carried out by trained search teams and forensic crime-scene investigators. Since the light was fading fast, the work could not begin until morning. The area containing the bones and clothing was placed under guard overnight.

The following morning Dr James Maloney met Detective Sergeant Tom Doyle at 8 a.m. at the crime scene in Killakee. Dr Maloney officially pronounced death, a legal requirement of the coroner's court. A short time later the deputy state pathologist Dr Michael Curtis and Laureen Buckley, a forensic anthropologist from the Forensic Science Laboratory, also arrived. They met Detective Superintendent Sutton and members of the Garda Technical Bureau. As Dr Curtis approached the cordon at the edge of the treeline the pathologist spotted the bones that had been retrieved by Millie and left on the pile of blocks by her owner. He identified three – a tibia, a fibula and a humerus – as being human, while the rest belonged to animals.

The white substance that Magali Vergnet had first noticed under the trees was adipocere and pointed to the spot where the body had lain after death. Adipocere is formed by the action of water on adipose tissue – body fat – over time. It occurs in anaerobic conditions where there is no oxygen in the body and a layer of water forms over the corpse. An examination of the remains found no soft tissue or organs, and moss was growing on some of the bones. The experts concluded that the body had been lying on its back when decomposition set in. The two forensic detectives were shown other bones and vertebrae that were strewn through the thick undergrowth. Each piece of bone was photographed and marked by a Garda forensic expert.

Laureen Buckley's hunch was that the remains were those of a female but this could only be confirmed by closer post-mortem examination. Members of the Garda search team combed the area and recovered between 60 and 65 per cent of the remains of a human skeleton, which they placed in seventeen individual evidence bags. Apart from the lower jawbone, the rest of the skull and the hands were not found. Identification of the corpse would be achieved with the help of DNA sampling and dental records. At 2.15 p.m. the remains were transported to the city morgue under Garda escort.

Less than three hours later on that Saturday afternoon, around 5 p.m., Roundwood Garda James O'Donoghue returned to the spot where Billy Fegan had retrieved the odd collection of objects. This time he climbed down the embankment beneath Sally's Bridge and walked along the dry beds to the waterline but could see nothing because the winds were still causing silt to cloud the water. He resolved to return when the weather was calmer.

The next morning, 15 September, the Sunday papers carried reports about the finding of the body in Killakee and the belief that it might be that of a woman. Inevitably the news sparked speculation that it could be one of three women who had vanished without trace during the 1990s. Jojo Dollard, Annie McCarrick and Deirdre Jacob had been the subject of an investigation by a specialist Garda team called Operation Trace, which had lasted several years without a breakthrough. The team's conclusion was that the women had been abducted and murdered, possibly by a serial killer. The media speculation was further fuelled by the fact that Annie McCarrick, who vanished in 1993, was last seen alive at Johnny Fox's pub, a short distance from Killakee. As part of the process of elimination the investigation team sought the DNA profiles of the women.

In the city morgue Dr Michael Curtis began his post-mortem examination with the assistance of Laureen Buckley. He was unable to ascertain the cause of death from the skeletal remains, so he recorded it as 'undetermined'. An examination of the tracksuit bottoms found beside the remains showed they were size 18 and had been bought in Dunnes Stores.

Ms Buckley then examined the remains to determine gender and approximate time of death. To her trained eye, the structure, texture and density of the various bones confirmed her earlier belief that this was a female. Ms Buckley then applied a standard technique for estimating the age of skeletal remains, the Suchey-Brooks method. This looks at changes in the texture and shape of bones consistent with specific stages of human development. Fusion of the first and second sacral vertebrae was complete, suggesting that the individual was over twenty-seven years old but under forty. She then focused on how long the woman had been dead. Bone marrow was still present, and allowing for the partial preservation by adipocere she estimated that the woman had died about one year earlier and no more than two.

Meanwhile, Dr Buckley found evidence of stress on the spine with slight compression and degeneration of the vertebrae. This finding was consistent with the person being overweight or obese, and it was corroborated by the size of the tracksuit bottoms found at the scene.

The Gardaí had been standing by for a preliminary report that would provide a starting point for the investigation. They now knew that the body was that of an overweight female, aged between twenty-seven and forty, who had been dead for between one and two years. This immediately ruled out the possibility that it was one of the three missing women from the 1990s. The files on all females reported missing since 2012 were scrutinized. The details of one woman in particular stood out as a likely match for the findings of the post-mortem. Her name was Elaine O'Hara, and she had disappeared just over a year earlier and was presumed to have drowned herself in the sea.

The Gardaí decided to compare Elaine O'Hara's dental records with the recovered human jaw. On Monday morning, oral surgeon Dr Mary Clarke attended the city morgue to examine the mandible found in the woods. Earlier, Gardaí had collected Elaine O'Hara's records from the Dublin Dental University Hospital. She had undergone extensive dental treatment there between 2006 and 2012, attending on forty-seven occasions. The initial examination indicated that the jawbone matched the dental records.

The O'Hara family, who had been in limbo for thirteen months, was now informed that the body was Elaine's. By this stage the Gardaí on the case had concluded that the cause of death was unlikely to be suicide: someone had brought her to the spot in Killakee before she died. This came as a bolt out of the blue for the family. While there was some comfort in knowing that she had not taken her own life, Elaine's father and siblings were now faced with an even more harrowing scenario.

With confirmation of the corpse's identity, detectives opened up the original investigation file. Investigators would have to trawl through every piece of information from that enquiry for clues to the killer's identity. The statements of everyone who had assisted in the initial investigation, including family and friends, would have to be studied and further, more in-depth interviews carried out. Now that a body had been found, every aspect of the case would be reviewed with different eyes. Something that had seemed unimportant or insignificant in 2012 could provide the all-important lead to solve the mystery. So far there was only one crime scene and no evidence as to the cause of death. The fact that the body had been left at the mercy of the elements for the past thirteen months meant the chances of finding any significant forensic evidence seemed practically non-existent.

That same Monday, James O'Donoghue was rostered to commence his shift in Roundwood Garda Station at 4 p.m. The items taken from the reservoir were still playing on his mind. It was a calm, sunny day, so he decided to pay a third visit to Sally's Bridge. This time the water was crystal clear and he immediately spotted something shining. It was a pair of handcuffs. He climbed down the embankment beneath the bridge and as he stepped into the water his boot sank into the silt.

The water turned brown and visibility was zero. He lost sight of the handcuffs and began rummaging with his hands.

A few inches under the muddy bottom his fingers felt something and he pulled out a set of keys. Among the assortment of car and house keys were two supermarket loyalty fob cards, one for Dunnes Stores and the other for Superquinn. The Garda continued his touch search and located a leather mask, a large kitchen knife, an inhaler, a rope and a rusty chain with a metal ring attached. Garda O'Donoghue brought the items back to the station and bagged them along with the rest of the recovered gear. He contacted Dunnes Stores customer services and asked for the details of the loyalty card. He was told that someone would phone him back with the information.

Garda O'Donoghue was off duty the following morning when a Dunnes manager, Aidan Kelly, phoned him at 9.30. He said the loyalty card belonged to a customer called Elaine O'Hara of 97 Belarmine Plaza in Stepaside, County Dublin. O'Donoghue contacted the Garda Information Service Centre in County Mayo and requested that the name be run through the PULSE computer system. It confirmed that Elaine O'Hara had been missing since 24 August 2012 and that her remains had been found three days earlier on the other side of the mountains.

O'Donoghue contacted Dundrum Garda Station, where the investigation into Ms O'Hara's disappearance had been moved since the closure of Stepaside. His extraordinary discovery gave the fledgling investigation a new impetus. It meant that someone connected to Elaine O'Hara's death had travelled to Vartry to dump her keys and other belongings in the expectation that they would never be found. And the discovery of the bondage gear alongside her keys suggested an extremely strong probability that Elaine's death was connected to her interest in S&M. A remarkable combination of weather, human instinct and coincidence had just blown the case wide open.

The unfolding situation technically involved three Garda divisions – the Dublin Metropolitan's Southern and Eastern Divisions where, respectively, Elaine O'Hara's remains were found and she went missing, and the Wicklow Division where the items were found in the reservoir. To ensure a coherent focused investigation, senior Garda management decided to pass the case over to the Eastern Division, as this was where Elaine was last seen alive and the likely location where she met her killer.

An incident room was set up in Blackrock Garda Station. The officer in overall charge was the divisional chief superintendent, Diarmuid O'Sullivan, and the commander on the ground was the district officer, Superintendent John Hand. Detective Inspector Brian Duffy and Detective Sergeant Peter 'Pecker' Woods of the Blackrock District Detective Unit were appointed as the senior investigation officers (SIOs). They would later be joined by Detective Superintendent Kevin Dolan, who was appointed as the head of all serious crime investigations in the Eastern Division. Detective Sergeant Woods, a hugely capable and experienced officer, would lead the investigation. Detectives in Shankill and Stepaside had done a considerable amount of legwork during the missing person enquiry in 2012. This would provide a starting point. Now the Blackrock team would set about unravelling the mystery of Elaine O'Hara's death.

Back in Roundwood, Garda O'Donoghue was instructed

to return to Vartry Reservoir and seal off the Sally's Bridge area as a crime scene. Very quickly it became a hive of activity as detectives and senior officers began arriving. Scenes of Crime Officer Wayne Farrell could see items in the water and used a shovel to retrieve a Nokia 1616 mobile phone, two sets of handcuffs and a black-handled knife. By then he was up to his knees in mud and the water had turned to murk. He stood back on the shore, waiting for the silt to clear and the arrival of the Garda Water Unit. Divers Lorcan Byrne, Brian Moore and Gerry McGroarty began searching the water on their hands and knees. They found a second knife, a red and black rucksack, a leather collar, two sex toys and a roll of black insulating tape. Also among the disparate array of objects retrieved from the muddy reservoir bed were the sawn-off barrels of a shotgun, a desktop computer, a large camera lens, a Dire Straits CD, a pair of shorts and a dressing gown bearing the Real Madrid crest. The material was taken away to the Garda laboratories for further analysis.

When the corpse had been officially identified, Gardaí had sealed off Elaine O'Hara's top-floor apartment in Belarmine Plaza, making it the third crime scene. AIB, which had been pursuing Elaine over her payment arrears when she went missing, had since repossessed the apartment. The bank had been unsuccessful in selling or renting it out, so it remained unoccupied. On 19 September, forensic detectives began a search of the apartment. It consisted of a bedroom, bathroom and a kitchen/living room leading to a small balcony. Over the year, Elaine's father had removed cutlery and other appliances. A TV, a decoder box and an exercise bike remained where Elaine had left them. The bedroom was bare, apart from a rug on the floor under the double bed. There were no bedclothes, except for a sheet on the mattress.

When Detective Garda Brian Berry pulled back the sheet, he noticed puncture marks and bloodstains on the mattress. The officer and his colleagues took the bedding away for forensic testing. It was a stroke of luck for the investigators that the apartment had not changed hands and its contents, especially the mattress, had not been dumped. Fate was yet again on their side.

3. The Man in the Shadows

When detectives gathered for the first full case conference on 18 September, they were still absorbing the incredible series of coincidences that had brought them together. A vital connection existed between the crime scenes in Killakee and Vartry Reservoir: if one location had been found without the other, there would have been substantially fewer pieces of the jigsaw on the board. The investigation team reviewed what they knew so far and agreed that the murder had not been a spontaneous act, the result of a moment of madness. Rather, it seemed clear that Elaine O'Hara's disappearance had been carefully planned and choreographed.

The bondage gear found in Vartry Reservoir, coupled with Elaine's interest in BDSM, indicated that this was how she had met her killer. And what they knew about her troubled history suggested that she might have taken risks and would have been vulnerable to being targeted by someone with a predatory interest in her. Even at the outset the team was strongly of the view that Elaine must have known and trusted her killer, unwittingly going along with a plan that would end in her death.

The shadowy figure running through the minds of the detectives had convinced his victim to leave behind the essentials she carried with her everywhere – iPhone, cigarettes, an inhaler – giving the impression to her family and the police that she had no further use for them. He had demonstrated the intelligence, meticulous planning and attention to detail of a serial killer. It was therefore reasonable to suspect that the perpetrator could have been successful in the past. There were enough missing women in the Leinster area to support such a hypothesis. It added to the sense of urgency about the mission at hand.

Apart from finding Elaine O'Hara's killer, the investigators faced another massive challenge: the post-mortem could not establish how Elaine had met her death. Short of a confession from the killer, it would probably never be revealed. Under Ireland's common law system, someone can only be convicted of a murder if the State proves that the *actus reus* (guilty act) combined with the *mens rea* (guilty mind) to constitute criminal liability. It must be proved beyond all reasonable doubt that the accused person had premeditated the murder and then carried it out. In the past, individuals against whom there was considerable evidence of intent had been acquitted on the grounds that there was no evidence relating to the cause of death. What this meant was that once the investigators identified a killer, they would have to construct an almost impenetrable wall of circumstantial evidence around that person to secure a conviction. So as they proceeded, not a sliver of evidence or detail of corroboration could be overlooked; absolutely nothing could be left to chance.

Scotland Yard, which pioneered police investigative methods, had first introduced a system for organizing a major crime enquiry that was adopted by the fledgling Garda force established after independence. Despite the evolution of new methodologies and the use of advanced technology, the basic principles still apply. An investigation requires control, direction, coordination and focus. The documentation of everything at the scene and statements from witnesses are as crucial now as they were in 1900. Chief Superintendent Diarmuid O'Sullivan and his staff would have to exploit every available investigative tool. Unmasking the perpetrator in this murder would require a combination of many skills: old-fashioned detective work alongside the latest technologies in the fields of forensic, psychological and electronic analysis. So the investigation adopted an interdisciplinary approach, involving a core of over forty Gardaí pursuing dozens of lines of enquiry. Experts and analysts, including civilian staff, from the Computer Crime Investigation Unit, the Garda Analysis Service, the Garda Telecommunication Section, the Forensic Science Laboratory, the Technical Bureau, the Crime and Security Branch and the Criminal Assets Bureau were all mobilized. Detective Superintendent J. J. Keane and officers from the National Bureau of Criminal Investigation (NBCI) were sent to Blackrock to assist. Detective Inspector Duffy and Detective Sergeant Peter Woods selected the team of detectives and set about coordinating the many lines of enquiry. Even with all this expertise in the team, investigators would also need an ingredient that all cops pray for in every serious investigation: luck. And, so far at least, luck had been with them.

In the incident room, detectives closely studied Elaine O'Hara's original missing persons file. Her killer was lurking somewhere among the pages of statements and reams of data lifted from her phones and computers. The first fleeting glimpse could be found in the statement Frank O'Hara had given following Elaine's disappearance. Her shocking outburst four years earlier when she had boasted about her interest in S&M had stood out in her father's mind. She talked about her involvement with a married man, 'an architect from Foxrock' who tied her up. She said she had asked this man to kill her but he had refused. At the time her father suspected that she was trying to shock him, which she had succeeded in doing.

The same mystery man was mentioned in the original Garda statement of Stuart Colquhoun, Elaine's therapist at St Edmundsbury Hospital. On 30 August 2012 he had told detectives about Elaine's history of self-harming and her interest in BDSM. She had shown Mr Colquhoun the 'significant but superficial' wounds to her stomach, arms and legs. 'Elaine admitted to harming herself and that a fella would call around and do some of it,' he said. The cuts ceased when she apparently stopped seeing the man, whom she again described as being married with a child. She never mentioned a name or divulged any further information about him.

When Mr Colquhoun's statement was read with fresh eyes, the investigation team decided to re-interview him in the hope that he might find more details in Elaine's records that related to this shadowy figure. The therapist found an entry in his files from 11 July 2011 when she revealed that she was involved with the same man again. Elaine said she had tried to end the relationship by email on a number of occasions but never sent them.

Other witnesses also came forward. On 17 September, Edna Lillis was watching the RTÉ six o'clock news at her home in County Meath when it featured a report concerning the discovery of Elaine O'Hara's remains. The woman's name meant nothing until her picture appeared on the screen.

Elaine stood smiling. She was wearing a stylish blue dress and had a fascinator in her hair. It looked like she was at a wedding. Edna Lillis immediately recognized her and phoned the investigating Gardaí. A few hours later she met detectives in Dublin to tell them what she knew.

The women first met six years earlier as inpatients in St Edmundsbury and quickly became close friends. Elaine, she said, was a lonely woman who lacked self-esteem and had no friends. She often spoke of the immense sadness she still felt at the death of her mother, Eileen. Edna and Elaine had lost contact in early 2012, about five months before Elaine's disappearance. But there was something she had confided during their last encounter which greatly disturbed Edna Lillis and she was anxious to share this with the police.

It was over coffee in St Edmundsbury that Elaine had first mentioned being involved in a relationship with a man she had met through the Internet. Edna Lillis specifically remembered Elaine saying that the man had children. 'He was an architect and he was married and it was a purely physical relationship in which he would inflict pain on her by cutting her,' Edna Lillis recalled. Elaine showed her four cuts on her stomach, each one about three inches long, which appeared to have been caused by a knife.

She warned Elaine that she was playing 'a very dangerous game' and advised her to keep his details written down in a safe place. 'She promised me she kept notes of the relationship, so they have to be somewhere,' she urged the detectives. Elaine knew her friend didn't approve of the relationship and Edna Lillis reckoned that was the reason why she subsequently ceased contact. Edna Lillis was so anxious to assist that she gave the officers permission to access her phone and medical records if it would help track down the exact date of the last meeting. She wanted justice for her friend.

Rosetta Callan, a nurse in St Edmundsbury for over forty years who had known Elaine since her first admission at the age of sixteen, was also interviewed by detectives. The night before Elaine's discharge the nurse called in to her room to see how she was. As she sat on the edge of the bed, Elaine told her she was 'pissed off' with a man who had been 'constantly calling to her and getting her to take part in bondage games'. The mystery man had a key to her apartment and she got the feeling that Elaine was afraid of him. When Rosetta Callan advised her to go to the police, she said she didn't want to because the man had children. 'She kept telling me that she loved kids and she didn't want the kids to get hurt. It was unusual for Elaine to divulge so much, because she was normally cagey enough about giving any information,' the nurse told the officers.

On the same day other members of the investigation team re-interviewed Caroline Nugent, who had worked with Elaine in Ken's Newsagents and had known her for twelve years. She also recalled Elaine talking about a relationship with a married man she had met on the Internet. The mysterious man, who Elaine said was from the country, was into sex games and had been messing her around. He wouldn't contact her for weeks and then he'd suddenly pop up and she'd take him back. The girls who worked with Elaine were aware of her mental health issues and never knew whether to believe her when she came out with such things. Caroline Nugent never saw her with a man.

Another colleague in Ken's Newsagents was the owner's daughter, Emma Robertson. Emma too recollected Elaine talking about meeting men on the Internet and revealing that she was involved with a married man. On one occasion she saw images of handcuffs, whips and restraints on Elaine's phone.

On 18 September, Sergeant Kevin Duggan was given responsibility for reviewing 219 days of CCTV footage from Elaine's apartment block at Belarmine Plaza. The almost 5,300 hours of footage covered the period between 18 January and 26 August 2012. It had been recorded on ten cameras covering the four entrance doors to the block, the parking area outside and an underground car park. The recordings were contained in two hard drives that had been seized at the time of Elaine's disappearance. In the initial missing persons enquiry the Gardaí had only checked the two days between her final departure from the apartment and when she was reported missing.

Sergeant Duggan collected the hard drives from the Computer Crime Investigation Unit in Harcourt Square in central Dublin and brought them to a designated room in Dundrum Garda Station. Gardaí Robert O'Keeffe, Mark Bergin and Michael Lynch were initially recruited to assist in the mammoth task, but over the following weeks up to eleven officers were required to view the mountain of material. At first the footage was not in chronological order and parts were missing. On 20 September an engineer who had set up the original CCTV system installed software to reconfigure the footage and this enabled the team to begin their search. Each officer scanned sections of the footage, noting any sightings of interest in a logbook. There was nothing exciting about the job; it required patience and concentration. They were looking for a needle in a haystack but there was a strong possibility that among the blur of faces they would find the killer. The stars of the banal film were the tenants of the thirty apartments in the block, their visitors and maintenance workers, all of whom were featured entering and leaving thousands of times.

The next day, Garda Lynch logged a man who had caught his attention. On 23 June 2012, Elaine had arrived home at 6.54 p.m. and taken the lift to her apartment on the top floor. Ten minutes later, at 7.04 p.m., a man entered the lobby of her apartment block, a small bare space with cream walls and grey floor tiles. There was a row of postboxes facing the camera, and the lift was to the left in the footage. The man drew the Garda's attention when he covered his hand as he pressed the call button for the lift. He then kept his back to the camera and looked towards the postboxes. It seemed that he was trying to avoid the camera overhead as he waited for the lift to arrive. There were no cameras upstairs to record which apartment or floor he was visiting. He could be seen leaving again at 8.18 p.m. The officer decided to keep an eye out for the mystery man as he continued sifting through the acres of security footage.

On the same day, 21 September, the Gardaí conducted a search at a second site in Killakee about 500 yards from where Elaine's remains had been discovered. Frank Doyle had alerted officers to the spot, which seemed to have been the venue for some strange activity. There the officers found a large number of objects, including hacksaw blades, insulation tape, various lengths of twine, fishing line, cable ties with bulldog clips and some with screws, denim shorts, grey trousers and harness equipment. The detectives suspected that this spot had been used for bondage sessions and that

Elaine O'Hara might have been brought here first by her killer. A shovel was also located in the undergrowth. They suspected Elaine's killer might have intended to bury her body. However, the mesh of tree roots under the surface would have made that job extremely difficult and he had obviously abandoned the idea.

4. The Text Trail

In the early days after the discoveries in Killakee and at Vartry, the focus of the murder hunt switched from its nerve centre in Blackrock to an office in the HQ of the Garda National Support Services in Harcourt Square, home to the Computer Crime Investigation Unit (CCIU). In addition to the information readily available on Elaine's laptops and phones, investigators knew that there would be much more to find in her devices' hidden recesses.

In the digital age every electronic interaction, either by mobile phone or online, leaves a traceable imprint and forensic analysis of such data has become an important investigative tool. When data is saved by a computer operating system it is indexed and stored in allocated space. But when a file is deleted, either by the computer or manually by the user, the discarded information is consigned in clusters to unallocated space. This is the computer equivalent of an afterlife for deleted information. But the files remain undead, so to speak, forgotten but never quite gone. This information can be resurrected using forensic software.

The job of excavating the hidden material to convert it into a readable form fell to Detective Garda Brid Wallace and her colleagues in the CCIU. Wallace and Detective Sergeant Alan Brown extracted over 4,000 SMS messages from the hard drive of Elaine's Apple MacBook. Of these, well over half – 2,639 text messages, 2,344 of which were readable – were between Elaine's number, 086 3xx xxx7, and an unidentified number, 083 1xx xxx4.

The unidentified number had been entered in Elaine's contacts under the name 'David' on 26 March 2011. It turned out that the phone to which the number had been assigned was purchased from the Three Store on Grafton Street in Dublin city centre at 1.26 p.m. on 25 March 2011. The number was pre-paid and the handset a Nokia 2730 that, together with a €40 top-up voucher, cost €99. The name entered in the registration form by the purchaser was 'Goroon Caisholm' with a date of birth in 1992 and a home address at 'Oak Lawn, Clerihan, Tipperary'. The contact number given for the new owner was 086 2xx xxx7. The records showed that the phone had been used for the sole purpose of contacting Elaine O'Hara's phone. It was last activated on 12 July 2012 and had not been detected on any telecom network since then.

It appeared that Elaine O'Hara had heeded Edna Lillis's warning to keep safe the details of the man who came around to cut her. The nature of the messages between her phone and the Goroon phone made it clear that he was the man she had described to Edna, and in backing up her phone she had captured his messages to her. These messages told a story that was so grotesque and macabre that even hardbitten detectives were horrified by their content. The texts were a dialogue between a master – the man on the Goroon phone – and his slave, Elaine O'Hara. They included graphic exchanges about punishment, rape, stabbing, bloodletting, pain, abduction, suicide and murder. Above all, Elaine's mysterious master continuously expressed his wish to stab her to death. Significantly, Elaine had last backed up her phone to the laptop on 15 May 2012, not long after her final meeting with Edna. Consciously or otherwise, she had left a trail to her killer.

After purchasing his new phone, the man called Goroon had wasted no time in contacting Elaine O'Hara. Just under two hours later he texted her, pressing the send button at 3.22 p.m. on 25 March. It was obvious from their first exchange that they had been involved in a BDSM relationship that he was now anxious to re-establish:

GOROON: Hi Elaine hope you are keeping well.
ELAINE: Who's this please.
GOROON: Sorry I may have the wrong number, is this Elaine O'Hara?
ELAINE: I dont have your number programmed in, who is this?
GOROON: This is an old friend :-). We used to play together and I miss it terribly. Would love to catch up.
ELAINE: Did I see you in the shopping centre the other day?
GOROON: Do you live near me, I have others.
ELAINE: Possible last week. I didn't go over . . . tried to get you out of my mind but can't.
GOROON: David
ELAINE: Yes it is you, I knew it.
ELAINE: I'm not into blood anymore.
GOROON: Yes, rang you from a call box to see if you were alive.
ELAINE: I'm alive and kicking so what can I do for you?
GOROON: Would love to start over, have you a partner.

ELAINE: No you're still doing . . . saw you with you know who looking at a restaurant menu the other day.

GOROON: :-) There's a girl in USA asked me to do something you asked me. Want to chat?

ELAINE: Sure, not today. I'm working in shop at five so you pick when.

GOROON: Great. Tomorrow? What time suits?

ELAINE: I'm working till 2.30. I don't live where I used to. So where?

GOROON: 3 then. I've been watching your old place. Figured you moved. Do you still smoke? Still have dark thoughts? Your place?

ELAINE: Yes I still smoke. I always have dark thoughts but I'm able to cope with them now. You can come but not in . . . Still smoke. I did give them up but back on them, they're addictive.

GOROON: I got this phone and sim just in case, can't be traced. Still chains?

ELAINE: No still have mine, market shop belarmine plaza, 3.Text me if not coming I'm not wasting my time.

GOROON: See you then. Missed you. X

ELAINE: Just to let you know I'm not promising anything.

GOROON: Hopefully. Do u ever think about me.

ELAINE: Honestly yes, I do, but then I remember the blood.

GOROON: Did u ever think I would surprise you and end it all.

ELAINE: No i knew you wouldn't. You'd never come near me with anyone around.

GOROON: If u ever see me again I don't bite. See you tomorrow x

ELAINE: You have me frazzled now. I never expected to hear from you again.

The flood of subsequent communications revealed how quickly Elaine had fallen under the influence of her master after that first meeting and her willingness to resume her role as his slave. In BDSM terminology she had been a submissive, or 'sub', for a number of years. Her preference was to be restrained and tied up in chains and cuffs. But the texts revealed that the mystery man's interests were more extreme. His predilection was for knives, blood and murder. So, though Elaine did not want to indulge in 'knife play' again, and he initially promised they didn't have to go there, the texts made it clear that he reintroduced a knife and regularly stabbed her during sex sessions.

Now that he had her in his grasp again the master did not hold back. Between March 2011 and July 2012 he bombarded her with terse commands and threats in words that left nothing to the imagination. The texts between them proved that Elaine had not been lying in the shocking outburst to her father in 2008 – Goroon constantly reminded her of the time in their previous relationship when, in the depths of despair, she had asked him to kill her. On that occasion he had refused, but three years later he was eager to help her end it all. He blamed her for awakening the murderous desires that consumed him.

GOROON: It's your fault I want to kill and you won't let me stab you.

ELAINE: I never thought me wanting to die would lead to this.

Like a cat playing with a mouse he toyed with her in the hope that he would bewilder and exhaust her. One text read:

> Hope you are feeling better today. Have thought a lot about your situation, and can adjust my kind offer to hang u in your apartment so u would be found and buried properly etc? less covering up to do for me as well. I could take cuffs off after. I would prefer the other way of course but just something to think about.

On several occasions Elaine tried to fight back against his demands, accusing him of merely using her and being selfish. She complained that he didn't give her what she wanted, which was to be tied up in cuffs and chains. When she said she wanted to find real love in her life, Goroon taunted her that she would never get anyone because she was 'old and fat, a smoker, disobedient and needy'. When she complained that she could never find a proper partner because of the stab wounds and the bruising from being punched, he would unleash another cascade of abuse about her appearance.

Exploiting Elaine's wish to be a mother was key to his approach. He kept reeling her in with the promise of a baby. In August 2011 it appeared that they had agreed to go their separate ways.

> GOROON: Sorry to lose you but will take you up on offers of play and murder. Did you say I could kill u as long as I didn't say it was coming?
>
> ELAINE: I don't think I said that sir. I will miss you Sir.

She added that if she was ever going to find anyone to give her kids she needed to be 'free of stabs'.

ELAINE: Unless you want to give me a child Sir?

When he didn't reply she texted again fifteen minutes later:

ELAINE: Didn't think so

GOROON: I would but I won't be around to raise or support it.

She told the master that she really wanted a child, despite him 'giving out all the time about the one in Donegal' and that for her the man was just a means to an end.

GOROON: I'll give you a child if you want but they can't ever know who I am.

They discussed when she might get pregnant and how she'd fit a baby in with work and college. He instructed her to start taking folic acid and stop smoking to prepare for a pregnancy. But the trade-off he demanded was extraordinary.

GOROON: OK a life for a life. Help me take one and ill give you one.

ELAINE: OK, you set it up.

The next day she texted again:

ELAINE: Did you mean what you said yesterday Sir?

GOROON: Yes. It's your reward for helping me stab a girl to death.

On another occasion when she dismissed his offer of 'play' because she feared he would cut her, Goroon replied: 'What about baby? Clock is ticking :-)' The texts showed that her spells of recalcitrance were always short-lived. It was never long before she would apologize and resume her submissive attitude. One of her texts to the Goroon phone read: 'Yes sir. Sir I'm your slave. You can use me for what you want. I have committed to you. I don't have to like it.' The master always got what he wanted.

From the very beginning of their renewed relationship, Goroon's texts showed that he felt secure and untouchable behind the anonymity of his unregistered phone. Three days after resuming contact with Elaine, on 28 March 2011, they exchanged texts from 7.42 that morning to 3.31 that afternoon. Goroon had no inhibitions.

ELAINE: Should have seen you walk to your car. You had an amazing happy walk.

GOROON: Woman next. Stabbed to death.

ELAINE: Easier said than done sir.

GOROON: I know. We have to work on it. Getting my car back friday and can give u money. How much do u need?

ELAINE: I don't know yet. Let me know during week.

GOROON: I wish i had kept the clip of the stabbing. All that blood! :-)

He sends another text shortly afterwards.

GOROON: I have a recurring dream, where u txt me to say u have a present for me at your place, and when i get there it's a naked girl gagged and bound tied to a chair and you have all my knives laid out.

ELAINE: Not going to happen sir!!!!

GOROON: It's a nice dream tho.

ELAINE: That it is a bit like the dreams I have about being in chains and serving a master.

GOROON: We are all doing our best.

ELAINE: I know sir. Sure that's life!!!!

GOROON: Yup. Life is short! Especially for u! Ha ha

Later that afternoon Elaine contacted the master again.

ELAINE: Sir you know I hate getting money but I do really need it. What kind of payment plan would you want? I pay interest.

GOROON: You can repay me in blood. 50 euro per stab!

ELAINE: Nice try. I'm not giving blood sir. For anything.

GOROON: I might just snap and stick u anyway against your will!

ELAINE: Every time you come near me that scares me!! Forget it.

GOROON: You love it! You enjoy me stabbing the shit out of you if it makes me happy?

ELAINE: I want you to be happy sir yes. But I don't want you sticking me.

GOROON: I love your knife scars. Happy memories. We better stab someone else then, but who?

ELAINE: Whoever. I've got other problems.

GOROON: What problems?

ELAINE: Never mind. I'll talk to you

GOROON: Tell me. Ok. Just say the word and I will end all your problems.

Two days later, on 30 March, the discussion centred on a fantasy to kill an unnamed female in the USA, the one he had referred to in their first text exchange. He told his slave that he couldn't afford the cost of going to the US to kill the woman.

GOROON: That will cost thousands, can't wait that long to sink my knife into flesh and see blood pour.
ELAINE: Well sir, you might not have any choice, you might just have to wait, you're not getting me. Never again.

And another exchange:

GOROON: I want you to pretend you want me to stab you or someone. It turns me on. You can send me texts like that to arouse and excite me, ok?
ELAINE: OK I'll think about it.

The dialogue was peppered with his threats to kill her if she didn't help him find a random woman to murder. In a series of communications he identified a potential victim, an estate agent. The fantasy involved him and his slave abducting the woman while posing as potential house buyers. Elaine even suggested that he could kill her sister, but when he immediately began plotting to stab and rape Ann Charles, she quickly withdrew it – 'just kidding,' she texted.

Goroon constantly cajoled and goaded Elaine.

GOROON: Help me with satisfying my stabbing fetish, find me someone or some way of doing it or offer your own flesh.

ELAINE: To kill sir? Or just stab?

GOROON: If its u just stab unless u want to die? If it's a stranger then she has to die so she can't identify me.

Another typical text informed her: 'I want to stick my knife in flesh while I'm sexually aroused and see pain. Blood turns me on and I'd like to stab a girl to death sometime.'

Goroon played on Elaine's insecurity and she responded by trying to please in any way she could. While she was studying for exams he texted her with this request: 'I really need to masturbate, can you text me something I can read to turn me on ASAP. Rape and stabbing.'

She responded with a story about her being alone in a park on a cold dark night after leaving a library. Elaine described being grabbed by somebody and pulled into the bushes. The fantasy ended with her being raped at knifepoint and then stabbed. Later, she texted her master's phone asking: 'That's it. Hope its OK? Did it help?' He replied: 'Excellent thanks.'

She told him her dreams:

ELAINE: I had a dream last night. To me scary dream to you probably a good dream.

GOROON: What was the dream?

ELAINE: I dreamt about standing on that stool the way I was and you walked out of the apartment. I slipped and choked myself. Then it changed. I was standing there and you brought in a girl removed my blindfold and made me watch you stab her to death.

GOROON: I would love that.

ELAINE: I guessed you would sir.

Goroon asked for more than stories and dreams. On 20 June 2011, Elaine O'Hara received an excited request.

GOROON: I want u to do something for me tonight. I want a photo of the largest kitchen knife u have as far up ur cunt as possible. Don't cut yourself, try to impress me.

ELAINE: Yes sir. I will try.

GOROON: Good girl. I want to see your hand gripping the blade as if u stabbed it in deep. Use ketchup if u think it would make a more exciting picture.

The following day Elaine asked whether he had got the photographs. 'Got them both, very very nice! X,' he replied.

Elaine even asked Goroon for advice on another liaison. His response was typically manipulative:

ELAINE: One of the masters I was txting before Christmas has been in contact again what should I do?

GOROON: You can have him. I'm thinking of quitting being a master to concentrate on killing.

ELAINE: Sir I don't want him I want you as a master.

GOROON: We will see getting bored I guess.

ELAINE: Is there anything else I can do sir? You're the best I have come across in my search. Everyone else is so soft. You were right sir. Don't know how to get someone for you to kill sir. I am not good at that kind of thing.

For Goroon, killing was never far off the agenda. In an exchange shortly after the resumption of the relationship Elaine told him:

ELAINE: Sir, just to let you know, I don't expect you to answer all my texts. I also wanted to let you know you can use me for what you want but I am going to use you for what I want. I'm different and I don't expect anything from you anymore. Just the above. Hope you had a good day.

GOROON: Thank u. Makes it easier to enjoy each other. Can u get me key and text code? I like the idea of lying in wait! Ur lucky punches hurt not stab wounds

ELAINE: I've terrible bruises on my wrists from the cuffs. Killing me. Can't wear my watch.

GOROON: Ok will try and do u tomorrow. I will get plastic knife and you get me key. Looking forward to the violence! I will try to keep your cuts and bruises under your clothes :-)

ELAINE: Cuts, what cuts!! No cuts sir please you promised!!

GOROON: You know what I mean. All marks. No cuts

ELAINE: Only joking sir! I know what u mean. Don't know if I have to get keys tomorrow sir but will try.

GOROON: No hurry. This means you have to stop putting on the deadlock so I can slip in while u sleep and rape/stab u.

ELAINE: I will try to get the keys. Sir you always said you would do that and only once did. Even then I knew you were coming.

GOROON: I will do it for u. It's the least i can do to thank u for all the stabs.

ELAINE: Looking forward to tomorrow's games! If I let you in.

GOROON: I promise I will slip in and attack you as soon as I have key.

Sometime later the same day:

ELAINE: Sir would you mind if i play with someone else. Sir i have to be honest. There is a guy. It's very early in the relationship at the mo. But I would in the end if it comes down to it choose him over you. Hope you don't mind.

GOROON: Like waiting for the 46a lol. I don't mind as long as he always wears a condom. I don't have to wear one if I pull out. He can't use my knife, balaclava and he can't know about me in case I need to end u someday.

GOROON: You deserve a full time master. I'm your secret killer.

ELAINE: Thanks and trust me he won't know about you. That's a cert. Thanks sir.

GOROON: The more male DNA and fingerprints in your flat the better. Get his prints on your kitchen knife!

ELAINE: He is definitely not into those kind of things. He's dead nice. We have played once on Tuesday.

Kind of weird he was very gentle. No chains unfortunately, no pain so I'm still thinking.

GOROON: Maybe you need him to give you things I can't. String him along and reveal your needs slowly. If he gives you any trouble we can kill him.

ELAINE: No killing. The other I will think about. Got to go.

GOROON: See u tomorrow, my urge to rape stab kill is huge. You have to help me control or satisfy them. This untraceable phone will be off normally between 5pm and 8am unless we're planning stuff. In case you get no replies later. Glad to have u back!

ELAINE: Control sir, not satisfy. Talk tomorrow.

GOROON: Acting them with you helps a lot.

In April 2011 there was more talk of the master's killing fetish:

GOROON: Woman stabbed last night in Dublin, guy got away clean.

ELAINE: Was it you? We will have to see sir. They just might not be saying anything.

GOROON: I'm watching the case with interest. She's still alive. Big mistake leaving a witness. I would love to have been the one knifing her. Can you imagine the knife going in and out of her, all the blood. Must have been a fantastic feeling for him, lucky guy x

ELAINE: You are sick v sick

GOROON: So are you, I know you wouldn't want me any other way. I'm going to do it, you have to help me or it will be you.

ELAINE: No you're not, you've been talking about it for so long and no action. You are never going to do it

GOROON: It sounds like a dare! I have to do it now to impress my sub.

ELAINE: I'm not your sub. I'm just someone you use.

GOROON: You are my sub, I'm training you . . . I'm always in your head.

With the master pulling the strings, Elaine was never allowed to stray too far from her suicidal thoughts. In the following exchange he explained how he would help her to die. He began by asking: 'When will you be ready for it?'

ELAINE: Don't know. Hopefully never. But that will change

GOROON: I can't see you as an old lady somehow. If you do decide one day, u have to promise me that I will send you off.

ELAINE: I don't know about that! Of course I will try, but you know that when someone wants to do it it's very quick like they do it then and it's all the planning that you want that is off putting. When I wanted to do it before you kind of didn't make it easy

GOROON: Wasn't ready before at short notice but am now with this untraceable phone. All you have to do is get in the car and I will take care of the rest! And it will be painless.

ELAINE: How would it be painless?

GOROON: You would be unconscious while I am killing you

ELAINE: You would choke first?

GOROON: Or use chloroform or sleeping tablets

ELAINE: Ok, thats good. It's the pain that puts me off.

GOROON: I would bind you in car once u make decision, u should write goodbye note. After, I would leave your car, clothes, note by the sea. Maybe I can smuggle you out in a suitcase next time you're tied up.

ELAINE: When I'm tied up I don't really have a say. You may have to gag me though as I would prob scream.

GOROON: With duck tape or you could be unconscious when I put you in case?

ELAINE: You couldn't do that sir. Actually fit me in a case

GOROON: How else could I get you out of ur apartment against your will?

ELAINE: I suppose . . . But will you tell me when so I can prepare myself for it.

GOROON: Really? Tell u before I do it? Before I kill you against your will?

ELAINE: Oh sir you will never kill me against my will. You've left too much evidence in my place. I'm not great at cleaning.

GOROON: I am though! :-) But yes, I will tell you before I do it.

ELAINE: Like to see you try to kill me. I wouldn't let you. Not against my will.

GOROON: What if I did it next time ur tied up?

ELAINE: Yeh sure sir, you wouldn't.

GOROON: I would like to think it was possible.

ELAINE: I would like to see you try sir.

GOROON: Sounds like a challenge, you're on.

ELAINE: Sir I learnt my lesson a long time ago not to challenge you.

GOROON: Hee, hee!

ELAINE: Does that mean you're still going to do it sir?

GOROON: Going to do what?

ELAINE: Take me out in a suitcase as a test run? As I said before I really don't have a choice do I sir?

GOROON: Not really.

So much of their dialogue showed Elaine giving in to Goroon's demands, engaging – however reluctantly – with his talk about stabbing or killing. But from time to time in the midst of this horror, she would reveal her heart's desire. Not only was Elaine O'Hara vulnerable and troubled, but she was also profoundly sad and desperate for love.

GOROON: If you ever want to do something nice for me u can let me stick u.

ELAINE: Sir I always want to please you.

GOROON: Then u should always let me stab u or find me someone else to do it to.

ELAINE: All the time sir? Between the punches and the stabs I will never find my true love.

GOROON: If u want to be collared u have only me.

ELAINE: I know but I can always dream sir. I still want kids even if its only one. And I want someone to care for me and love me. That will never change sir. I can still have it can't I sir?

GOROON: We will see.

In contrast to Elaine's lack of guile and her fragility, Goroon was manipulative and showed no empathy or emotion towards her. His one and only desire was to satisfy himself. To inflict pain or worse.

As they read through the texts, the Gardaí were sure that they had found Elaine's killer. They also recognized that he had all the characteristics of a sociopath. Their hope was that he had left enough electronic DNA to be tracked down and brought to justice.

5. A Killer Unmasked

As each tranche of information was brought to the surface in its raw format it was difficult to read. Members of the CCIU began the time-consuming task of translating the text exchanges into a readable form and organizing them in chronological order. Sarah Skedd, a civilian crime and policing analyst attached to the Garda Analysis Service in Garda HQ, conducted cell site analysis to pinpoint the locations of the Goroon phone when messages were sent. By cross-referencing the text traffic and the transmission masts used by the device, the investigation team could work out a rough geographical location for the phone as well as its direction of travel. The list of dates, times and places could also be used as a guide for locating sites where CCTV cameras might have captured an image of the suspect. This information would prove vital if – or when – the Gardaí identified him.

As it was sorted, the material was immediately dispatched to the incident room in Blackrock for further action. Initially the dates and times were absent from a lot of the restored material. Civilian experts attached to the Criminal Assets Bureau set about developing a programme that would resolve that problem.

Records of call credit purchases for the phone showed that it had used €100 worth of credit – including the initial €40 top-up – between March 2011 and July 2012. A top-up voucher for €10 had been purchased in Jones' Deli on

Baggot Street in central Dublin on 22 November 2011. The last voucher for €10 was bought at a Centra supermarket in Cornelscourt Village in South Dublin. The cell site analysis identified the phone as being most active in these two areas and travelling between both. It was an important new piece of the puzzle.

At the same time, detectives were tasked with compiling a list of all males in South Dublin bearing the names Gordon or David Chisholm, or David Gordon, in a process of elimination against the name in the Goroon phone registration. When they checked the Oak Lawn in Clerihan, County Tipperary, they found it didn't exist but that there was a small estate in the village called Oak Park. Apart from the address, there appeared to be no obvious connection with the phone, which had never been used in the area.

In his texts Elaine's shadowy master had left a string of clues that gave the enquiry team confidence that they would uncover his earthly shape. The messages had revealed that the owner of the Goroon phone had keys to Elaine O'Hara's apartment. The ongoing cell site analysis gave them time indicators to help them navigate through the mass of CCTV security footage from her apartment building.

The team assigned to examine the material had found more images of the mystery man they had first spotted entering the building on 23 June 2012. Over the following days the investigators made a significant breakthrough when the footage showed him entering the apartment block in the company of Elaine O'Hara. The pair were picked up by the camera entering the lobby at 5.02 p.m. on 9 July. The mystery man and Elaine briefly exchanged glances as they stood feet apart, waiting for the lift. He was dressed in dark clothes with his hands stuffed into his pockets and his head down as if to avoid the camera. He re-emerged in the lobby thirty-eight minutes later and left. He was again spotted entering the block on 11 July at 5.34 p.m. As usual, he tried to hide his face and this time took the stairs instead of the lift. The Gardaí reckoned he might be the killer and the painstaking research for a clearer facial shot continued.

Back in Harcourt Square, Detective Garda Brid Wallace started the painstaking task of constructing a picture of what might have happened to Elaine from her computer records and online activity. Wallace and her colleagues had trained at the Digital Forensics Investigation Research Department in University College Dublin. She had been involved in several major international investigations, working alongside Interpol to search out paedophile rings using the Internet. Now she hoped to pull together the disparate strands of Elaine O'Hara's life by dredging through the recesses of her computers: an Apple MacBook, a Compaq computer, an HP notebook, and a Dell laptop she had previously given away. Wallace waded through the available and deleted files, including still and moving images, and began tracing Elaine's Internet and email usage to build a picture of how she met her killer.

When Wallace delved into the Apple MacBook she found three sets of movie files. One included sixteen downloaded pornographic movies featuring BDSM content. A second set contained videos of family gatherings and sporting events. And the third set consisted of mainstream TV series, including *CSI: Crime Scene Investigation*. She discovered pictures of Elaine taken in various poses when she was clothed, semi-clothed and naked, some clearly taken by herself and the rest by another party. A number of the images featured close-ups of marks and healed scars around Elaine's torso.

Brid Wallace also recovered a PDF document titled *Serial Violence: Analysis of Modus Operandi and Signature Characteristics of Killers*, a book written by US academics William J. Birnes and Robert D. Keppel. In the book the authors analysed the signature crimes of several high-profile US serial killers, and it included graphic images of mutilated bodies and crime scene pictures. It also devoted a chapter to the Ripper murders in London's Whitechapel area between 1888 and 1891 and described the killer's signature: piquerism. Piquerism is a form of sexual perversion, mainly male, in which sexual satisfaction is derived from piercing or stabbing another, sometimes to the point of death.

Another document, created in April 2009, was a first-person story about being abducted by a man on the way to work, locked in the boot of a car, then held in chains, whipped and knifed. The writer graphically described how the pain 'sent shivers down my spine' and how she could hear blood dripping. 'All he could do was laugh and he started whistling,' it continued, with the author adding that she 'must have been unconscious' before she turned up at home two months later. The editing time on this document was forty-four minutes, suggesting that Elaine O'Hara had been its author.

Wallace also found a document titled 'Outline of slave', which set out a 'contract' for slavery. It was created at 7.54 p.m. on 18 September 2010 and had been modified two minutes later, which suggested it had originated elsewhere and been transferred to the computer by email or USB. It read:

> I'm offering 24/7 sadistic and brutal treatment for masochistic slaves. Slaves are property, possessions, meat. They are loved as a pet or as a cherished car. They are not a wife or a mistress. Slavery is a hard lifestyle to endure; you are not just a sex toy but a complete package. You will be offered an annual slavery contract with no early release for any reason. You will either be kept in a heavy duty steel cage or a locked cell in my cellars. If you're good and collected merit awards, you will have a real bed with steel collar and chained in the room. Agreed limits will be in your contract and adhered to. I prefer bi-sexual or bi-curious slaves but again if your sexual orientation is straight, you won't be forced into bi-sexual roles. I'm looking for a poly-slavery arrangement.
>
> After initial training to my standards you will be expected to work as a slave part-time in my restaurant. If you're a UK National (Citizen) class 3 NI stamps will be paid. You will be bought slutty outfits and a couple of dress outfits for formal occasions. I will not stand for breaking objects in a tantrum. It is the only thing that will result in a very, very severe flogging.
>
> I have plenty of Dom friends so expect occasionally to have no holds barred heavy use. My limits – no sex with children or forced use of drugs. Nothing will be done that will result in your death or very serious injury. Slave or not, you are a person with just one life to live and you're entering a consensual relationship. Having said that, unless listed on limits within your contract. Expect piercings, breast skewering, branding, breast suspension and maybe even a cattle prod

> on your cunt (and that's just for starters). I have most equipment and toys and can build more to suit individual sizes.
>
> I'm not here for online fantasies but the real thing. If you have a fantasy you would like fulfilled I will work out a practical way to achieve it. My aim is to create the perfect obedient masochistic slave. Slavery is about domination and control, sex is just part of it.

This so-called contract echoed the bizarre document Gardaí had found at Elaine's apartment after she went missing, 'The Gorean Lifestyle: A Woman's Right is Slave'. It explained a lifestyle based on sexual master–slave relationships between men and women. The Gorean lifestyle was inspired by a 1960s series of misogynistic science fiction novels set on the imaginary planet of Gor. The series' author, John Norman, described a society in which the natural order is 'that men have a natural drive to dominate women while women have a strong desire to submit to men and give up their rights. Women are either free or enslaved, but free women can be enslaved at any time.' The printout went on to explain that the novels were the inspiration for a number of sex cults in the UK and the US. Though they had been banned from libraries and bookshops in the US during the 1980s because they were deemed to be so offensive to women, interest in the novels and the Gorean lifestyle experienced a revival in the Internet age.

A partially written document called 'mystery' had been created in November 2011 at 9.37 a.m. It was another first-person story, this time about the narrator being given a lift home from a party by a man who stopped the car, slapped her in the face and grabbed her hair. The driver told the woman, 'I own you,' before throwing her in a cellar where she was whipped and chained. The document's properties showed the author as 'A&D Wejchert'. A four-page essay on helping children with dyslexia to read, titled 'dyslexiaand-reading', was created and modified on 29 November 2011 also by A&D Wejchert.

Within the downloads folder, a subfolder called 'Read this' contained three PDF documents. The first, labelled '21 techniques', included four chapters – 'Manual Weapons', 'Spike', 'Knife' and 'Nunchaku' – from a book outlining techniques for silent killing by Master Hei Long. The second, 'Hidden Weapons', was a 35-page booklet describing various weapons. The third PDF, 'Murder Inc the book' by 'Jack the Rippa', outlined methods of picking a target and killing people.

On Elaine's other devices there were pictures of mutilated bodies and saved Google Maps images of Killakee Wood and Vartry Reservoir. A subfolder called 'Killing' on one of the computers contained a series of photographs depicting dead women, most of whom had been hanged. One such picture was labelled 'Raped, murdered Hindu woman found in Bangladesh'. There were pictures of a crime scene that included a naked female victim and another of a naked woman found hanged in Mexico.

There was also plenty of evidence of a tormented and confused woman. In the first of a number of diary entries on 12 November 2010, Elaine wrote:

> Dear Diary, I'm just after doing a day's work and I'm knackered. I want to cry and I don't know why. I am pissed off and angry because I'm really lonely, I can't talk to anyone because they will say it's my fault because I haven't done enough to

get out and make friends. Its easy for them to say. I watch and see the way they interact with people, because that's the only way you'll learn isn't it? If you observe you will learn, practice makes perfect and I try but I just seem to put my foot in it all the time. I just wish I could cry then it would be ok. The urge to cut is great. I know its still there as is the need to smoke. Why can't they just leave me alone. I want the physical urges to go away. I want to cut and my mouth waters at the thought of a cigarette, and the smell. I just want it to go away.

In a second Elaine began:

Dear Diary, Oh my God I am angry and tired and I want to cry again because I am tired of everything going on in my head. I just don't know where I am anymore. Half of me is going one way and half is going in the other. I just don't know where I am anymore. It's not only in my head, it's everywhere – emotions, etc.

Brid Wallace also retrieved a letter from Elaine to her therapist, Stuart Colquhoun, that she had drafted on 1 April 2010, in which she referred to her anger issues. She wrote: 'I'm too angry now to do anything. All my thoughts are negative. I just don't have the energy to do anything positive. When the anger goes down I will make contact. This has to be done by me.' In a June 2012 email to Mr Colquhoun, she again spoke about feeling angry.

Dear Stuart

I'm sitting here and I'm so mad at you. I know you're only doing your job, but I'm so fucking mad. Every day people have to make small talk, superficial talk. I do it every day and I understand why people have to do it. I always talk about the weather and how terrible it is, and how the summer is now over, and the children back at school in their coats . . . 'Are you having a good day giggle giggle; how was your weekend?; how is your mother doing?; did you go to the Westlife concert; that photo's lovely, she is so cute.'

See I can do it, but I am scared to go any further. I know what I do is wrong. I know, I am not stupid, but I don't need people shouting at me, making me mad. If you want to help that's fine but you're sounding like my dad, and sister, Sheila, my brother. You're just imaging [*sic*] them and that makes me mad.

I don't need that – I've had that all my life. When I get mad it makes me want to hide away and cut myself to release the anger. Every Tuesday I go to the Red Cross and volunteer . . . I volunteered to help out in the Tall Ships in August.

I didn't like your tone when you said I have to get out there and meet people because as you can see I am doing that, but it takes time. I don't know what you want me to do otherwise, but making me mad won't help me and I want to hide away.

Is it worth me going back?

Well as I find it hard to speak when I'm mad I thought I should write it down as sometimes I can't explain it. I hope you don't mind.

Elaine O'Hara

Brid Wallace's next step was to build a picture of Elaine's involvement in the BDSM world through her visits to fetish websites and interactions in chat rooms and by email. It appeared that she had three online profiles – 'submissive391', 'suborslaveforyou' and 'helpmelearn36/f' – on the fetish website Alt.com, the earliest of which dated back to November 2006. On her second profile, created in October 2008, she was listed as a 'silver' member. Her third profile, helpmelearn36/F, was accompanied by a picture of a female bent over and tied up.

For this last profile Elaine had written: 'I hate these things as you don't know someone until you meet them. I have been a sub on and off for a while. I have learned a lot but I still have a lot to learn.' She said that her fetish was bondage and she wanted to serve a master. 'I would love a 24/7 relationship but I have no expectations.' She listed her ideal person as someone who would train her to be the 'best submissive slave I can be' and said that she wanted someone 'trustworthy, caring and strict to a 24/7 slave'. To indicate her preferences she ticked the boxes for bondage, collar and hands/leash, kidnapping, knife play, mummification, sensory deprivation, spanking, slap in the face and verbal humiliation. It would later transpire that this profile had been viewed almost 10,000 times.

Brid Wallace found an online group that Ms O'Hara had joined called 'degradedcunthouse' where her profile had been viewed 776 times and featured on eleven 'hotlists'. She also found emails from a website called Extremerestraints.com, where Elaine had purchased BDSM-related paraphernalia.

From the nature of the content Wallace was uncovering, it was reasonable to suspect that Elaine might have met her killer as far back as 2007. It was also a fair assumption that some of the material that had been downloaded on to her computers had been the work of the shadowy figure who, as the texts already revealed, had a key to her apartment. So Wallace began the process of tracing people Elaine had met in chat rooms and through various BDSM websites.

By Friday 27 September, day ten of the murder hunt, though much of the computer work and analysis was still a work in progress the investigators were confident they already had enough to lead them to the killer. In Blackrock a team had been assigned to scrutinize the context of the phone messages for clues. Two exchanges were of particular interest. This one on 24 May 2011:

GOROON: Hi. Was lying low and leaving phone off in case stabbing was investigated. It isn't! Animals have picked carcass clean! Yay!

ELAINE: How do you know sir?

GOROON: I was up flying on Sunday and had a peek. Skeleton ribcage where Knife went in. Rest of sheep moved, no call to Club from farmer or Gardaí. I want to do a woman next. It was fantastic feeling the knife go in and watching blood spurt out. So happy. X

And this one on the morning of 13 June 2011, after Elaine had texted Goroon asking how his weekend had been:

GOROON: Terrible, 15pc pay cut and came 5th in flying.

ELAINE: Sir, welcome to reality. Fifth is good. Sir, where were you flying?

GOROON: Wiclow [*sic*]

Detective Sergeant Peter Woods had detailed members of the team to draw up a list of all registered pilots in the country, especially those living in South Dublin, where cell site analysis indicated that the Goroon phone had been most active. They were also looking for flying competitions around the country. The detectives had begun compiling details of fly-fishing competitions, too.

That Friday afternoon, Woods and Detective Gardaí James Mulligan and Colm Gregan were still studying the references to flying in the texts. So far the pilot register and flight competitions had thrown up no obvious leads. They were also drawing a blank with fly-fishing competitions in the Wicklow area at the relevant time. Then Colm Gregan had a brainwave. He remembered seeing people flying model aircraft while he was out walking on the Sugarloaf Mountain in County Wicklow. He googled model aircraft flying and found a website called maci.ie, the official website for the Model Aeronautics Council of Ireland (MACI).

The detectives had already worked out that 'flying on Sunday' in the first of the exchanges referred to Sunday, 22 May 2011. The detectives checked the events calendar on the MACI website and found that a 'Fun Fly' event had taken place on that day in Shankill, County Dublin. They also knew the date referred to in Goroon's '5th in flying' text from the second exchange was likely to have been 11 June 2011. The MACI website event calendar listed a competition in Roundwood, near Vartry Reservoir. And there was a link to the June edition of the MACI magazine *Flightlines*, which included a report on the Roundwood event. The fifth-place finisher in the competition was a Graham Dwyer.

The name rang a bell. While searching the computer using

the Goroon number, Brid Wallace had found a diary entry for 30 June 2011 that read, 'Graham's phone number 083 1xx xxx4.' The name – Graham – and number had also appeared in a telephone book seized from Elaine's apartment after she had originally gone missing.

The discovery caused a frisson of excitement in the incident room. 'I think you're on to something there, lads,' Peter Woods told the officers. The team gathered around his desk as James Mulligan ran a search for any Graham Dwyers in the Garda PULSE computer system. He made an instant connection. A Graham Dwyer had been recorded as having his bike stolen from outside his place of work – a company called A&D Wejchert with offices at Lower Baggot Street. His home address was 6 Kerrymount Close, Foxrock, in South Dublin. The cell site analysis had found that the Goroon phone mainly used the mast at the ESB HQ in Fitzwilliam Square, near Lower Baggot Street, and the one at the Rochestown Lodge Hotel in Cabinteely. The Dwyer address was close to the Cabinteely mast. The same Graham Dwyer had also been involved in an incident in Ballyshannon where his former partner had called the Gardaí following a row, but no further action had been taken.

Peter Woods did a Google search of A&D Wejchert and found that it was a firm of architects in which Graham Dwyer was a partner. From the *Flightlines* magazine Woods downloaded a picture of the Graham Dwyer who had come fifth in the flying competition. It bore a strong resemblance to an image of the mystery man's face found by the team trawling through the Belarmine CCTV footage.

The investigators dug out the registration details for the Goroon phone when it was purchased in the Three Store on

Grafton Street – a short walk from Lower Baggot Street. Peter Woods obtained Dwyer's work mobile phone number, 087 2xx xxx7. The contact number for the Goroon phone was exactly the same, but with an 086 prefix. Further checks revealed that Graham Dwyer was married and that his wife had given birth to a daughter in March 2011. The birth of a baby had been referred to in texts just after the event. There was silence in the team until one of the detectives said what they were all thinking: 'Fuck, I think we've found him!'

6. Murder by Design

There was nothing about Graham Dwyer's appearance to connect him to the sociopath Goroon with whom the detectives had become familiar from Elaine O'Hara's text records. Dwyer was a small man – just five foot five inches in height – with a bit of a pot belly. His face was boyish and unremarkable, apart from a distinctive downward turn to his mouth. He had short mousy brown hair and the beginnings of a bald patch. Neither did the initial facts Gardaí could establish about him suggest anything other than middle-class respectability. Dwyer lived in a substantial timber-clad detached house at the end of a mature, tree-lined cul-de-sac in the heart of Foxrock, one of Dublin's most affluent suburbs. His wife, Gemma, was also an architect – they had met in college – and they had two young children.

Even experienced Gardaí were taken aback by the contrast between the man they had anticipated finding and the man who was now their prime suspect. One of the investigators recalls: 'As a detective the first thing you learn on the job is never judge the book by the cover; everyone wears a mask and some have better ones than others. But when we started to look at this guy in the flesh you couldn't but be struck by the fact that there was nothing in his appearance or social context to suggest what he was capable of. In a lot of ways it was actually unbelievable. The stuff in the texts was so outrageous that you expected a monster with horns, not a little guy who likes flying model aeroplanes.'

Dwyer's identification as the prime suspect sent the murder investigation into overdrive. Now the priority of the investigation team was to 'house' the suspect, which in Garda parlance meant placing him under discreet surveillance and monitoring his phones. Gardaí skilled in surveillance techniques were deployed to sit on Dwyer. Wherever he went, the undercover cops shadowed him.

The officers were more accustomed to tailing organized crime bosses and terrorists, who often deployed counter-surveillance tactics. Compared to them, trailing Graham Dwyer was a doddle. Nevertheless it was imperative that nothing happened to arouse Dwyer's suspicion. In the unlikely event that Dwyer smelt a rat and tried to get out of the country, he would leave the police with no option but to arrest him. That could jeopardize any future prosecution because, in the absence of a cause for Elaine O'Hara's death, they needed time to build a case. Chief Superintendent Diarmuid O' Sullivan warned everyone that any mistake could result in a killer escaping justice. It was all going to be a matter of precision timing.

The Gardaí were equally concerned that if their suspect realized they were on to him, he might murder his own family in a fit of panic. One officer recalls: 'At this stage we had no way of knowing what this man did in the past and what he was capable of doing if under pressure.'

For fear that anything might leak out, Dwyer's identity was kept a closely guarded secret, known only to the core members of the investigation. They then set about circling their target, probing from the outer edges of his life to avoid raising his suspicions. As they watched and listened from a distance he appeared completely unperturbed by the ongoing murder investigation. Although there had been media reports that items linked to Elaine O'Hara had been found in Vartry Reservoir – including her keys, a rucksack, handcuffs, restraints and a phone – Dwyer did nothing to suggest that he was worried by the confluence of events at Vartry and Killakee Wood. In the weeks that followed, Graham Dwyer seemed blissfully unaware that he was now the one being stalked.

What made this murder investigation unusual was the killer's single-mindedness over a seventeen-month period as he had planned to end Elaine O'Hara's life. It was murder by design. The text messages were his blueprint and he approached his plan in the measured way he might a building project. Each stage was carefully slotted into place as the project progressed towards its completion – murder. The man on the Goroon phone had displayed both the appetites and calculation of a serial killer. References in the messages set off alarm bells – the Gardaí had good reason to suspect that Dwyer might have killed before and could strike again – and this added to their sense of urgency.

In August 2011 Goroon had informed Elaine O'Hara that he had found someone they could target to abduct and kill, a female estate agent he had spotted while walking on the street. 'We need to plan it,' he texted her. 'We need new untraceable pay-as-you go phone. You make appointment to see estate agent at remote cottage. Need fake names and just say we are teachers.'

Later that day he sent her another text: 'I found empty house close by. Pretty attractive young female estate agent,

Rowena Quinn.' He sent Elaine the woman's work number, instructing her to arrange an appointment for them to view a house: '8 Willow Park, Druids Valley, Cabinteely. We must check escape route for cameras.'

But when Elaine protested that it was too dangerous and they could get caught, he replied: 'I think it will be okay. Non-traceable phone. Fake names and off we go. Hammer her while her back is turned. Cover her head. Drag her into a back room. Gag, rape her. Stab her over and over. Stomach, chest, side, tits. Turn her over and stab her back and slit her throat. Then go back to yours and celebrate. Knock you up.'

Elaine asked if they could stop discussing it on the phone.

ELAINE: I don't want to get caught.
GOROON: We will be fine, don't worry. I am going to enjoy it.
ELAINE: I know. Technology is the killer now, sir. Sorry.

Detectives discovered that an estate agent called Rowena Quinn actually existed. The potential target, an attractive woman with blonde hair who bore a marked resemblance to Dwyer's wife, had been in the real estate business for several years. In the summer of 2011 she was a managing partner in Hunters Estate Agent, which she had established along with her partners in 2010. The company headquarters was on Baggot Street.

When Rowena Quinn was subsequently interviewed by detectives she confirmed that she had handled the sale of the house in Cabinteely in the summer of 2011. Her records showed that sixteen people had viewed the house, none named Graham Dwyer or Elaine O'Hara. Nor could she remember anyone matching either of their descriptions. It seemed most likely that Dwyer had first spotted Ms Quinn at her office, which was close to where he worked. (The text exchange about Rowena Quinn led to a subsidiary investigation with a view to charging Dwyer with conspiracy to murder.)

When Elaine O'Hara dissuaded him from targeting Ms Quinn, Goroon continued to bombard her with messages about murder. But she rebuffed them, reminding 'Sir' that he could be caught by the police.

GOROON: No one was ever caught for Raonaid Murray or the homeless woman in the Phoenix Park.
ELAINE: True . . . hope for your sake you won't
GOROON: I won't. It'll be all over the news. Can I trust you to keep mouth shut?

This exchange also made investigators sit up and take notice. In September 1999 seventeen-year-old schoolgirl Raonaid Murray was murdered in a frenzied knife attack in the early hours of the morning near her home in Glenageary in South Dublin. Despite intensive investigations in which over 8,000 people were interviewed, the murder weapon was never found and no suspect was identified. The case remains one of Ireland's highest-profile unsolved crimes. Coincidentally, Raonaid had attended the same school as Elaine O'Hara, St Joseph of Cluny. And it so happened that the investigation of her unsolved murder was the responsibility of the team now investigating Elaine's murder.

The second victim Goroon referred to was a fifty-year-old

homeless Romanian woman called Eugenia Bratis, who was found stabbed to death in the Phoenix Park in August 2009. Like Raonaid Murray, she had also suffered horrific injuries and her murder remained unsolved.

Analysis of the text messages suggested that Elaine's killer had done nothing more than fantasize about killing. But at this stage in the enquiry nothing could be ruled out or left to chance. The files on the unsolved murders and the cases of missing women were consulted. It was decided that as soon as Gardaí had a sample of Dwyer's DNA it would be compared to evidence from every outstanding murder case in the Garda files.

In the meantime the phone found in Vartry Reservoir had been brought to the Forensic Science Laboratory at Garda HQ. The Nokia handset had been severely water-damaged and was covered in mud. Sergeant Niall Duffy took it apart and cleaned the circuit board and SIM card with solvent, water and a fibre brush. The phone and the SIM were then placed in a warm incubator to dry. The number of the recovered phone was 086 17x xxx1. It had just one number in the contacts: 086 17x xxx6, which was saved under the name 'mstr'. This second phone had not yet been located. Gardaí discovered that both numbers were purchased, together with two Nokia handsets, at an O2 store on Grafton Street at 4.30 p.m. on 30 November 2011. They believed that Dwyer bought the two phones and gave one of them to his victim on the same date. The detectives concluded that he bought the two phones as part of his ultimate plan to murder her and was covering his tracks.

The investigating team concluded that the recovered

phone was most likely the one seen in Elaine O'Hara's hand when she left her apartment for the last time on 22 August 2012. Cell site analysis and the record of where credit top-ups were bought were consistent with Elaine's neighbourhood. On the day she went missing she had recorded the 'mstr' number in her iPhone as 'David S 2 phonr'. In doing so, Elaine had left another clue.

Phone records showed the Nokia phones had been used for the sole purpose of contacting each other and a total of 1,369 text messages were exchanged between them up to the day Elaine vanished. 'Mstr', the investigators concluded, was short for 'master' and this was the phone likely to have been used by Dwyer. Phone analysis also showed that the contacts between the Goroon phone and Elaine O'Hara's iPhone dwindled after the purchase of the new phones. Investigators downloaded the text traffic on the phone found in the reservoir but only a small number of texts were recovered because, unlike smartphones, the Nokia handset could not store a large amount of data. To complete the picture the Gardaí needed to find the 'master' phone and its SIM card.

On the same day that the officers in Blackrock Garda Station identified Graham Dwyer from the text messages, another important piece of corroborative evidence landed on Peter Woods' desk. Crime and policing analyst Sarah Skedd's role was to sift through all the evidence and information gathered so far in the investigation for connections that might throw up important new leads or suggestions as to where Gardaí might look. This included the collection of texts, emails, cell site data, CCTV footage and phone bills. She focused on the use of phone masts to narrow down who had been using the Goroon and 'master' phones.

Skedd noticed that on 4 July 2012 the 'master' phone was picked up on a mobile phone mast in Galway City in the morning and in South Dublin later that afternoon. There was a gap of two hours and eleven minutes, suggesting that the owner had used the motorway. That meant the owner would have had to pass through toll booths on the M4 and M6 motorways. On 25 September she contacted Detective Superintendent J. J. Keane with a request. She wanted the toll data covering vehicles travelling from Galway to Dublin on 4 July 2012 between 12.30 p.m. and 2.15 p.m. He contacted the toll companies.

When she received the data on 27 September, Sarah Skedd began checking the details of every car that passed through the M4 toll at Enfield, County Kildare, one hour after passing through the M6 toll at Ballinasloe in County Galway. Having already established that whoever was using either the Goroon or 'master' phone was most likely living in South Dublin, she ran each registration plate through the Garda database, looking for anyone with a South Dublin address. A blue Audi TT, number plate 99 G 11850, was the only car that met her search criteria. The car was registered to a Graham Dwyer of Foxrock, County Dublin. Skedd arrived at her conclusion about the same time as the main investigation team in Blackrock: when Peter Woods phoned J. J. Keane to let him know that the team had a suspect, Keane asked whether it was a Graham Dwyer, as Sarah Skedd had picked him out from toll data twenty minutes earlier.

Once Graham Dwyer had been identified as a suspect, Sarah Skedd began looking at the data with new eyes. Armed with Dwyer's work phone details, she quickly established a direct connection between that phone and those in the hands of Elaine's killer – the Goroon and 'master' phones. She found that wherever Dwyer's work phone went it was shadowed by the two unregistered phones. In the two areas where the Goroon and 'master' phones recorded the heaviest traffic – central Dublin and South Dublin – they used the same transmission masts as Dwyer's work phone. The most used cell site for the work phone and the two unregistered phones was a mast at the ESB HQ building in Fitzwilliam Square, 400 metres from Dwyer's workplace at 23 Lower Baggot Street. In one period the work phone used the same mast 952 times while the 'master' phone used the same mast 941 times. The shops where call credit top-ups had been bought for the various phones were close to either Dwyer's office or his home.

Sarah Skedd then isolated the unregistered phones to see if they could be found using any other mobile masts outside Dublin. On 5 and 6 July 2012 – the two days after Dwyer's trip to Galway – the 'master' phone and his work phone were both detected using masts in Ballyshannon and Bundoran in County Donegal. A similar analysis of the toll road traffic showed his Audi TT going through the barriers at the same time as the phones.

On 7 and 8 July the 'master' and work phones were recorded pinging off masts in Bandon, Limerick Junction and Tipperary. Dwyer had travelled home to see his parents and stayed overnight, and the following day he attended a model aircraft event in County Tipperary. The evidence was piling up.

*

Over the days following the initial breakthrough the team examining the CCTV footage at Belarmine Plaza had identified Dwyer in ten clips on dates in January, April, June, July and August 2012. There was the one in which he was in the company of the murdered woman. In two clips, from 13 and 15 August 2012, they identified him arriving and leaving with a rucksack that looked identical to the one retrieved from Vartry Reservoir. And now the cell site analysis of the phones also confirmed a connection between the 'master' and work phones and Dwyer's arrival at Elaine's apartment building. One eagle-eyed officer viewing the footage noticed that on one occasion the phone in Elaine's hand lit up as she was walking from the lift. When the date and time of the clip was cross-referenced with the cell site analysis, it showed that she had received a text from the 'master' phone, which was using the nearest mast to Belarmine Plaza. The message said that he was a few minutes away. Dwyer could then be seen walking into the lobby.

While phone records could be used to determine the location of the phones, and the frequency of traffic between them, only the 'master' phone and its SIM card could reveal the texts that it sent and received. Chief Superintendent Diarmuid O'Sullivan authorized the Garda Water Unit to conduct a second, more intensive, search of Vartry Reservoir. A five-member team returned to Sally's Bridge on 7 October and this time carried out a fingertip search along the bed of the reservoir with the aid of an underwater metal detector.

Within an hour of the search commencing, the metal detector pinged. Garda Lorcan Byrne found the cover of a black Nokia mobile phone, two mobile phone batteries, a black single-opening ski mask and two black anal plugs. The search continued and a short distance away Garda Eoin Ferriter found several items, including a Nokia mobile phone, a SIM card and a pair of glasses. The members of the investigation team keeping watch from the bridge above were sure it was the 'master' phone. It was put into a tamper-proof evidence container and rushed to Garda HQ. The murder enquiry had just made another major breakthrough.

On the same day, Detective Garda Paul Kane, one of two officers whose job it was to build the investigation file and compile the book of evidence, made another important discovery. He had been analysing the bill records for Graham Dwyer's official work phone – 087 2xx xxx7 – between 2006 and 2012. As he studied the data he found that between 1 January 2008 and 4 December 2009, a total of 847 text messages were sent from Dwyer's work phone to Elaine's personal number, 086 3xx xxx7. While the content of the text messages had long since evaporated into cyberspace, it meant that Graham Dwyer could not deny knowing Elaine O'Hara.

A technical investigation of an entirely different complexion that was central to the case was an investigation into Dublin's BDSM subculture. It was a first for the Gardaí involved, and quite an eye-opener. What they found was a thriving community of fetishists across Dublin. They discovered the scene had its own vernacular and was populated by people who categorized themselves as masters and doms, slaves and submissives. The slaves or subs preferred to be tied up, chained, gagged and humiliated; the masters and doms did the tying up, chaining and abusing. In the BDSM world, conventional sex was labelled 'vanilla'. The officers met ordinary people – the vast majority middle-class and upper-class professionals – from all walks of life, including the worlds of politics, public service, medicine, the law, the media and academia.

The officers sometimes found it difficult to hide their amazement at what people in powerful positions of responsibility and influence liked to get up to in their free time. It was striking that their investigation was taking place at a time when, on foot of the phenomenal global success of the *Fifty Shades* series of erotic novels, the imagery and language of BDSM had become mainstream. The E. L. James novels depicted a love affair between a naive young student, Anastasia Steele, and a charismatic business tycoon, Christian Grey, that revolved around Anastasia's initiation into and partial acceptance of Christian's BDSM sexual practices. For some the massive appeal of the books suggested that behind the drapes in quiet suburbia there existed a huge appetite for unorthodox sex. Others argued that the novels were simply old-fashioned romances with a lot of kinky sex thrown in. Whatever the case, it was undeniable that the novels had taken BDSM out of the world of sex shops, specialist clubs and fetish sites and brought it into the public gaze.

The Internet revolutionized the world of alternative sexual practices. Before its advent it was difficult for those with marginal or extreme sexual preferences to meet like-minded individuals. They were forced to suppress their inclinations and remain underground. The digital age changed that and meant that those interested in BDSM could form networks with rules of engagement and indulge fantasies that would otherwise have gone unrequited. Now those who shared specialized interests could meet in private settings where there were agreed safety measures and accepted limits of behaviour. Inevitably, however, given the amount of role play and fake violence that was part of many BDSM 'play' scenarios and relationships, it allowed someone with real murderous desire to hide in plain sight.

Despite the language that participants in the scene liked to use – they spoke of lifestyle choices and freedom of expression – the officers could not help but think that there had been no protection for a vulnerable woman who was looking for love and attention. Elaine had strayed from the crowd and into the path of a predator.

From what the cyber detectives in the CCIU could establish online, it appeared that Graham Dwyer became involved in the BDSM scene through dedicated websites as far back as July 2005. It seemed that he had been secretly pursuing his interests in more extreme forms of sexual activity from early in his marriage and hooking up with women online to meet for bondage and S&M sessions. He found Elaine O'Hara in 2007. Detectives were of the view that he had been stalking the websites until he found a candidate – a suitably vulnerable, malleable individual – with the potential to fulfil his darkest fantasies.

Elaine O'Hara's online participation in Dublin's BDSM world could be traced back to 2006. As Detective Garda Brid Wallace had searched Elaine's computers, she identified several men Elaine had encountered in chat rooms and through websites, especially Alt.com. She passed their details to the investigation team in Blackrock. The men interviewed by the Gardaí were traced through emails they had exchanged with Elaine or their numbers being found on her phone. Among these were the eight men who had already been interviewed after she went missing in 2012. All the men who were approached agreed to give statements. In their statements the previous year two men had described meeting Elaine but backing away when they discovered she was into more extreme acts of bondage and sadomasochism than they were. In this more extensive trawl the Gardaí did not find anyone else who had met her.

Brid Wallace concluded from her investigations that Graham Dwyer had used two profiles on the Alt.com website, 'architect77' and 'architect72' (Dwyer was born in 1972). She noticed that Elaine had viewed the 'architect77' profile on 25, 26 and 31 October in 2007, and again on 7 and 11 November of the same year. In Elaine's eircom.net account she also found references to fetishboy@gmail.com, gdwyer@gmail.com and submissive391@gmail.com. In a subfolder called 'Google local search history' she found searches for 'Graham Dwyer architect', 'Wejchert', and the same name spelled incorrectly. Using the email address submissive391@gmail.com, Elaine had emailed 'architect72' at fetishboy@gmail.com.

An email from 'fetishboy' to 'submissive391' dated 19 September 2008 contained the kind of language that was now familiar to the investigators. Although the words were soft, they were undoubtedly written by the man who had used the Goroon phone. Four years before Elaine's death, 'fetishboy' was gently offering to help her end it all.

> I hope you are keeping ok. I've assumed you are trying to get better and trying to stay away from what we do together. Just so you know I'm always thinking of you and hoping you are safe and not suffering too much in the inside.

Anytime you want, I will gladly carry out what I promised I would do, regardless of the consequences. All you have to do is ring me from a call box and say where and when, even if it's months or years away. I am always waiting. Get in touch any time you want to for a chat or even for the simple, harmless things you want to do. Take care x Sir.

7. 'Go Down to Shore and Wait'

Though it had lain in mud and water for over a year, the phone taken from the bed of Vartry Reservoir on 7 October was not destroyed. The specialists attached to the Garda Telecommunications Unit at Garda HQ succeeded in resuscitating the phone and getting its SIM card working. It was confirmed as having the number 086 17x xxx6, the number that had been saved as 'mstr' in the contacts of the first phone they had found. When it was switched on the phone had just one number saved, that of the first phone, which was listed in contacts as 'slv', or slave.

Phone records had already shown them that a total of 1,369 texts had been sent between the 'master' and 'slave' phones between December 2011 and 22 August 2012. The content of the vast majority of the messages had long since evaporated into cyberspace. Text messages are stored in two places on a mobile phone: on the SIM card and in the memory space in the actual phone handset. Generally SIM cards retain only a small number of texts and the built-in memory of the 'master' and 'slave' handsets had much more limited storage space than smartphones. Investigators could only recover a total of 268 texts from the two phones and the SIM cards. Nevertheless, the retrieved texts provided vital evidence as they recorded the exchanges between Dwyer and Elaine in the days leading up to her disappearance.

They provided the chilling narrative for the end of Elaine O'Hara's life.

On 20 August – two days before she was due to be discharged from St Edmundsbury Hospital after a five-and-a-half-week stay – Dwyer was checking in, making sure that she was ready for their reunion.

MASTER: Morning slave, looking forward to seeing you Wednesday.

SLAVE: I'm not being stabbed.

MASTER: Ok, but you must take some sort of punishment.

SLAVE: I know.

MASTER: What kind of punishment would you like? Choices are hard anal with stabbing and choking. Whipping till bleeding. Chained overnight in forest. Choked unconscious. If you don't pick one then it's all four.

SLAVE: I don't know sir. Sorry doc came in. Sir u know I can't make choices.

MASTER: Ok overnight in woods.

SLAVE: Sir, I'll take stabbing.

MASTER: Ok but I must see blood.

SLAVE: Ok.

MASTER: And I want to do it outdoors.

SLAVE: Please sir, indoors.

MASTER: Why?

SLAVE: I'm afraid if outdoors you might kill me.

MASTER: I won't kill you. If I was it would be indoor hanging once you are chained up.

SLAVE: I know, I mean that's it, nothing else?

A few hours later Elaine texts the master informing him that she is attending the Tall Ships Festival. She also has a request.

SLAVE: I was wondering if you could keep the visual marks to a min sir, please?
MASTER: That's a big request. But Ok.
SLAVE: Thank you sir, I appreciate it. I can cover wrists and arms, it's the neck sir.
MASTER: Don't worry I wont stab you in the neck.
SLAVE: Maybe not but you want to.

On Tuesday, 21 August 2012 at 10.27 a.m.:

SLAVE: R u mad at me sir?
MASTER: No but you must be punished for trying to kill yourself without me and for being unavailable for so long.
SLAVE: Yes sir, I know. Master needs to punish slave.
MASTER: I'm going to get blood on my knife for this alot of blood then we can move on.
SLAVE: Yes sir.
MASTER: That's my good slave. Master is very horny and needs to put his cock in his slave.
SLAVE: Master, may I ask you something?
MASTER: Yes but don't upset me before I am about to cut you.
SLAVE: Do you go by the Gorean way and is it just a fantasy Gorean I mean?
MASTER: It's a real lifestyle that people really live by. Yes you are my slave but I need you to be serving me

not stuck in hospital. I wish I could fuck you on my lunch break.

SLAVE: How do we do that master?

MASTER: You need to get out of hospital and serve me.

SLAVE: Yes master im out tomorrow sir. It will be after lunch as the doc wants to see after lunch at 2.30 b4 I go.

The master then brings the conversation back to the subject of suicide.

MASTER: Are u happy going on like this forever?

SLAVE: Sir, please stop. You want me to be in here forever! Can't we just have a normal master slave relationship without this please sir.

MASTER: Ok but you must promise me next time you fall down that I end you. Hopefully you will be Ok though.

SLAVE: Ok, I promise sir.

MASTER: I mean it now. I will get into trouble if I don't do it at this stage

SLAVE: What do you mean? How could you get into trouble? It's suicide. It's fucking suicide. Don't be troubling yourself. It's suicide! No one will look into it

MASTER: I want to watch as well and be there for you so you won't be lonely.

SLAVE: Shit. That's shit. I am lonely all the time and you're not there that's how I get like this. You just want a hard on. You're being fucking selfish!

A few minutes later she resumes her submission.

SLAVE: Sir, sorry. Just get angry talking about it. I just want to try again. Be a good person/slave/friend and I want to try and have a normal life without talking and thinking about that. Please let me try.

MASTER: Ok.

Later that afternoon:

MASTER: It's up to me and you have a big punishment coming up, getting knifed in the guts

SLAVE: I know sir. I better be tied up good sir. Please not outdoors, please

MASTER: I know. You will be well bound and gagged and tied to a tree deep in the forest. I have a spot picked out.

SLAVE: What if we get caught?

MASTER: We won't get caught.

SLAVE: I'm not leaving my apartment. You will have to drag me out.

MASTER: You will do what you are fucking told. I want outdoor play and you are going to follow instructions or I will double punishment or hang you.

SLAVE: How do you know we won't get caught.

MASTER: I found a really really remote place. No one will find us

SLAVE: Sir, do I have to be naked!

MASTER: It's very deep in the forest and yes you do. I don't want blood over your clothes.

SLAVE: Now I'm terrified!

MASTER: Trust me it will be exciting.

SLAVE: Sure sir. So what time do u want me from tomorrow sir? I was going to go see my niece before I went home as they are hols next two weeks!

MASTER: 5.30.

SLAVE: Yes sir.

SLAVE: Do I have to drive sir?

MASTER: A bit yes.

SLAVE: Now I'm really scared and I have to meet my counsellor.

MASTER: Don't be scared look forward to being reunited with master.

SLAVE: I'm trying sir. Just in case ur wondering sir you never came up in conversation with counsellor.

MASTER: That's good no one should know about me.

SLAVE: They don't know specifically about u. Just in general.

MASTER: Like what?

SLAVE: Like I meet people for BDSM.

MASTER: Ok that's cool they would still find me way back in your emails and alt history if you went missing so relax.

The last text on 21 August is sent from the 'master' to the 'slave' phone at 5 p.m.

MASTER: I'm heading out to the spot now to double check.

The cell site analysis showed that both Dwyer's work phone and the 'master' phone were initially detected on the mast on the ESB building in Fitzwilliam Square and sometime later on a mast in the Killakee area of Rathfarnham.

22 August 2012: Elaine O'Hara is due to be discharged from St Edmundsbury at 11 a.m.

SLAVE: This place although a pain in the ass at times is safe because I know what's coming and I don't want to leave.

MASTER: It will be ok. Trust me. When you say you know what's coming what do you mean?

SLAVE: Well tonight and the talk about killing and stuff but at the mo mainly tonight I'm just so scared. Did you know sir that I'm scared of you. You have this hold over me that terrifies me.

MASTER: That's good for you to feel owned and that your life is in my hands every time you submit to me. I love that, thank you. Do not fear death

SLAVE: Sir can I ask a favour?

MASTER: Yes.

SLAVE: Please don't mention killing for a while until I settle back to life. Please sir.

MASTER: Fine. But tonight's punishment will be like me pretending to do someone for real ok?

SLAVE: Ok thank you Sir.

MASTER: And it's important to me that you feel like it is my right to take my slaves life if I want to.

SLAVE: Yes Master, it is your right.

MASTER: Good slave. Every time I stab or strangle you, I want you to think this is it. And every time I let you live you owe me your life and are grateful and worship me.

SLAVE: Yes Master. Can you stop talking about it. I know my life is in your hands every time we meet that's why I am scared every time you come, even when your not there, please sir.

MASTER: Ok. Looking forward to tonight. X

A few hours later:

SLAVE: Got out earlier than expected so on way home now. It's official I'm out.

MASTER: Well done, I'm delighted.

SLAVE: Any instructions sir?

MASTER: Have a bath, make sure cunt is shaved, no under wear not even a bra, loose clothes, footwear for bit of mud. Make sure you are fed, take painkiller at 5pm.

SLAVE: Sir. Can I do what I want until I am needed?

MASTER: Like what?

SLAVE: I don't know yet, just anything I want to do.

MASTER: Sure enjoy a tiny bit of freedom. You will be in a lot of pain later and next few days.

SLAVE: Sir, it's going to be that bad? I'm really busy next few days with the Tall Ships. Please don't make it really sore. Please.

MASTER: You will have stab wounds you know the drill. Last few didn't bleed but these will.

SLAVE: Sir how many?

MASTER: As many as I like.

SLAVE: Yes sir.

At 12.50 p.m. the CCTV footage at the apartment block showed Elaine O'Hara walking back into the lobby after dumping something in the bins outside. At that moment the master texted her again, telling her where to go later.

MASTER: I want you to park at Shanganagh Cemetery at 5.30, leave your iPhone at home just bring slave phone and keys. You will get further instructions there.

SLAVE: Sir are we doing this if it's raining? And Sir are you coming to apartment after as if so I need to clean.

MASTER: Yes if it's raining and no I won't be back at your place.

SLAVE: Yes Sir. No offence sir, but do we have to do it in rain. It's cold.

MASTER: Yes we do.

MASTER: Don't worry, it's never as bad as you think it's going to be. :-)

SLAVE: Yes it is Sir.

There was a break in the text exchange, during which time Elaine O'Hara spent her last few hours in the company of her father and her niece. At 4.24 p.m. Elaine drove her car into the parking lot under her apartment building. As she was walking inside she received another reassuring message from the master.

MASTER: Just don't be nervous and enjoy being told what to do.

SLAVE: Easier said than done sir.

MASTER: Just empty yourself and become nothing.

> You are property, a piece of slave meat. Your only job is to serve.

At 4.55 p.m. Graham Dwyer's work phone was last detected pinging off the mast on the ESB building close to his office. It appeared to have been switched off.

> SLAVE: Can I wear socks with my runners and can I bring my inhaler. Didn't have time to eat Sir. Will we be late back Sir?
>
> MASTER: Yes to socks, you can leave inhaler in car. You should be back at car about 8. More painful getting stabbed on empty stomach, suit yourself. See you in a bit. X

At 5.05 p.m. the CCTV cameras recorded Elaine leaving her apartment for the last time. As she hurried back to the car for her dreaded appointment, she sent another text to the master.

> SLAVE: Sir do they close the recycling place in Shanganagh?
>
> MASTER: Stay in outer bit on way in.
>
> SLAVE: Sir alot of the kids I work with live around here.

At 5.22 p.m. Elaine parked her car as instructed on the road leading into Shanganagh Cemetery. Cell site analysis placed the 'master' phone in the area of the park at this time.

> SLAVE: Here Sir. Please let me take my inhaler sir.

MASTER: Ok, take only keys and slave phone make your way on foot to park next door and text from middle.
SLAVE: Ok.
SLAVE: Ok sir is the park with playing fields. The top park or bottom?
MASTER: Ok cross railway bridge into next park near cliffs.
SLAVE: I'm lost I'm in football field now.
MASTER: Look for railway footbridge.

It was here that Elaine approached jogger Conor Guilfoyle in Shanganagh Park to ask for directions to the footbridge. He remembered how she appeared distant and preoccupied.

SLAVE: OK here. Sir where's the park?
MASTER: Cross bridge and head for opposite end of park near steps to sea.
SLAVE: OK on the footpath yes no?
MASTER: Yes.
SLAVE: Steps here.

At 6 p.m. Elaine O'Hara received the final text:

MASTER: Go down to shore and wait.

After that last terse command both the 'master' and 'slave' phones went dead. The Garda investigation team believed that within an hour of that last message Graham Dwyer had achieved his ultimate fantasy and Elaine O'Hara lay dead on the floor of a damp forest, having sustained an unknown number of stab wounds. Those six words were the culmination of a story told through 2,612 text messages spread over seventeen months.

It didn't take a clairvoyant to figure out what had happened after Elaine received her final instruction. On the other side of the footbridge over the railway, a footpath skirts around the outer rim of the park. The path leads to an exit between the arches of an old railway bridge. Beyond the exit a short lane ends with steps that lead down to Shanganagh beach. A small road called Quinn's Road is the only access point. Graham Dwyer would have been keeping watch from his car, and when the coast was clear he went to the shore and beckoned his victim. Elaine got into the car and he drove off towards the mountains, using a route he had reconnoitred to ensure he wasn't picked up on CCTV cameras. Avoiding detection was something he often referred to in his texts. In Killakee, because the gate was locked, they most likely walked into the wooded area, a spot they had probably visited before.

Apart from Graham Dwyer, no one will ever know what passed between them, or exactly how many times he stabbed Elaine or how she died. The only thing that is sure is that it happened within a three-hour time frame. Dwyer's work phone, which was last detected in the city centre at 4.55 p.m., pinged back to life at 8.59 p.m. when it used the mast closest to his home in Foxrock.

As they continued to build their case, members of the investigation team drove all the available routes between Shanganagh Park and Killakee Wood, to establish roughly how long it had taken him. The journey from Quinn's Road to Killakee would have taken about thirty minutes. The return journey from there to his home in Foxrock, across the mountains via Vartry Reservoir, would have taken another fifty-five minutes without stopping. They concluded that his long-anticipated murder ritual had probably lasted no longer than one hour.

Towards the middle of October 2013, the Gardaí began planning Dwyer's arrest. The investigating team had uncovered a huge amount of evidence – albeit circumstantial evidence – that would have to be put to Dwyer. They believed that they had enough evidence to sustain a murder charge but recognized that a lot would ride on how the interrogation was conducted and how Dwyer responded. The undercover Gardaí who had been shadowing Dwyer noted that he was still showing no signs of pressure. Despite the ongoing publicity surrounding the case, including the fact that Gardaí had recovered the mobile phones he had dumped, he continued to appear totally detached from what was unfolding. One detective recalls, 'He really was as cool as ice and was showing no reaction of any kind. Normally even the coolest customer will display some sign of pressure or be nervously trying to cover his tracks. Not with Dwyer. Even from a distance we could see the arrogance and confidence in him that he would not be caught. He was a textbook psychopath.'

In the weeks before they made their move, a Garda who was a qualified psychologist worked on a profile of Dwyer for the investigators and those who would be assigned to interrogate him. With all the evidence and available information about his demeanour, she allayed the detectives' fears that Dwyer might turn on his family if he felt he was in danger of being caught. She said that Gemma Dwyer was a 'trophy wife', the key to Dwyer's respectable façade, and he would not do anything to jeopardize that relationship. She also told her colleagues she was confident that his wife had no knowledge of her husband's predilections and dark secrets. She advised them that Dwyer was a narcissist who would consider himself to be much smarter than the cops when he was arrested.

Chief Superintendent Diarmuid O'Sullivan convened a conference with the investigation team and they decided they had enough to arrest Graham Dwyer. The plan was to lift him on the morning of 17 October 2013 – one month after the investigation had been launched.

8. Arrest

Around the time the Killakee landowner Frank Doyle had called the Gardaí to report the presence of human remains on his land, down in the city a couple were leaving their house for a night out. And by the time Gardaí were draping blue-and-white crime-scene tape around the clearing in Cruagh Wood where the remains lay, the couple had taken their table in a trendy Mexican restaurant on George's Street in Dublin city centre. It was a mutual celebration because that Friday night – 13 September – was the date of both their birthdays. Later that night, as a Garda stood watch over the scene in Killakee, Graham and Gemma Dwyer had a few after-dinner drinks in town and then took the Luas home. Now, just over a month later, the days of arranging babysitters and sharing celebrations and swapping happy memories over dinners in town were about to come to a shattering end.

In the three weeks since Dwyer had been identified there had been intensive preparation for his arrest and on this the appointed morning the officers had gathered at six o'clock for a final briefing. This was their D-Day; they were finally going to come face-to-face with the man in the shadows. Over forty members of the investigation team were present in the incident room in Blackrock, where a large picture of Elaine O'Hara was pinned to the wall as a constant reminder of what all this was about.

Every aspect of the impending swoop had been planned

with near military precision. The assembled group was subdivided into three separate teams. Detective Sergeant Peter Woods and Detective Garda James Mulligan were to carry out Dwyer's arrest. Sergeant Brian O'Keeffe and nine Gardaí were assigned to conduct a search of Dwyer's home. An eleven-member search team under the command of Sergeant Kevin Duggan – including Detective Garda Brid Wallace and Cliff Cullen of the CCIU – was to be dispatched to search the offices of A&D Wejchert. The previous day Sergeant O'Keeffe had obtained two search warrants in Dun Laoghaire District Court.

Chief Superintendent Diarmuid O'Sullivan emphasized to the gathering that the searches were vital to the next stage of the investigation. The man they were about to confront was considered too dangerous to be released pending further enquiries. So the searches had to be meticulous and nothing could be overlooked. They needed to find evidence that corroborated material in the various phones, as well as any DNA traces that might connect Dwyer to his victim. The whole investigation now hinged on what would happen in the next twenty-four hours.

Other pairs of detectives, all trained interviewers, would approach potential witnesses after 9 a.m., once Dwyer was in custody. No witnesses had been contacted before this for fear Dwyer would be alerted. Officers were on their way to Donegal to approach Dwyer's former partner Emer McShea and their son Sennan before they went to work. Any information gleaned from the searches and the interviews was to be relayed back to Blackrock station, where it could then be put to the suspect. Gardaí had also traced a number of cars Dwyer had sold in the past two years – one of his hobbies was buying and selling high-performance cars. As soon as the arrest was out of the way the new owners were to be approached and the vehicles seized for forensic examination. Tow wagons had been booked for 9 a.m.

The squad sent to arrest Graham Dwyer and search his home for evidence arrived at the end of the leafy cul-de-sac in a small convoy of unmarked squad cars at 7 a.m. on Thursday 17 October. There were no sirens, blue lights or screeching tyres. The dozen members of the investigation team stepped out of their cars quietly, trying to avoid waking up the neighbourhood where people would soon be heading off to work and school. The only evidence that they were police were the jackets they wore, with 'Garda' emblazoned in yellow letters across the back. There was no rush because they knew the suspect was inside. The undercover surveillance officers had secretly escorted him home the previous evening and he had not stirred out since. There would be no forced entry, shouting or brandishing of weapons. But as Detective Sergeant Peter Woods and his colleagues opened the wrought-iron gates and walked silently towards the house, their presence was just as dramatic and calamitous for those inside as a full-on raid.

As Peter Woods and Brian O'Keeffe stepped up to the locked patio doors at the front of the house, some Gardaí went to the back and the rest stood around behind their two sergeants. They wore latex gloves and they held bundles of evidence bags under their arms. Their instructions were that the search operation would go on for as long as it took. A tow truck had also been ordered to take away the family's two cars for forensic examination.

Peter Woods rang the doorbell at 7.06 a.m. A couple of minutes later Graham Dwyer appeared in pyjama bottoms and T-shirt. He produced keys and opened the door. Detective Sergeant Woods held up his Garda badge and identified himself.

'Can I come in?'

Dwyer appeared confused and nodded: 'Yes, come in.'

'Are you Graham Dwyer?'

When Dwyer nodded, the detective looked into his face and put a hand on his shoulder. 'Graham Dwyer, I am arresting you on suspicion of the murder of Elaine O'Hara on 22 August 2012. Do you understand?'

Dwyer seemed stunned. 'I don't know what you are talking about.'

'You are not obliged to say anything unless you wish to do so and whatever you say will be taken down in writing and may be given in evidence against you.'

Gemma Dwyer came to the door and asked her husband what was going on. Their two children were asleep upstairs. Sergeant O'Keeffe and Garda Jennifer Quinn then entered the house and showed Gemma Dwyer a warrant authorizing them to search it. She took the document in trembling hands and tried to focus on what it said.

Peter Woods told Dwyer to get dressed because he was taking him to Blackrock Garda Station. The sergeant escorted Dwyer upstairs and waited as he dressed in silence and used the bathroom. Downstairs the search team began filing into the house. As they were leaving, Dwyer remembered his wallet and phone. Woods brought him back to the bedroom to get them and then held his hand out for them, telling Dwyer he would look after them until they were finished. After a moment of hesitation, Dwyer handed them over without protest.

'Is there anything in the house connected with the murder?' Woods asked.

'No.' Dwyer seemed astonished.

Woods brought Dwyer to the back garden to open the combination locks on two sheds so they could be searched. Peter Woods and James Mulligan then escorted him to a waiting squad car.

On their way to Blackrock, Woods sat beside Dwyer. He broke the silence by advising the suspect that he needed a solicitor and asked if he had one. The architect said he knew none.

'You're under arrest for the most serious crime there is. You need to contact a solicitor and you need to instruct them,' he said.

'I can't afford one,' Dwyer replied gruffly as he looked out of the window. Woods said the officer in charge at the station would get him one.

Meanwhile Gemma Dwyer, who was still in shock, got her children up and dressed. The detectives were courteous and sympathetic but they needed them out of the house while the search was going on. They initially approached Mrs Dwyer with caution. They could not tell her what was going on until she sat down with them to give a statement, which she agreed to do. She organized care for the children and was then brought to a location away from Garda stations where she was to be interviewed by specialist officers over several hours. Though the psychological advice was that Gemma Dwyer was extremely unlikely to know about her husband's dark side, the detectives needed to confirm this. But Gemma

Dwyer was distraught and it became clear very quickly that she knew nothing. She made arrangements to stay with family members. (She would never return to the house at Kerrymount Close. When she learned the full details of what her husband was accused of, her marriage effectively ended. Graham Dwyer would not see her again until she gave evidence in his trial. He would not see his children again.)

When the first keyholder arrived at the offices of A&D Wejchert, he was met by Sergeant Kevin Duggan and his search team. Duggan produced a warrant and ten Gardaí filed in, asking to be shown to Graham Dwyer's work station. Over the following hours the officers took away two laptops, memory sticks, computer towers, mobile phone records and reams of documents. Dwyer's business partners were also shocked and stunned. He had been due to make a presentation later that morning to important clients.

The Gardaí and Dwyer arrived at Blackrock station at 7.41 a.m. where he was formally detained by Sergeant Gordon Woulfe, who opened a custody record. 'Graham John Richard Dwyer,' Dwyer replied when asked for his full name. Dwyer seemed to have recovered from the shock of his arrest and came across as cocky and confident. As Sergeant Woulfe made out the custody record, Dwyer twice ignored him when he asked if he had any aliases or nicknames. Eventually he said: 'Smiler' – a name likely inspired by his distinctive downcast mouth. When asked his height, he said 'Five feet ten' with a sneer; he was clearly nowhere near that height. But Woulfe duly entered in five feet ten. When asked had he consumed any alcohol, Dwyer said: 'One rum last night.'

Sergeant Woulfe then contacted a local legal-aid solicitor, Jonathan Dunphy, on Dwyer's behalf. Woulfe read Dwyer his rights and informed him that he was being detained under Section 4 of the Criminal Justice Act 1984 and could be held for an initial six hours. He was then brought to another room to be searched. His belt was removed and his pockets emptied. Sergeant Woulfe arranged to have him photographed and fingerprinted and to have a cheek swab taken for DNA analysis. Dwyer asked if he could phone his office to inform them he wouldn't be in for work but Peter Woods refused permission.

Dwyer was brought to a holding cell until his solicitor arrived. At 8.20 a.m. Woods met Jonathan Dunphy in the station but declined to give the solicitor any details of the Gardaí's evidence against his new client. He did not want Dwyer forearmed with any knowledge of what they had uncovered, and it was up to Dwyer to instruct Dunphy, not the Gardaí. He brought the solicitor to the holding cell and introduced him to his new client. Woods handed Dwyer a cup of coffee and left him to have a consultation with the solicitor.

At 9.30 a.m. Dwyer was brought into an interview room by Peter Woods and James Mulligan. Woods was the obvious choice to lead the questioning. He was a Level 4 interviewer, the highest qualification a police interrogator can achieve, had attended several internationally accredited interrogation courses, and he lectured young detectives in interview techniques at the Garda training college. The role of a Level 4 interviewer is usually to act as overall supervisor to the trained detectives conducting interviews, the most experienced of whom are classified as Level 3. But this was an unusual case, and as the officer coordinating the mammoth investigation he was the one most familiar with all the evidence gathered so far. James Mulligan was a Level 3 interviewer who had been at Woods' side since the investigation began. The interview plan was that he would assist in the questioning by taking memos of everything that was said, which would also be recorded. The custody sergeant, Gordon Woulfe, gave Mulligan tapes to put into the audio-visual recording equipment. Before the interview commenced, Woulfe read Dwyer the legislation authorizing the electronic recording of interviews. This procedure would be carried out before each interview session. They would make three copies of each set of recordings: a master copy that would go into a sealed bag; a copy that would be provided to Dwyer's solicitor; and a copy that would be used by the Gardaí. As there was then no right for a suspect in Ireland to have a lawyer present during questioning, Jonathan Dunphy was not in the interview room.

It was likely that Dwyer had no idea that Elaine had backed up the vital text messages or that the phones he dumped in Vartry had given up their secrets. The messages had been assembled into several volumes. Sarah Skedd had drawn up extensive diagrams and charts outlining the cell site analysis and the connections between the various phones. The CCTV stills featuring Dwyer at Elaine's apartment block were also printed. Everything had been prepared to present to Dwyer and organized in the order that it would be revealed. The intention was to unveil the information to him gradually as the interviews progressed.

Woods' plan was to adopt a conversational style to put Dwyer at ease and gradually pry out the information needed to corroborate the evidence. He asked Dwyer if he knew why he had been arrested and told him that he could be held for a maximum of twenty-four hours.

'That's unlikely,' Dwyer said.

Peter Woods asked the first question: 'Did you know Elaine O'Hara?'

'I didn't kill anybody,' Dwyer snapped back.

Woods: 'So you didn't kill anybody?'

Dwyer: 'No . . . I know what you're getting at . . . I don't want to kill anybody. I'm worried about my wife and job.'

Peter Woods asked if he had read anything about the murder in the media.

'I did. I read papers and breaking news online so I am aware of it,' he said.

Woods asked him what he had heard.

Dwyer said: 'The various things they found, a woman's body and stuff. The body was found in Rathfarnham and the other stuff in Roundwood, I think. She had been missing. I would have read everything about everything. I wouldn't retain it.'

He said he had read the coverage 'every day' since the discovery of the body but then 'it died a bit'.

'You're not a person who comes into contact with the guards?' Woods continued in his conversational style. Dwyer said that he sometimes drank in the company of guards and mentioned the names of officers he knew from growing up in Cork and through his wife's family.

Peter Woods asked him about his son in Donegal. Dwyer said that Sennan lived in Letterkenny and that he had been up there on different occasions for work and to visit. He described how he had first met Emer McShea in college and how their relationship had become 'quite adversarial'. He said they were last in touch in 2007 or 2008, 'around the time Sennan got cancer'. He said he stopped paying maintenance when his son left college.

The conversation moved on to his finances. Dwyer said that he and his wife were 'deeply in debt'. They had bought the house in Foxrock with a view to renovating it and then the economic crash happened. 'Gemma lost her job and I had huge pay cuts,' he said.

Woods and Mulligan discussed with Dwyer his love of cars and the type of cars he owned, his workplace, his office routine, IT training and projects he had worked on – including in Poland. He gave the dates when his son and daughter were born and their routine at home. All apparently innocuous chat. It must have seemed like small talk to Dwyer. But the questions were designed to elicit corroborating information.

For instance, he volunteered that his sister lived in County Tipperary and that he sometimes popped in to see her on his way to Cork. Woods asked his sister's address. 'Oak something, I'm not sure. Clerihan,' he said. Oak Lawn, Clerihan, Tipperary, was the address 'Goroon' had provided when he bought the phone in March 2011.

Woods asked: 'What's your hobby?'

Dwyer said it was flying model aeroplanes and that Roundwood, Shankill and Laois were the main three clubs to which he was affiliated. It was a subject he was comfortable talking about, and he said that he had travelled around the country to various competitions and was 'progressing well'. Woods asked whether it was expensive. 'I haven't had a crash,' Dwyer replied.

Peter Woods probed more about his family, his educational

background and how he had started studying architecture. He moved back to the subject of pay cuts, which had also preoccupied the Goroon phone owner.

'They started when I bought the house. I took pay cuts every three months; the last was ten grand in January 2013,' Dwyer said. He talked about the property tax and Woods asked if he looked at Myhome.ie, to which he said: 'A little bit.'

'Do you know any local estate agents?' Woods asked.

'No,' Dwyer replied.

Peter Woods asked the suspect what sort of private work – 'nixers' – he took on.

'House extensions, friends or people I'm recommended to; sometimes you get paid and sometimes you get vouched.'

Woods asked Dwyer again about his planes and whether he had done well in any competitions.

'Second or third, a few events this year,' he said.

Woods asked him about the previous year.

'Very little,' he said.

Woods asked if Shankill was his first club. Dwyer said that it was his main club, and more recently Roundwood, for the longer runways.

'Are there sheep in Roundwood?' A text from the Goroon phone was about the thrill of stabbing a sheep to death close to his flying club.

Dwyer: 'No, the odd deer . . . my fear is to crash.'

Asked about work projects, Dwyer described working in Mullingar, Leopardstown, Carlow and a private house in Galway, which corroborated several aspects of the cell site analysis. In all these locations Dwyer's work phone had been shadowed by either the Goroon or 'master' phone.

Detective Sergeant Woods began discussing investigative

techniques with his suspect, including DNA and genetic codes.

'I would love to know why I am connected with this,' Dwyer said.

Woods: 'Do you have a twin brother?'

Dwyer: 'Unless my parents haven't told me, I don't know. You probably know I don't have a twin brother.'

Woods continued to talk about DNA evidence and its importance in a case. Dwyer became uncomfortable. 'I understand all of this. I didn't kill anybody so why am I here? I want to know why I am here and when I can go home. I don't mind giving my DNA, I didn't kill anybody.'

The detective sergeant then talked about the gathering of soil samples. He explained forensic anthropology and how pathologists could date how long a body had been lying in a particular place and how marks made on bones by bullets and knives could establish cause of death.

'It's all fascinating but how does it affect me?' Dwyer said.

'Every contact leaves a trace,' Woods said, adding: 'We will not judge you, Graham.'

'I still don't know what you want to know,' Dwyer said. 'I believe this and I believe the stuff you say, all that is doing is making me concerned about why I am here. When can I go home? I didn't kill anyone. I am not going to be dressed up to match your profile. I am concerned about why I am here. I didn't kill anybody.'

Peter Woods let him calm down and then looked into Dwyer's eyes. 'Do you think we would have arrived at your door without being prepared?'

Then, to pave the way for the introduction of the CCTV

footage later, Woods moved on to Belarmine. He asked Dwyer if he had ever visited the area.

'I know it, I have been to the shop there, the one in Stepaside, the one beside a playground,' he admitted.

Woods: 'Why would you be up there?'

Dwyer: 'Driving around, buying a bottle of Coke.'

Woods: 'Is that Belarmine?'

Dwyer: 'Yes, the playground is there. Look, I would do anything to help you but the advice I got was: "If you didn't kill anybody, say you didn't kill anybody." I'm worried the newspapers will say: "Architect arrested for murder." I don't know if you are doing some sort of psychology, I didn't kill anybody . . . I had nothing to do with it. I want to go home.'

Woods: 'I think maybe you should talk to your solicitor again and if you did know Elaine O'Hara you should tell me . . . Are we going to connect you?'

Dwyer: 'I don't know, I do know I didn't kill anybody. I don't want to be associated with it. Will I have a wife if I am associated with it? Who will employ me?'

Woods offered some advice: 'You have big decisions to make. Don't make them based on your standing in the community.'

'I know,' he said.

Peter Woods told Dwyer that the Gardaí had a clear picture of Elaine O'Hara's mental health and her hopes and plans at the time she vanished. Woods said it was 'sad her body was found in such a place'.

'It's tragic,' Dwyer said.

Woods told Dwyer that they also knew a huge amount about Elaine's sexual history. 'What Elaine O'Hara did sexually is her own business. We don't judge anyone,' Woods said, before repeating: 'Everything leaves a trace.'

Dwyer suddenly seemed interested: 'I'm listening.'

Peter Woods said that the Gardaí had compiled a full list of the dead woman's contacts and who she met through her interest in BDSM.

'Somebody's private life should be their private life,' Dwyer said.

Woods then asked him if he knew what had been recovered from Vartry Reservoir.

Dwyer went into defensive mode: 'I don't want to be on any tabloids. If I was even remotely associated with this I would jump in the river, if I wasn't able to have my wife's trust and my job.'

Woods: 'Does your wife trust you?'

Dwyer: 'I'm a very lucky man, I want to keep it, I have had bad relationships and I want to keep Gemma.'

Woods: 'We have very strong evidence. How do you think we came to your door?'

Dwyer: 'I wouldn't like to guess, I have made my decision. I didn't kill anybody.'

By 12.53 p.m. Dwyer had been in custody for nearly six hours. Peter Woods suspended the interview and left the room to ask Superintendent John Hand to extend the detention by a further six hours under Section 4 of the Criminal Justice Act 1984. James Mulligan then read a memo of the interview to Dwyer and asked him if it was correct. Dwyer said: 'I would say so, yeah, that is pretty good.'

He was asked if he wanted to add anything, which was his right. Dwyer said: 'A lot of it isn't relevant.' He could not have been more wrong.

Dwyer was returned to his cell and had a McDonald's meal and a chocolate bar, washed down with a Diet Coke. At 1.40 p.m. his solicitor arrived and spent nearly an hour with him.

Throughout the morning Dwyer had the demeanour of a man mystified and deeply aggrieved that he could be associated with such an appalling crime. He had seemed concerned only with the implications his arrest would have on his life: his marriage, his job and his reputation. As he tried to convince his interviewers that he didn't know her, he displayed no concern for or interest in Elaine O'Hara. To an experienced investigator like Peter Woods this strongly indicated that he was talking to a guilty man. An innocent man would at least look for more detail about the person whose death had led to his arrest, and how that death had happened, and be anxious to clear up the misunderstanding.

Woods had investigated many murders and pried the truth out of many killers, including some of the hardest criminals in the business, but he had never encountered the likes of Graham Dwyer. There was an element of condescension in his attitude, as if Gardaí were further down the social food chain than he and didn't quite understand his position, and he seemed confident that they had nothing on him. But for Woods and his colleagues that first interview was just the warm-up before the match proper.

9. 'That's Not My Phone'

When the second interview began at 2.30 p.m. Dwyer was angry. 'I'm not happy, I spoke to my solicitor and my wife has been asked to go to a Garda station and my family have been contacted and it's spread like wildfire. It has been in the media. I am upset at what I heard is being leaked from the case.'

'This is not a case, it is a murder enquiry,' Peter Woods said, adding that his wife had been taken to a safe location.

'I did not murder Elaine O'Hara . . . I did not murder Elaine O'Hara,' Dwyer said.

Peter Woods asked Dwyer if he had been at a construction site in Leopardstown a lot. Dwyer said 'varying times' but that he could clear this up with his work diary.

'We have probably lost that job now it's out. I would like to know how my life has been ruined by this case. How can I help you?' Dwyer asked.

Woods asked if he remembered where he was on 22 August 2012.

'No,' Dwyer replied.

Peter Woods and Dwyer talked freely about holidays and Dwyer's fortieth birthday, which had fallen three weeks after Elaine's disappearance. He asked him if he had got 'anything big'.

'We are very poor. I got a guitar and we all chipped in for the meal,' he said.

Woods asked if he had been in a band.

'Yes, I was in a rock band,' Dwyer said.

Was he any good?

'No.'

What kind of music did he like?

'Depeche Mode, all kinds of bands.'

'U2?'

'Yeah.'

'Dire Straits?'

'Not so much.'

In further casual conversation Dwyer volunteered that he had bought a bicycle under a government tax incentive scheme. The owner of the Goroon phone had informed Elaine O'Hara that he had bought a bike so that he could 'get fit for murder'.

Dwyer said there were time sheets in his workplace that showed what was on every day and where everyone was. Peter Woods asked whether it would show if he was missing from work.

'No, but if I went flying she'd call me,' he said, referring to the office manager, adding the record would show he had taken a half day.

Dwyer said he occasionally socialized with his colleagues and at lunchtime would 'wander down Grafton Street', naming several shops he'd visited. This was another useful circumstantial detail – the 'master', 'slave' and Goroon phones were all bought on Grafton Street.

He said his daughter was 'lovely' and that he was 'very close' to his younger son.

He told Woods that he had been visiting an 'old school friend since junior infants' who lived in Stepaside and maintained the friend was 'the only person I know up there'.

Peter Woods then produced a picture of Elaine O'Hara.

'I see that,' Dwyer said, adding: 'I won't tell any lies and I won't give any mistruths, I'm not a killer, I'm not a saint.'

Woods told Dwyer that they were there to help him tell his side.

'If my family and job are not the same I've nothing to live for,' Dwyer said.

Peter Woods talked about the role played by mobile phones in major criminal investigations and how they could be tracked. He gave the example of Joe O'Reilly, who was convicted of the murder of his wife Rachel in 2004. The case against O'Reilly had rested largely on evidence about the movement and locations of his mobile phone on the day of the murder. Woods presented a report that had been compiled by analyst Sarah Skedd, which showed how the five phones at the centre of the investigation – Elaine O'Hara's phone, Dwyer's work phone and the 'master', 'slave' and Goroon phones – had been tracked through cell site analysis.

'When did she go missing? Where was my phone that day?' Dwyer said.

Woods then produced a series of stills from the CCTV footage at Belarmine Plaza taken on 23 June 2011. In the clip Dwyer had entered the apartment complex ten minutes after Elaine O'Hara had arrived home at 6.54 p.m., and left again at 8.18 p.m. Woods put the stills on the wall of the interview room for Dwyer to look at. On the opposite wall he placed a large diagram containing the phone analysis of that evening. It had images of five generic phones, representing the five phones that were in use at various times, and arrows indicating the connections between them and the location of the devices at various times.

'I'm glad I'm not murdering anyone in any of those pictures,' Dwyer said.

'Where did you think your phone was?' Woods asked, referring to the Skedd document, which had a record of him making a call on his work phone just after leaving Elaine O'Hara's apartment block.

Dwyer: 'I've no idea.'

Woods: 'Belarmine Plaza . . . less than two minutes after you leave the building.'

Dwyer: 'I didn't kill anybody. Is anyone else on the CCTV?'

The detective referred again to the phone records and CCTV analysis and said that Dwyer's phone pinged off a mast in Stepaside. He produced yet another still from 23 June, showing Dwyer leaving after over an hour.

'They are meaningless to me, I didn't murder anybody,' he protested.

Woods showed him a further CCTV still from that evening, this time of Elaine O'Hara entering Belarmine Plaza.

'I'm not going to remember these,' Dwyer continued, as if it were a nuisance.

Woods then showed him a still from another date. It showed a man he maintained was Dwyer leaving Belarmine Plaza at 8.02 p.m. and told him his phone was pinging off the mast at Tree Rock in the foothills of the Dublin Mountains at the time.

'What's that mean?' Dwyer said.

Woods: 'It means it [Dwyer's work phone] was in the area and you said it's with you all the time. Remember I told you that every contact leaves a trace? We can follow you when your phone is switched on.'

Dwyer: 'I'm sorry I said that now if you're going to do this.'

Detective Sergeant Woods asked him if he should get more advice from his solicitor.

'I told you I'd been up there . . . I never denied being up there or Belarmine Plaza. Has anyone else been arrested for murder?' Dwyer said.

He said that he had been in the shop at Belarmine 'more than once' even though it was off the beaten track.

Peter Woods returned to the cell site analysis and Dwyer's work phone pinging off the mast at Stepaside station at the same time as the Goroon and 'master' phones.

'How far apart are the masts? Where's the closest mast to my house?' Dwyer asked, peering closer at the wall chart.

Detective Sergeant Woods raised the purchase of the Goroon phone – 083 1xx xxx4 –bought in a Three Store on Grafton Street on 25 March 2011.

'I've never had that phone,' he said.

Peter Woods told him that the device had been bought by a Goroon Caisholm, who gave the address Oak Lawn, Clerihan, Tipperary, and also gave the number 086 2xx xxx7 – just like Dwyer's number but for one digit in the prefix.

'That's an 086 . . .That's my sister's address. I don't know what to say to that.'

He denied knowing anyone called Goroon Caisholm.

Woods told him that the Goroon number also pinged off a mast at Belarmine Plaza as well as one at the Rochestown Lodge Hotel, the mast his work phone used when he was at home. He asked Dwyer about the purchase of the 'master' and 'slave' phones from the O2 shop on Grafton Street on 30 November 2011.

'They're not my numbers,' Dwyer said.

Woods then asked Dwyer if he had visited adult websites and if he had contacted Elaine O'Hara through one.

'I can see why you knocked on my door, that's better . . . I didn't kill anyone.'

Avoiding Woods' question about contacting Elaine O'Hara, Dwyer said he knew from media reports that she had been in hospital. Both directly and indirectly he was maintaining the position of knowing of her only through media coverage of the case.

Peter Woods said he believed that Dwyer had had one of the phones and Elaine O'Hara the other.

'Absolutely meaningless to me. I can see why I'm a person of interest. You're making huge assumptions. I would like you to use your phone technology to see where my phone was.'

Woods probed Dwyer about where he went in his cars and about the locations where several top-ups were bought for the unregistered phone numbers.

Dwyer complained again that his arrest was being reported in the media and that he had been missing from work for the day.

Woods said: 'Just because you're arrested doesn't mean you're guilty, Graham.'

Dwyer: 'I didn't kill anybody.'

At 7.03 p.m. Peter Woods left the room to talk to Chief Superintendent Diarmuid O'Sullivan. O'Sullivan was keeping an open line to the Director of Public Prosecutions' office. He and other key members of the investigative team had been monitoring the interviews on a screen in Woods' office. The interview was going to plan: Dwyer had already confirmed several important details that would go a long way to convincing the DPP to charge him. The response to each innocuous question provided another block in the wall of evidence. The chief superintendent authorized Dwyer's period of detention to be extended for another twelve hours once the initial twelve hours had expired. Dwyer was informed of this by the custody sergeant, Gordon Woulfe.

'Do I have to stay the night here?' Dwyer looked aghast. Sergeant Woulfe explained that he would be entitled to suspend his interviews for sleep for eight hours. The following morning the eight hours would be added to his detention period. Dwyer wasn't happy and asked to see his solicitor. In the meantime he had another McDonald's meal and a twenty-minute walk around the station yard.

Shortly before the third interview commenced, Jonathan Dunphy met Peter Woods and complained about the continuing media coverage of his client's arrest – the story was all over the news. The solicitor said he was learning more about his client's detention from media coverage than from the police. Woods stuck to his guns, informing the lawyer that the law did not require the Gardaí to give him a briefing on the evidence they had against his client. He told Dunphy that it was a matter for Graham Dwyer and Dwyer's conscience.

For a third time James Mulligan put new tapes into the recording equipment. They were expecting this to be the final interview of the night. Again they cautioned him. Dwyer confirmed that he had spoken to his solicitor four times since his arrest and that he understood why he was being held. Woods asked if he wanted to say anything.

'No, not at this time,' he said. The detective sergeant then asked if he wanted to say anything in relation to Elaine O'Hara.

'No, not at this time but you know . . . no, not at this time.' Dwyer hesitated momentarily, as if unsure of what he wanted to say.

Woods presented him with a document detailing the top five cell sites used by his phone, the Goroon phone and Elaine's phone.

'Do you see a pattern?' Woods said.

'I don't,' he replied.

Woods asked him about his phone pinging on certain masts, including in Cashel in County Tipperary and Three Rock in South Dublin, on specified dates.

'I would like to know how big the areas are,' he said.

Peter Woods drew his attention to the phone diagram on the wall and read out the numbers of the 'master' and 'slave' phones.

'Do you know anything about master and slave?'

Dwyer shifted in his seat. 'Not at this time . . . I am thinking about my wife and kids. I didn't kill anyone. I know that.'

Peter Woods read over cell site information from 7 and 8 July 2012 and put it to Dwyer that on those dates he was flying in Carron, County Tipperary.

'We know you were there,' Woods said, adding that the 'master' phone was detected at the same time in the same area.

'I do know that is not my phone.'

Peter Woods told Dwyer that Elaine O'Hara had backed up her iPhone, including her text exchanges, to a laptop the Gardaí had seized. When he began reading the lurid messages, Dwyer tried to hide his shock. It looked like the penny had finally dropped and he realized what all the small talk had been about in the previous two interviews.

Detective Sergeant Woods read the texts from 'sir' to Elaine in which he referred to the birth of his daughter. Woods suggested that it was an extraordinary coincidence that the mysterious master's wife also gave birth to a daughter with the same name at the same time.

'That's not me . . . that's not my phone,' Dwyer said, growing more agitated.

Woods started reading the hundreds of text messages the investigation team had assembled specifically for the interrogation.

'Jesus. That's not me . . . that's not my phone,' he said over and over, like a mantra, as if trying to fend off what he was hearing.

When Woods read the texts outlining the plot to abduct and murder the 'young female estate agent' Rowena Quinn, Dwyer recoiled.

'Who is this supposed to be? Who is this supposed to be from?'

Peter Woods looked at him hard. 'It's you,' he said, before looking down to continue reading the material. He told Dwyer that the number of the Goroon phone was entered in Elaine O'Hara's diary next to 'Graham's number'.

'It's not me . . . I can't explain that, that is my name . . . it's not my phone, it doesn't make sense,' he said.

The detective sergeant read another text about an Asian woman who lived in an apartment next to Elaine's in which Goroon had described strangling her unconscious in a lift and then burying the body.

'I am sorry, guys, that is not my phone.'

Peter Woods decided to raise the tempo some more: 'You have a stabbing fetish, don't you?'

'Oh my God, that is not my phone.'

Woods read a text from the Goroon phone describing a meeting with the Polish ambassador. In the earlier interview Dwyer had spoken openly about meeting the diplomat and having worked extensively with the Polish embassy.

'You did ask me that, yeah.'

Woods read another text in which Goroon advised his victim to wear polo necks to cover up her stab wounds.

Woods: 'Aren't you wearing a polo neck?'

Dwyer: 'Everyone who knows me knows I wear polo necks.'

A text from the master including the line 'I would have preferred you died by knife' made Dwyer wince.

'That is awful stuff.'

Another including the words 'Killing is my new goal' made him gasp.

'Jesus.'

Peter Woods was getting into his stride. Dwyer shifted around in his seat, putting his head in his hands as if trying to block out what he was hearing.

'Look, that isn't me, please stop. It's not me . . . I'm mortified, it's awful.'

Since the early-morning raid the Garda computer experts had been searching through his phone and computers for more evidence. They discovered that the previous night Dwyer had been watching a snuff movie depicting a woman being stabbed to death. So Peter Woods asked him what he had been watching at home the night before. Dwyer appeared surprised at the question.

'Horror movies,' he said meekly.

Woods: 'I wouldn't say it was horror . . . describe it to me.'

Dwyer: 'Horror scenes from horror movies. Erotic horror, it's sort of art to do with horror. Please stop. I am thinking of my wife and kids. My private life is my private life, please stop. I'm mortified to describe it. I didn't kill anyone. I'm not guilty of any crime.'

Woods: 'How could you get sexual pleasure from that kind of material?'

Dwyer: 'I don't know, I believe you are trying to shock me, upset me.'

Woods resumed reading the text messages. Dwyer continued to express horror. Then he quipped: 'This is really not turning me on . . . do you want to check?'

The detective sergeant continued reading. When he got to the one where 'sir' is telling Elaine of his plan to stab her to death and then bury her, Dwyer began to crack.

'Fucking hell, that's nuts . . . Oh my God, who is that from? That's not me . . . you are trying to disgust me. I can't explain these things.'

After hearing further material from this exchange, Dwyer erupted again. 'You said it excites me, do I have an erection? I don't want to hear any more about rape and murder. There are some things I can't explain.'

Woods looked up. 'Do you like blood?'

Dwyer: 'No, not particularly . . . I'm not commenting on my sex life. Anyone who knows me knows I wouldn't hurt anybody.'

Woods pressed harder, asking him to explain BDSM and the role of master and slave. 'Do you see yourself as a master?'

'This is the most private thing. I can't talk about it. Please respect that. I would be very uncomfortable. I would like to preserve my marriage, thank you very much.'

Woods and Mulligan, and those watching on the monitors elsewhere, noticed how Dwyer still completely ignored Elaine O'Hara. It was as if she had never existed.

Woods resumed reading the texts, ignoring Dwyer's pleas for him to 'stop, please stop'. His strategy was working out just as he had planned: Dwyer was clearly feeling the pressure.

'These phones are masking your phone . . . they are both together,' Woods said.

Dwyer: 'Oh my God, that's not my phone. Please stop, they are not relevant.'

Woods: 'They are very relevant.'

Dwyer: 'You are trying to shock me.'

Woods: 'Is it a shock that we have them? What does "assume the position" mean?' This was a reference to a line that appeared hundreds of times in the texts as the master instructed Elaine to be ready for his arrival at her apartment.

Dwyer: 'I am upset. I really don't want you to read any more. I have asked you a hundred times to stop.'

Peter Woods' plan was all about timing. And as the night wore on he had an ace up his sleeve. The visit to Dwyer's former partner Emer McShea earlier in the day had thrown up a powerful piece of evidence. When she had talked to the detectives that morning, Ms McShea had shared some devastating information about Graham Dwyer. She told them that when she and Dwyer were living together in Dublin in the early 1990s after the birth of their son, Sennan, Dwyer had told her that his fantasy was to stab a woman while having sex. After that he began bringing a kitchen knife into their bedroom during sex. At first he would leave it on the floor but then he began holding it. She told the officers that while he never actually stabbed her, having the knife close by appeared to be the only way that by then he could achieve sexual gratification.

The sudden appearance of the detectives on her doorstep had allowed Emer McShea to unburden herself. She had been living in fear of her former boyfriend for twenty years. Everything she told the cops corresponded with the profile of Dwyer the detectives had assembled from his text messages to Elaine O'Hara.

Emer McShea and her son had both identified Dwyer in the CCTV stills taken from Belarmine Plaza. They said that he hated smoking, a recurring theme of the Goroon and 'master' texts, and described a row he had had with Sennan about smoking on his fifteenth birthday that led to the police being called. They confirmed that he had visited Sennan in Donegal in early July 2012, confirming the cell site analysis showing the 'master' phone and Dwyer's work phone using masts in Ballyshannon and Bundoran on 5 and 6 July 2012.

When Peter Woods told Dwyer about the interview with his former girlfriend he looked uncomfortable.

'She wouldn't be friendly to me,' he said, as if to discredit her statement in advance.

Woods began reading from the lengthy statement that set out Emer McShea's experiences with Dwyer during their four-year relationship. When he arrived at the part about Dwyer bringing the knife into their bed, the architect flinched.

'Oh my God.'

Woods stopped reading and looked across the table: 'Do you want to say something?'

Dwyer: 'I'd say she enjoyed that, she's delighted I am in trouble.'

Woods: 'Is she telling lies about you pretending to stab someone during sex?'

Dwyer: 'Ask my wife . . . er . . . Don't ask my wife . . . please, please get back to the murder.'

As the third interview neared its conclusion, Woods produced the rucksack and other BDSM paraphernalia found in Vartry Reservoir. He then showed Dwyer a still from the CCTV footage in which he could be seen leaving Elaine's apartment block with the same type of bag. Dwyer implied that he knew who owned the bag but would say nothing more.

'How stupid of you,' Woods said. 'You thought you had committed the perfect crime.'

There was a final shock in store for Dwyer. Earlier in the evening the Forensic Science Laboratory had phoned the incident room in Blackrock to say that the DNA sample taken from Dwyer that morning matched a semen stain on Elaine O'Hara's mattress. When Peter Woods told Dwyer they had found a match for his DNA in Elaine's apartment, he tried to bluff it out.

'I can understand how it could be there but I didn't kill anybody.' He spoke as if he were being backed into a corner. 'I wouldn't be surprised if you find my hair or fingerprints there but nothing of a sexual nature. I'm not an innocent man but I'm innocent of murder. I really don't want to talk because of my wife and family. It's not sexual, it's not the stuff you are reading out, people are planning stuff. I'm confident I didn't kill anybody and I'm relying on that.'

Woods told Dwyer that the sample came from a semen

stain from Elaine's mattress, a mattress that had multiple puncture holes. He had been caught out in a major lie: throughout the interviews his position was that he didn't know Elaine O'Hara, but here was compelling evidence to the contrary. How could he continue denying that he knew her? The self-assurance that Dwyer had first carried into the interview room had all but disappeared.

'I will not air my dirty laundry here, if it's going beyond here. I think I know what's coming next. I don't want my wife hurt. I know I didn't murder anyone.'

Woods: 'I cannot make you any promises or give you any guarantees about that. But I still want you to tell me.'

Dwyer: 'What do you think is the likelihood of my laundry being aired? I am terrified of all this being aired. I didn't kill anyone.'

Peter Woods advised Dwyer that he should talk to his solicitor. At 11 p.m. he had asked the custody sergeant to ring Jonathan Dunphy and request him to come to the station. At 11.20 p.m. James Mulligan began reading over the memo of the interview. When Mulligan finished reading and asked Dwyer if he had anything to add, he objected to the inclusion of the text messages.

'The stuff in the middle was unnecessary,' he said.

For the first time since he had first spoken to Dwyer nearly seventeen hours earlier, Peter Woods allowed himself to show a brief flash of anger. He stared at Dwyer and snapped: 'That stuff in the middle was absolutely vital.'

Outside the interview room Peter Woods spoke to Dwyer's solicitor and informed him that he was invoking inferences under Section 19A of the Criminal Justice Act 1984 as amended in the Criminal Justice Act 2007. This occurs where a suspect fails to mention a fact that he may later wish to raise in his defence. The fact was that Graham Dwyer had known Elaine O'Hara and had failed to mention it.

At 11.51 p.m. Dwyer declined an offer to have his questioning suspended for the night. It appeared that he just wanted to get the nightmare over with. He still seemed confident that he would be going home and that the police had nothing on him. Dwyer's decision was unexpected and upstairs Chief Superintendent O'Sullivan got on the phone to the on-duty lawyer in the DPP's office. He told the lawyer to stand by because they would need a decision on charges sooner than anticipated.

10. Murder Charge

At 12.57 a.m. James Mulligan installed fresh tapes in the recording equipment and he and Peter Woods started their fourth interview with Graham Dwyer. Woods cautioned Dwyer, reminded him of the reason for his detention and asked if he had anything to say. Dwyer said: 'I didn't do any murder, I didn't kill anybody.' But there was a noticeable change in his demeanour. After hours of jousting with Peter Woods it finally seemed to be dawning on him that he was out of his depth.

Woods asked him about the extreme acts described in the texts and if that was part of his lifestyle.

'Rape and murder? No,' Dwyer said.

Then came the first crack in his façade. Woods returned to the CCTV footage of Dwyer carrying a rucksack out of Belarmine Plaza on 13 and 15 August 2012. Dwyer said it was not his, but added: 'I know who owns the bag.'

Woods: 'So you said you know who owns the bag . . . who?'

Dwyer: 'Elaine O'Hara owns the bag. That is Elaine's bag. She used to keep BDSM gear in it, she used to meet men for BDSM things.'

He admitted then that it was him in the CCTV stills hanging on the interview room wall and that he was carrying the bag from the reservoir. This was a significant admission. Dwyer had now linked himself to the material found in Vartry Reservoir. In another office in Blackrock station

Diarmuid O'Sullivan was phoning the on-duty lawyer in the DPP's office to explain the most recent admissions. The lawyer said he would review the material and get back to him. In the meantime he wanted to be informed of any more developments.

Meanwhile in the interview room Peter Woods asked Dwyer what he was doing at Belarmine on 15 August. Dwyer said: 'She was in hospital, yes? She may have wanted to move it while she was in hospital because she was afraid her father would find it.' Dwyer could not explain how he got into Elaine's apartment and denied he had a key.

Detective Sergeant Woods asked him how he had met Elaine. 'Through BDSM websites. I'm not a big part of the scene. I didn't want to say because of my wife,' he said.

Woods asked when he met her.

'A long time ago on Alt.com when I would have been called "architect". People on it were honest and genuine.'

Woods: 'Did you go to fetish nights?'

Dwyer: 'No . . . I am mortified over this.'

Woods: 'Was Elaine a slave?'

Dwyer: 'A slave would like to wash my shoes and I don't think she wanted that. I believe she had some mental health problems. I became aware she was heavily scarred, she had been cutting herself with a box cutter. I remember I would say "not for me" . . . she wanted to be chained all the time. She was deeper into it than me. She was deadly serious about not wanting to have any control over her situation.'

Woods: 'What would you meet her for?'

Dwyer: 'I suppose I wanted to meet her because I was stuck. We met a few times over the years. She wanted to be chained up. I was hoping to try sex, but she wasn't very attractive. She would start to describe what she wanted to do and I would do it. She wanted to be chained up, tied up. There came a point when she cut herself and there was fresh blood. I am fascinated with all that, but it's not a turn-on.'

Woods: 'It's not?'

Dwyer: 'It's not for me. For a long time I wouldn't describe it as part of my character. I would be fascinated by it and horrified too.'

Dwyer said he would not cut anybody and was not into bloodletting. 'It's fantasy, make-believe,' he insisted. He said he only contacted Elaine through his work phone and continued to deny any connection with the other phones.

He said: 'The ultimate thing with Elaine was she wanted to be kept all day in a cage with a bowl of water . . . she was scarred from head to toe.'

Woods: 'Did she ask you to do anything else?'

Dwyer: 'At one stage she asked me if I would kill her . . .I know she was sad. It was a cycle, there were patterns of depression.'

Woods: 'When she asked you to kill her how did that make you feel?'

Dwyer: 'She asked that if I did kill her, if she could be hung so her father would find her. It's a big ask. My father always said if he suffered a stroke to push him off the Old Head [of Kinsale].'

Woods: 'She asked you to kill her?'

Dwyer: 'Years ago.'

Woods: 'Is that a fantasy of yours.'

Dwyer: 'I would say no, it's in the horror movies, it isn't in BDSM. We have safe words, we didn't use them. She didn't like sex, made it clear that sex hurt her. All she wanted was to be in a position of no control. If you do something to a girl and she isn't signed up, you are in big trouble. I am here in big trouble and I didn't do anything.'

Woods: 'What was in it for you?'

Dwyer: 'It's a perfect scenario, you wouldn't have to go through all the bullshit of dating.'

Woods: 'What did you do?'

Dwyer: 'Did I have sex? Yes.'

Woods: 'It wasn't vanilla?'

Dwyer: 'It kind of is but she is incapacitated.'

Woods: 'Are you totally dominant?'

Dwyer: 'I'm not in general but you would be expected to be. To me it's fantasy, a short-term thing, but to Elaine, she wanted it full-time.'

Woods: 'Surely it is acting out the fantasy?'

Dwyer: 'I know you are trying to connect my horror movies but it's not, it's a game, it's like acting, there is a sexual element but it's not all about sex. There are specific powers in play where Elaine can be completely helpless. It's escapism, that's what I call it, that's what she wants.'

Woods: 'Is it sadism?'

Dwyer: 'I was very vanilla, I did all that weird stuff but it's not me.'

Peter Woods read through the texts leading up to Elaine's disappearance, including the one from the master on 21 August 2012 in which he said he was going to check out the 'remote place' he had found for their 'play' and that he wouldn't kill Elaine because he would still be found way back in her emails and Alt.com history.

'Who would they find on the Alt.com history?' Peter Woods asked.

'Lots of people. But that's not me.' Dwyer said.

Referring to the text 'I'm heading out to the spot now to double check', Woods told Dwyer that his work mobile had pinged off masts at Edmondstown Golf Course and a GAA club at Cookstown. 'They cover the area of Killakee, the area where Elaine's body was found.'

'That's a huge leap. Where did you get to the bit where you say I kill somebody?' Dwyer said.

The detective sergeant read the text that referred to 'tonight's punishment', which the master said would be 'like me pretending to do someone for real'. And he read the text in which Elaine asked how many stab wounds she would be getting. Woods asked Dwyer what she meant.

Dwyer: 'That's awful. I'm not into stabbing. Who said that?'

Woods: 'Your ex-partner did.'

Dwyer: 'I think there was some key words dropped to her [McShea], there was a lot of hatred there.'

As Woods continued to read the texts Dwyer fell back on his default refrain: 'That's not me. Please stop referring as if it's me.'

Woods read the texts instructing Elaine O'Hara to go to Shanganagh Park and across the footbridge to the shore.

'Your phone was turned off at the time,' Woods told Dwyer.

'I rarely turn off my phone, could it be my phone is not being used?' Dwyer asked.

Woods read the statement from the jogger who described Elaine seeking directions to the footbridge.

'You were the last person to see her alive,' Woods said.

'Now where did that leap from? How was I the last person

to see her alive if she was murdered?' he said. 'That's awful, it's nothing to do with me.'

Detective Sergeant Woods pressed Dwyer for an explanation of how Elaine's inhaler and glasses ended up with the rucksack in the reservoir.

'I don't know how anything ended up in any reservoir,' he protested. Woods then accused Dwyer of going back again to look at his victim's body. The psychologist had suggested it was likely, based on the fantasies expressed in the text messages, that the killer would have returned at some stage to view his victim and admire his work.

'Ah that's disgusting,' he said. 'Ask my phone, has my phone ever stopped at the reservoir?'

Dwyer confirmed that the knife recovered in the reservoir was part of the gear Elaine kept in the bag and that it was 'possible' he may have held it. Dwyer's admission about the bag and now the knife was hugely significant. It suggested this was the same bag referred to in a text from Goroon to Elaine in July 2011 instructing her to prepare to be stabbed during their next encounter: 'I want you to boil my silver folding knife, your black folding knife and the smallest one in the kill bag for tomorrow and make sure they are out for me when you assume the position.' It looked like he was becoming careless.

Dwyer accepted that the language used on the Goroon and 'master' phones was similar and agreed it was 'sinister'.

When asked how he used to get in touch with Elaine O'Hara's iPhone, he again said: 'I can't explain.'

Woods asked him if he had any alibi for Wednesday, 22 August 2012 between 6 p.m. and 9 p.m.

'I'll have to check.'

As the morning drew on Dwyer said that Elaine O'Hara had not known as much about his life as he knew about hers, but she would have known the names of his children.

'I would say you are looking in the wrong place,' he said.

Dwyer could not recall the last time he had seen Elaine. He did not think he had a key to her apartment and could not explain why he had left there with the bag on 13 and 15 August.

Woods asked him what he thought of Elaine.

'She had serious mental issues,' he said. 'I have to say that language, "Sir", would be her. She was definitely submissive, she wanted to be a 24-hour submissive.'

Asked again about material on his phone, he said it was 'horror mainly'.

Woods: 'Horror being knife wounds on females?'

Dwyer: 'Not specifically.'

Woods: 'Does cutting turn you on?'

Dwyer: 'No, I am interested in horror movies, I like serial killer, apocalypse, sci-fi.'

Woods: 'Is it the fear in you that you like or the fear in others?'

Dwyer: 'All my movies are fantasies, some are based on real events; Zodiac killer, things like that.'

Woods: 'How did the phones get into the reservoir?'

Dwyer: 'I don't know.'

Woods: 'Graham, you do know.'

Dwyer: 'I didn't really kill anybody ever.'

Woods: 'What do you mean by that last comment?'

Dwyer: 'I really didn't kill anybody.'

Woods: 'What did you do with the bag [rucksack]?'

Dwyer: 'I don't know, the bag would always end up back at her place.'

Woods: 'The bag ended up in the reservoir beside her car keys, glasses and the phones.'

Dwyer: 'I can't explain that. You have been suggesting stuff all day and I have been on my toes. I didn't kill Elaine O'Hara.'

The interview ended at 4.54 a.m. after the notes were read back to him.

Detective Sergeant John Colgan from the National Bureau of Criminal Investigation had been brought in to conduct the final interview with Graham Dwyer. As Colgan took his place, Peter Woods and James Mulligan joined Chief Superintendent O'Sullivan and the rest of the investigation team in the incident room. Woods phoned the DPP again and went through the evidence they had to sustain a charge. Across the four interviews Woods had built a wall of strong circumstantial evidence to support the charge of murder by stabbing. Dwyer had confirmed a large amount of the information contained in the Goroon and 'slave' phones. He had also confirmed that he knew Elaine O'Hara and was involved in BDSM with her, and had identified himself on the CCTV footage at her home. Crucially he had also admitted to having had possession of the rucksack that was found in the reservoir, which they now believed to be the 'kill bag' referred to in the text messages. He had described various trips he had taken, supporting the cell site analysis showing the unregistered phones shadowing Dwyer wherever he went. And he had provided his sister's address, which was so similar to the Goroon phone registration details, details that also included a contact number that was the same as his work number but with a different prefix. The DPP would have to consult with colleagues before making a decision. The clock was ticking. Dwyer would have to be released in less than one and a half hours.

Detective Sergeant Colgan's interview began at 5.47 a.m. on 18 October. He questioned Dwyer about material found on his work mobile phone. The initial items were from a YouTube app; the first was called 'Close up stabbing' and the time stamp was 26 May 2013.

'Whatever it says, I go along with that, I don't recall what it is,' Dwyer said.

The next was 'Woman stabbed prison guard', dated 23 April 2013. Dwyer said: 'If the machine says that, I would agree with that. It would be related to horror.'

Two more files were titled 'Stabbing' and 'Stabbing 3'. Dwyer said: 'If the machines say so, you would find that they are extracts from horror movies.'

Two others were titled 'woman strangled' and 'woman strangled yoga', dated 30 May 2013. John Colgan asked if he had accessed these.

'I wouldn't dispute it but I have to say I never strangled anybody,' Dwyer said.

When Colgan asked him about a clip titled 'Woman stab Live Leak', Dwyer said: 'That sounds like a real murder, I think it was a real murder in Russia.' And about a file titled 'Woman strangled by friend', dated 10 June 2013, he said: 'Again, that would be my movie interest, that would be a specific clip. I think it's all drama except the Live Leak stuff.'

Colgan produced a second document. It related to an entry

in the address book of Dwyer's work phone. Under the name 'submissive' there was an email address, 391@gmail.com.

Colgan: 'Can you explain who that is?'

Dwyer: 'Is it Elaine O'Hara?'

Colgan: 'I believe it is.'

Dwyer: 'I was asked for that earlier and I couldn't recall but it was Elaine's.'

A third document put to him contained two images of what appeared to be the same young woman from Lovelydisgrace.com. One was titled '17 year old girl immobilized, gagged and then killed on her bed with more than 80 stab wounds all over her body'.

Dwyer: 'I would have looked at these websites on my laptop, they are gore websites, again concerned with horror.'

Colgan: 'Why do you need to go on these sites?'

Dwyer: 'I can't explain, I know it's sick.'

He was then asked about four small snapshots that were downloaded from his phone. One was of a female breast with cuts and a screwdriver inserted into it. Dwyer said it was a 'horror picture', probably from the same source as the others, and he had not taken them. One picture was of a young girl and another was a 'semi-naked female covered in blood with somebody standing over her in blue shoe covers'.

Detective Sergeant Colgan then asked Dwyer if he had anything to add.

'I have two comments to make. First, I am not guilty of the offence I am being presented with, and second, from what I have heard today and from what I knew before today, there are other people you should talk to as well as me and that is not being done in my opinion.'

Colgan: 'What people?'

Dwyer: 'Anybody else like me who has been in contact with Elaine O'Hara.'

He was asked if he knew the details of any other person.

'I don't know the identities of the men, that is all I have to say,' he said.

The interview finished at 6.50 a.m. and the memo notes were read over to him. When he was asked if he had anything to add, Dwyer was clearly embarrassed and anxious to give an excuse for his extreme tastes.

'I want to record what I said earlier, that it paints a picture of what I look at as a proportion of what I also look at. Please don't present to people that that is all I look at.'

When the interview had ended, the custody sergeant, Gordon Woulfe, gave Dwyer what must have been the best news he had heard since opening his front door almost twenty-four hours earlier: he was being released. A few minutes before 7 a.m., as Dwyer's belongings were being returned to him, Diarmuid O'Sullivan's phone rang. It was the lawyer at the DPP's office. A smile cracked across O'Sullivan's face and with the phone still to his ear he made a thumbs-up gesture to Woods. Woods turned towards the public office. Graham Dwyer was walking towards the exit from Blackrock station at 7.05 a.m. when Peter Woods stood in front of him. Dwyer was going nowhere.

Woods arrested Graham Dwyer for the purpose of charging him with murder contrary to common law. Sergeant Woulfe made out a new custody record and read the prisoner his rights. Dwyer then spent half an hour consulting with his solicitor. At 7.49 a.m. Detective Sergeant Peter Woods formally charged Graham Dwyer with the murder of Elaine

O'Hara. When he asked Dwyer if he had anything to say, he replied: 'Not guilty.' He was returned to the holding cells. Around the same time the Gardaí recommenced the search of Dwyer's home, which had been suspended in the early hours.

Later that morning there was a large media presence outside Dún Laoghaire District Court for the arrival of the squad car bringing Graham Dwyer to be formally charged with the murder of Elaine O'Hara at an unknown location in Dublin on 22 August 2012, the day of her disappearance. Peter Woods gave evidence of arrest, charge and caution.

Dwyer did not speak during the brief hearing. An application for free legal aid was deferred. Woods said he was aware of Dwyer's financial background and had no objection to his application for free legal aid. Judge Bridget Reilly remanded Dwyer in custody to appear at Cloverhill District Court a week later. A few minutes later Graham Dwyer was ushered into a squad car by members of the investigation team. And for the second time in just over twenty-four hours he found himself sitting in the back seat beside Peter Woods, as the car sped off to Cloverhill Prison.

11. Horror Stories

As Graham Dwyer was coming to terms with his incarceration inside the walls of a remand prison, there was no relaxation for the investigation team. Having him charged with murder and locked up in a cell, for the time being at least, was just the second phase in the enquiry. Now they faced the herculean task of corroborating even the smallest, most insignificant pieces of evidence as they prepared the case against him. And Dwyer's success at managing two distinct personalities posed a challenge. They would have to scrutinize every aspect of his life since childhood in a bid to uncover his secrets – and to discover if there were any more victims.

Following her husband's arrest, members of the investigation team spent several hours, over a number of days, taking statements from Gemma Dwyer. What she was being told about him tying up and stabbing a woman while living a normal family life was clearly beyond her comprehension. She remembered nothing unusual or out of the ordinary about his behaviour on the night of Elaine's disappearance – 22 August 2012 – or any other night. Three weeks later she had organized her husband's fortieth birthday in Bandon. They had been in the audience of the *Late Late Show* three months after that. All the normal stuff of family life. She faced the realization that she had shared her aspirations and hopes, her trials and tribulations, her life, with someone she didn't recognize. The father of her two children was now accused of a savage crime. When the enormity of what he had been charged with began to sink in, she was traumatized and broken. The knowledge that her husband had been fantasizing about stabbing women to death while playing the role of a normal husband and dad at home made her physically sick. Her visceral reaction to what Gardaí told her confirmed that Graham Dwyer had not shared his predilections in the sixteen years they had been a couple.

The searches at his home and office uncovered a wealth of evidence to corroborate what the investigators had already put to Dwyer. A total of 219 individual exhibits were seized from the house, as well as a laptop, a badly damaged external Seagate hard drive and two media storage devices. Documents they found confirmed he had taken a 15 per cent pay cut in 2011, something 'sir' had mentioned in a text to Elaine O'Hara. They found a receipt for a bike bought under the Cycle to Work Scheme that tallied with the time and date of the text in which the master said he bought a bike because he 'must get fit for murder'. Invoices confirmed that he had paid almost €4,000 for repairs to an Audi A6 and to a Porsche that his wife said he called his 'baby'. In some of his texts Dwyer had mentioned problems with his cars and Elaine had also referred to one of them as his 'baby'.

This growing wall of evidence was about to be consolidated, thanks to the cyber detectives. The Gardaí shadowing Dwyer in the weeks before his arrest had seen no signs that the discovery of his crime had flustered him. And his demeanour for most of his interrogation suggested he was confident there was no evidence against him. However, Dwyer had taken one precaution after the discovery of Elaine O'Hara's body and the items at Vartry Reservoir: from a home computer he had erased data that he would have difficulty explaining if the Gardaí ever came asking awkward questions. He deleted a secret library of violent pornographic material he had been building for years. But just as he hadn't anticipated the consequences of a long hot summer when he dumped the bag of incriminating evidence off Sally's Bridge on a rainy August night, so he had underestimated the ability of the cyber cops to recover damning information from the depths of his hard drive.

Detective Garda Brid Wallace was unable to get at the hidden contents of the damaged Seagate hard drive. It was sent for repair to Critical Data Services, a specialist computer company. It took several days to fix and two gigabytes of data were eventually recovered. When it was returned to the CCIU, Brid Wallace began exploring Graham Dwyer's secret world. Mingling together in unallocated spaces, next to images of pregnancy scans and family pictures from weddings and christenings, there were clusters of videos and pictures of women being mutilated and strangled. And next to videos of Dwyer flying his model aircraft were scores of downloaded snuff movies featuring rape, bondage and murder. The two types of content told the story of Graham Dwyer's double life.

Brid Wallace found over thirty video clips that had been recorded on a camera phone on dates between 2007 and 2009. One opened with a naked Graham Dwyer looking into the lens of his phone. The camera turned to a knife on a table which he picked up and pretended to use to stab himself in the arm. The knife had a retractable blade and it appeared he used ketchup for effect. In another clip he looked dazed as he held the camera in front of his face and was obviously groggy as he spoke into the lens: 'I'm just after waking up from having knocked myself out with chloroform. I have very little recollection of what happened. I remember exhaling out and getting a warning sign as the blood rushed through my body and waking up with a pounding noise in my head, like a headache and a loud noise.'

Brid Wallace then found film clips featuring Dwyer having sex with various women, each of whom was tied up, chained and gagged. In all of the videos Dwyer stabbed the women during sex, either with a 'play' knife or the real thing. It appeared that none of the women was aware that he was filming them. At least four women, including Elaine O'Hara, featured in the clips. Elaine O'Hara featured more than any of the others. In one she was shown naked and gagged, bent face down on a bed, with her arms tied behind her back. Dwyer, who was also naked, was having sex with her while repeatedly stabbing her in the sides from behind. The gag in her mouth did not stop Elaine screaming in pain. In a clip showing another sex act between them, she was crying out as Dwyer stabbed her and rubbed the knife along her skin. There was a close-up of a male hand drawing a knife across her breast and squeezing as blood seeped from the cut. In another clip Dwyer, who was on top of Elaine, prodded her stomach with a knife during intercourse. He continued until he ejaculated and then said, 'Ssh . . . Now that wasn't bad, was it?' A further clip showed Dwyer kneeling behind Elaine before placing a clear plastic bag over her head and wrapping a cable around her neck to seal it. As she scrambled for breath he tightened the cable until she went limp and fell to one side.

The videos had names such as 'Blood2', 'Attempted breast stab', 'Bloodletting', 'Firststabbing' and 'Thirdstabbing'.

But the Seagate hard drive contained even more hidden horrors. As Brid Wallace continued her search she discovered a Word document labelled '4Darci' and titled 'Killing Darci'. It had been created on 2 March 2011 and edited for eighty-nine minutes before being saved. It appeared to be a fantasy written by Dwyer. (Its content is so extreme that a section is summarized here, rather than being reproduced verbatim.)

> Months had gone by and soon the day would finally arrive. From the first email I knew this one was special. I had always fantasized about killing ever since I was a teenager and I got hard every time I had a knife in my hand, wielding the power, knowing I could decide who lived and died just like my hero God.
>
> Every time I made love I closed my eyes as I pushed myself in, wondering how it would feel for a hard cold steel blade to push itself in destroying all in its path. Every time I came I wondered what opening a throat would feel like spraying and gushing forth death instead of life.
>
> My addiction grew, just like any addiction and soon I met girls who needed pain and suffering as much I needed to give it. Bondage, rape, slashing and stabbing soon became my hobby, acquiring two fine subs over the years, and having role play with many others. I was the lucky one and I knew there were over a hundred men like me for every girl like the ones I played with. Yet I always managed to win them over, partly because I knew exactly what I was doing, and partly because I could show the others what I was capable of.

The scenarios grew and grew and could not satisfy my blood lust. Around the time I first considered crossing the line, one of my subs came to me and asked for the ultimate, to help her die. This was discussed and planned at length, each of us having differing viewpoints. Ultimately, the decision would be hers unless I took that power away from her.

But the trail, the mess, the time, too many loose ends. How many times had our phones ping ponged at the same place at the same time? But yet, now I knew it was in me to do it and now I wanted to do it too.

I thought about stabbing a stranger to satisfy my lust for a while. To take a life in exchange for an orgasm, a memory, a video clip I would watch into my old age over and over again, wielding death.

Having been responsible for creating three lives, wasn't I at least entitled to take just one?

But who?

I considered finding someone suicidal or terminally ill, or both, someone with no ties, who needed the courage to die that I could provide. I knew there were many out there: 400–500 suicides a year in a small country with only 4 million people. Also, if someone takes their own life here, insurances don't pay out if a death by misadventure verdict is recorded. Why not become a random murder victim? You get to die, your family does not blame you, but me. You are free from the sin of taking your life and I carry the sin of killing – very appealing to some.

When she first came into my life I knew her only as 'Cassie'. I was later to learn the significance of this name which only made me fall deeper in love with her. At last I had found someone who ticked all the boxes. Beautiful, young, smart, clear about what she wanted, and critically wanted to die in the same way I wanted to kill. This was a rare marriage indeed.

For weeks we shared images, videos, ideas and worked out the details of how she would come to me and how she would die by my hand in my care, my responsibility, and worked out the details of how she would. It is not a responsibility I shoulder lightly, and I fully understand the depth of work in preparation that was necessary to send her off beautifully, in her finest pose. I have been posting her a few hundred dollars every month here and there, bank transfers, this did a few things for us.

Firstly she could settle her debts, tie up her loose ends, clear her conscience and her mind. Free from material possessions and indebtedness are the largest boulders she would shoulder and I was happy to give her this relief knowing the biggest was yet to come.

She would get a ticket to Boston and a ticket to Dublin and didn't have to work the last couple of weeks so she could visit her old friends, family and spend some time with her beloved dog her brother would take care of. She knew her departing would cause such pain to her mom, brother, and her dad, but it would fade in time and it was a fraction of the pain she carried around with her in her head 24 hours a day.

She came to me with a hand luggage suitcase so as not to arouse suspicion, and wore a silver chain I had posted her. Soon this chain would be mine again after I removed it from her ruined throat. She was happy she had no keys to carry, no phone to carry, no wallet, just some money in her pocket and her favourite outfit. Underneath she wore the special undergarments that would soon be blood soaked and in ribbons around her ankles.

She smiled at me and gave me a huge thank you hug outside the airport, grateful for what I was about to do to her. She rested her head on my arm all the way to the place I had prepared. She gazed at the beautiful green scenery as we drove through the mountains on the back roads.

The sun was setting as we arrived at the cabin. She knew she wouldn't see another sunset. We didn't say much. There was little to say. We had prepared everything in the greatest detail and it was like watching a movie that we had written and directed.

At the cabin we had a meal, one that would never leave her body and she tasted her last favourite food and her last drink. We were nervous, excited, but placid too; we knew nothing could go wrong now. I gave her every opportunity to turn around. She even had a return ticket but this was what she wanted.

I showed her my knife, and she played with it, stroking her skin with it and testing its sharpness. Meanwhile I used her computer to wipe our accounts and she posted her suicide video.

Many people were wondering where she was, that story she gave her family they now knew wasn't true, that she was gone about 12 hours now and people were starting to worry.

When they would see the video they would understand. They might realize she went to Ireland, but it was too late. I was planning to take her clothes and laptop to a popular suicide cliff the next day that she would be missing forever. Her family and friends would think she was somewhere across the Atlantic and think of her lovingly every time they looked out over the sea on the coast of Maine.

It was dark now but there was complete silence, just the wind outside. Without speaking she put on her Ipod [*sic*] speakers which was loaded with a playlist carefully chosen, and as she pressed play I closed my eyes, knowing the sequence and at which song to start the final act.

I carefully undressed and moved my clothes to a clean place in a plastic bag. She did not need to see the shovel, or bags of lime and bottles of bleach I had stored. I was trying to make it as perfect for her as I could. She knew the cameras were on us, but I had moved them back so they wouldn't interfere with what was going to take place.

The last time we embraced, we kissed passionately and made love in stark contrast to the brutal rape she would endure soon, and worse. She cried as she rode me and I stroked her hair and her tears away trying not to mess her perfect makeup. She was so beautiful, so perfect, she turned her back to me when we were finished, and I put on my mask and gloves.

She could hear what I was doing and I heard her fear when I opened my knife and stood behind her. I grabbed her arms roughly, she didn't resist and I tied her tight down over the mattress on the ground which was lying on a sheet of plastic. She knew this was to become her coffin and she rubbed her cheek on it as she squirmed in her underwear.

As my knife drew across her body slowly around her underwear she gasped and shook, afraid of what was to happen but not afraid of when it would end.

She knew He was watching and waiting to take her home to see her gran and her old dog. He did nothing to stop the events that led us here and who wouldn't have wanted such a pretty angel by his side. I knew she would look after me and watch over me after I killed her . . .

In the dozen paragraphs that follow here the author describes the rape, multiple stabbing and killing of his victim in meticulous and graphic detail. Among the actions the author describes is using one of the many wounds he has inflicted as a sexual orifice. After he has stabbed his victim's front so there is nothing but 'a ruined mess of guts and bloody burst organs', he describes her as 'finally free'. He then turns over the body to have sex with it again while repeatedly stabbing its back.

. . . I lay with her for hours as she went cold, her stab wounds didn't bleed as her heart had stopped soon after I slit her throat the first time. I fell asleep on her body like that for hours.

It was dawn when I woke and she was stiff, pale, her body was white with dark blue bruising around the stab wounds, which were pink and oval. All the blood was crispy and matted everywhere, so much of it I thought at least 8 pints.

I removed the silver necklace from around her neck and put it in an old tin box that would soon also contain the memory card from the camera to be kept in a very special place.

I took my last photos and took her body to the bathroom where I washed it lovingly and carefully and went over every inch examining every detail of every place the knife went in, and gazed into her lifeless eyes and into her gaping throat. She would have been proud of me and I hoped she was nearby watching from above. I soaked her body in bleach and laid it on a mattress where I covered it in lime.

I rolled the mattress around the body all sexy and stabbed; her throat slit, the knife gone. I tied her body into the mattress and wrapped the whole thing carefully in plastic and loaded it into the car.

It was a short drive to the spot where I had prepared her grave, a place I would visit many times, and ask forgiveness for what I had done.

THE END.

Brid Wallace found a photoshopped picture in the same folder as the document, depicting a blonde female who appeared to be dead, with multiple stab wounds and her intestines visible. The detective then found another story, this one titled 'Jenny's First Rape' (again, the most graphic content is summarized here):

> It was my first time in Newcastle. The day was sunny and fine. I had flown over to visit the local sites: The Angel of the North, that magnificent piece of engineering crossing the Tyne, but also to visit some of the more contemporary shopping centres and architectural developments to get some ideas from it for my new building back in Dublin.
>
> I also wanted to feed my lust, and was hoping to get to fuck one of Newcastle's finest before getting my flight home. Dressed respectably in casual clothes, no-one would suspect what was on my mind – rape. I had my little overnight bag packed with the usual things: socks, underwear,

spare shirt, laptop, chloroform, rope and of course my hunting knife.

It's difficult to get a knife past security since those pretty young Air hostesses got their throats slit open on 9/11, but I usually find a good hunting shop on my trips abroad.

I thought long and hard of my usual hunting grounds: drugs, girls, drink, in a nightclub, shoving them into my rental van in an underground car park. Speaking of long and hard, my cock was aching to be satisfied and I checked out everyone as a potential victim while walking on the street.

In a small 'burb, about nine miles out of the city, I stumbled upon a huge old bookshop several stories high. I thought, perfect. This is the perfect opportunity to find a timid little flower that will not put up a fight. I felt the scar I got from that wild cat I raped in the bushes of St Stephen's Green back home. I smiled. Happy memories. That will be the last time she will try to grab the knife from someone who is raping her, in fact the last time she would do anything.

I entered the bookshop, no one looked at me, or felt I was out of place in this intellectual mass maze of a building. I picked up a book and strolled around, glancing occasionally over the book at medium girls browsing, finally coming to the top floor. It was deserted except for a beautiful girl in the corner. She was lit beautifully by the window, her wavy long blonde hair falling on her sleek shoulders.

As I carefully browsed towards her, I could see the silhouette of her pert little breasts, and if I wasn't mistaken, the outline of her nipple poking from within her white, see-through blouse. She was engrossed in a book in the erotic fiction section – how ironic. I carefully browsed towards her. I noticed her blush with excitement as her tongue flicked over her lips, she was standing uncomfortably moving from one leg to another as if she needed to adjust herself down there with the heat between her legs. I glanced at the cover of the large book she was holding – the Marquis de Sade, a classic book filled with erotic cruelty, rape and murder.

I knew this girl is going to be my next victim. Steadily browsing my way over, I moved to the bookstand directly behind her so that we were back to back. She was so engrossed in her book she barely even noticed my presence. I put down my book pretending to take another while instead reaching carefully and slowly into my jacket for my six inch hunting knife.

Looking around to see the coast was clear, I also noticed there were no security cameras in the area. Sweet. Without warning, I drew my knife and turned around so that I was standing behind her. She dropped her book and squealed with surprise as I clamped her mouth shut and held the knife up in front of her eyes which were now wide with terror. Mmm.

'Don't make a fucking sound you little cunt,' I rasped in her ear. 'Do you understand me? I will slit you open in seconds and you will be lying in your guts if you scream. Play along and you won't get hurt.'

She nodded furiously. I took my hand away and she drew a large gulp of air in, trying to hold in her tears. 'Now walk slowly out of the building, if you try and escape I'll have this knife in and out of you 10 times before anyone knows what's happening.'

Shaking she led me out of the building as I watched her

> very carefully to make sure she wasn't making eye contact to warn anybody. But she must have believed my threat and soon we were outside. I walked her with my knife in my jacket down the street to my hotel and led her to the room. She was terrified and starting to panic. Suspecting she was about to try something stupid I removed a small plastic bag from my backpack, which contained a rag soaked in chloroform. I had it over her mouth as she went down and I dragged her into the room . . .

In the next paragraph the author describes undressing, tying up and gagging his victim, and anticipating what he's going to do to her.

> . . . This time the ball gag had air holes in it, learning from my past mistakes when the fun ended far too soon. I took lots of photos of her like this for my growing collection of rape victims. Thank god for digital photographs, these weren't the kind of photographs you could drop into Boots to develop. I could see her waking up and knew she would be groggy and disoriented. So I quickly got naked and grabbed my knife. I lifted her by her hair as she squealed and brought my knife under her throat . . .

The author then describes in detail how he further terrifies his victim, rapes her vaginally and anally, all the while gripping his hunting knife and being aroused by her cries of pain and terror.

> . . . I looked into her terrified face, contorted with pain, fear and rage, mouth open and stuffed with the ball gag and smiled, 'How was it for you, baby?' Ha ha ha ha.'

I could see relief creeping in her face but that changed into terror again as I picked up my hunting knife. As far as I was concerned the fun was only beginning.

The end

In the computers seized from Dwyer's office, Brid Wallace found more disturbing stories. There was a document written in the first person about a building inspector becoming sexually aroused at the prospect of murdering a female tenant. Dwyer continued:

> My fake clip board and pen, nearly forgot those. I locked my TT and headed across the road as she disappeared inside. I found it more difficult to conceal my erection than my knife when I rang the doorbell. When the woman resident answered the door I said: 'My name is Graham Dwyer from Reads Rains management. I'm here to inspect the roof. Shit, just realized I used my real name. That changes things slightly.'

Another fantasy featured a woman being raped in a cave and then stabbed to death after she tries to escape.

It took the detective several days to extract all of the material from its hiding places in the various hard drives. The videos and stories showed Dwyer was lying when he tried to distance himself from BDSM by saying: 'I'm not a big part of the scene.' They proved his fascination with blood, knives and murder. Dwyer's home movies also corroborated a suspicion held by the psychologist advising the team. Given the 'Killing Darci' story, which set out Dwyer's template for fulfilling his fantasy of killing a woman, she thought it was highly likely that Dwyer had filmed the murder of Elaine O'Hara. Of special interest was the line 'I removed the silver necklace from around her neck and put it in an old tin box that would soon also contain the memory card from the camera to be kept in a very special place.' The investigation team went back to Dwyer's empty house and carried out more searches, checking behind electrical fittings and cavities in walls. A memory card has never been found. Members of the investigation believe that it exists and remains hidden.

Detective Superintendent Kevin Dolan, who was supervising the ongoing enquiry, instructed the investigation team to try to establish the identities of the women in the videos and those referred to in the stories. Dolan was concerned that the stories might not be based on fantasy, and nothing could be left to chance. In a bid to trace the woman featured in the 'Killing Darci' story, the Gardaí asked their US counterparts for help in establishing if the woman existed, possibly in the state of Maine. They wanted to know if the woman was alive or dead or missing. The material in the story seemed too detailed and specific to be mere fiction and there was also a reference to an American woman in Goroon's earliest texts. A check with the US Department of Homeland Security showed that Dwyer had not been in the States but, based on the story, it was possible that the woman had travelled to Ireland. The investigators also gave the US authorities details of people who had been in touch with Elaine O'Hara and Dwyer via fetish websites, and asked for help identifying their IP addresses so they could contact them. They made a similar request to the Newcastle Police, asking them for any information concerning the person featured in the 'Jenny's First Rape' story, including any unsolved murders involving women over the previous years. They referred to a specific type of tattoo mentioned in Dwyer's story. No such cases were identified. But the exercise proved to be fruitful.

In spring 2014, with the help of the US authorities, the investigation team identified the woman referred to in the 'Killing Darci' story as a Darci Day from the state of Maine. In April 2014 she was interviewed on behalf of the Gardaí by Detective Ryan Brockway of the Major Crimes Unit of the Maine State Police. She acknowledged that she had been in contact with an Irish man called Graham Dwyer. She said she had met him online in 2011 through a website dedicated to suicide. She had been contemplating taking her own life at the time. In his emails Dwyer told her about Elaine O'Hara, who had also been suicidal, and how he had offered to kill her. She said Dwyer told her that he fantasized about killing her after first killing Elaine O'Hara. Ms Day said he described how, in his fantasy, he would drive her to a location where he would cut her throat as they had sex. 'His fantasy was basically wanting to stab a woman to death during sex,' she said. In July, Peter Woods and James Mulligan travelled to the US to take her statement.

12. Mr Average

Psychopaths rarely look the part. Those who secretly stalk and plan a victim's destruction for sexual gratification tend to be ordinary, educated people who have never before come to police attention. They hide in plain view behind a mask of middle-class respectability, like a metaphorical twig in the forest. People will stare long and hard at the photograph of such a killer after he has been exposed, searching for telltale signs of the evil that lies within, and seeking the reassurance of discovering that he is different in appearance from *normal* people. But men like the one who had just taken shape from the fog of texts, emails, stories, pictures and videos are gifted at camouflaging their true nature. The truth is that most predators only begin to look 'obviously' mad and bad after the truth of their horrific deeds has been laid bare.

Graham Dwyer was a classic example of the bogeyman hiding behind the mask of Mr Average. Dwyer was born on 13 September 1972 and grew up in Bandon, County Cork. He was the second of Seán and Susan Dwyer's four children. He had an older sister and two younger brothers. The family lived in a modest semi-detached former local authority house in the Deerpark estate on the edge of the town. His father worked as a tradesman and taxi driver to educate his family. Graham attended St Fintan's National School and was a member of the local Boy Scouts. He loved the outdoors and regularly went camping with his father and brothers. He then attended Hamilton High, a prestigious Catholic boys-only secondary school in Bandon. Known locally as the Hammies, the school has a proud reputation for academic achievement. Dwyer was described as a hard-working, bright student who excelled in art, music and English. He was also single-minded and focused in his quest to achieve his goals. Such was his determination to become an architect that when technical drawing was not available in his own school, he took classes at another school in the town, St Brogan's.

Those who knew him growing up saw him as an average, likeable chap. He certainly never revealed any hint of being capable of something as twisted and vicious as the killing of Elaine O'Hara. But there were behavioural quirks and incidents that, with the benefit of hindsight, were signs of another side to his personality, tiny cracks in the mask he wore in public.

After his arraignment, one individual approached Gardaí with a story about how Dwyer had tried to kill a younger boy when they were children. He pushed the child off the roof of a building while they were both playing, leaving him with broken bones. While the child was recuperating, Dwyer attacked him a second time. During the research for this book a friend of the witness revealed: 'The one thing that he [the victim] remembers is the look in Graham's eyes just before he pushed him off the roof – he said his eyes were dead and he knew that for no apparent reason Graham wanted to kill him. It was never mentioned again and was put down to an accident while the kids were playing. But that kid is now a man and he has never forgotten. He confided this to a few people but it never became relevant until the murder. The man grew up in the circle around Dwyer and couldn't really avoid him, so he continued to be a friend of his but secretly he hated him. When Graham Dwyer was arrested he went to the Gardaí and told them what he knew.'

As a teenager Dwyer played the left-handed bass guitar with a local band called Strangeways that gigged in the pubs around Bandon. He was a popular kid who was known as a charming lad-about-town and had a string of girlfriends. During the summer holidays from secondary school and college, he worked in a chicken factory. Here too there was odd behaviour that hinted at a darker side. Dwyer knew the trick for putting a chicken to sleep – tucking its head beneath one wing and then, holding it in both hands, swinging it gently from side to side for ten seconds or so. However, unlike the average fellow who might do this for a laugh, before waking up the bewildered bird, Dwyer would put a few chickens to sleep and then line them up and kick them to death. Not only did he find it funny to do this, but he would tell people, including fellow classmates, how entertaining he found it. 'At the time it was remarked upon but was generally forgotten,' a former co-worker recalled. 'Funny, it was the first thing that some of us remembered when he was accused of murder.'

In the summer of 1991, Dwyer passed his Leaving Cert exams with flying colours and earned enough points to study architecture at the Dublin Institute of Technology (DIT) on Bolton Street in Dublin's north inner city. Although he settled permanently in Dublin he still maintained close ties to his home town, regularly visiting his family and friends. Shortly after starting college Dwyer met Emer McShea from Ballyshannon, County Donegal. Emer was studying environmental health in Cathal Brugha Street, another DIT college.

She was introduced to Dwyer through her flatmates, who were in his architecture class. The couple started a relationship in January 1992 and two months later Emer discovered that she was pregnant. Her friends would later reveal that Dwyer was initially supportive throughout the pregnancy and he was with Emer when she gave birth to their son, Sennan, the following November. She then dropped out of college for a year to mind the baby.

When Emer McShea returned to her studies in Dublin in 1993, the couple and their son moved into a flat. But Emer ended the relationship a few years later and former friends describe how Dwyer was controlling and emotionally abusive. As she had witnessed his sinister proclivities at first hand, it was understandable that Emer McShea continued to live in fear of her former boyfriend.

Over the subsequent years Dwyer played a minimal role in his son's life. In 2007 Emer McShea was forced to call the Gardaí after Dwyer arrived unannounced at her home in Ballyshannon after hearing that his son was smoking. Dwyer was an implacable anti-smoker and he flew into an almost uncontrollable rage when he confronted the teenager. There was only sporadic contact after the Gardaí intervened and no further action was taken. Two years later, Sennan McShea was diagnosed with cancer, but luckily the teenager recovered his health after treatment. The 2007 incident was reported in the Garda PULSE computer system and appeared when the investigators first searched for a Graham Dwyer. It had provided a useful lead in their investigation.

Shortly after the relationship with Emer McShea ended, Dwyer began dating another architecture student, Gemma

Healy from Sligo. Dwyer was anxious to shake off his modest working-class background and his dream was to own a nice house in a fashionable Dublin suburb where he could rub shoulders with the right kind of people. Gemma Healy was everything the socially ambitious Cork man aspired to in a future wife. She was bright and beautiful and came from a family steeped in medicine. Her parents were both respected doctors – her father, Dr John Healy, was a trauma and orthopaedic surgeon and a former chair of the Irish Medical Council's fitness-to-practise committee – and some of her siblings were also entering the profession. As the investigating Gardaí would discover, Dwyer did not reveal his dark predilections to his future wife, perhaps fearing that he would frighten her off and he would lose the social status that she brought him.

Dwyer graduated from DIT in 1997 with a 2.1 degree and in 1998 became an associate member of the Royal Institute of the Architects of Ireland (RIAI). He worked in a number of well-known architecture firms, including Keane Murphy Duff, Oppermann Associates and Burke-Kennedy Doyle. In 2000 the 27-year-old appeared on the RTÉ home-makeover show *Beyond the Hall Door* in which he described a bathroom he had designed. The youthful-looking Dywer came across as confident, intelligent and articulate. 'The challenge here was to create an individual look around a standard white bathroom suite. The approach I took was a modern one and it creates a more private, focused space around each utility,' he said. 'The floor here is Gerflor. It's a simple, solid-colour lino. And effectively it's very hygienic and easy to wash.'

In the same year Dwyer and Gemma Healy bought their first home, an old fireman's house dating back to the 1880s, at Gulistan Cottages, off Upper Mountpleasant Avenue, between Ranelagh and Rathmines in upmarket Dublin 6. They married on 21 September 2002 and became a stereotypical golden couple of the Celtic Tiger era – young, educated, professional and going places. During the credit-fuelled property boom, architects were in high demand. In 2001 Dwyer had joined A&D Wejchert, a Polish-owned firm, and he studied part-time in UCD, where he completed a master's degree in urban design. Dwyer worked on several major projects and his diligence paid off when he became an associate in the company two years later and a full partner in 2006 – one of five in the company. His specialist skill was in 3D visualization and artist's impressions of projects and presentations, and he was recognized as a wizard with computers. At the same time Gemma Dwyer's career was also in the ascendant and she was working as a project director with another major architecture firm in Dublin.

Over the years the redesign and refurbishment of their cottage became the couple's pet project. When they put it on the market in May 2007 it featured on the front cover of the *Irish Times'* property section. The young couple, who had not yet started a family, were described as members of the 'trendy architect set'. The feature included a picture of them in their crisp white kitchen, both smiling warmly. She looked petite and pretty and he proud and protective as he stood behind her with his hands on her shoulders. The article detailed how they had snapped up the pint-sized two-bedroom cottage for €200,000 and spent €60,000 to turn it into a 'smart city pad', ideal for the up-and-coming Celtic Tiger cubs.

They sold the cottage for €590,000 and moved to a four-bedroom detached house at 6 Kerrymount Close in

Foxrock, which they bought for around €1 million plus stamp duty. When the economic crash hit Ireland a year later the couple found themselves in crippling negative equity. Gemma was made redundant and in the same year gave birth to their first child, a boy. Over the next few years Dwyer also suffered a succession of pay cuts as his company struggled to survive in the worst recession in the history of the State.

Dwyer's apparent all-consuming passions were fast, expensive cars and flying model aircraft. He bought and sold high-performance cars and at various times owned a Porsche 911, two Audi A3s, an Audi estate and an Audi A4. He was now driving a blue Audi TT and also owned a jeep. Dwyer's first love was his hobby as a model aircraft enthusiast. He became interested in model aircraft while in college and in 2000 joined the Model Aeronautics Council of Ireland, with the registered number IRL3543. He had passed two exams, one a certificate for the first level of competency and the other allowing him to fly in competitions abroad. He worked on the planes almost every day, regularly ordering parts from specialist websites, and flew them in races most weekends.

Shortly after moving to Foxrock he joined the Shankill Radio Flying Club, which had a small clubhouse and runways for the aircraft in the shadow of Sugarloaf Mountain. Ironically, that was the club Detective Garda Colm Gregan encountered while walking on the mountain, the memory of which ultimately led to Dwyer's identification. When detectives began making enquiries following Dwyer's arrest, members of the club recalled a dead sheep being found not far from the clubhouse one time. (Goroon claimed he had stabbed a sheep to death close to where he had been flying.) In 2011, when he had acquired the necessary proficiency,

Dwyer was invited to join the Roundwood Model Aeronautical Club, for advanced enthusiasts. The club grounds were situated on twenty acres of land a short distance from Vartry Reservoir and Sally's Bridge. Dwyer regularly took part in competitions at the club and would fly his model aircraft there at least once a month.

Everything about Graham Dwyer and his life looked normal, including the struggle to juggle the bills in recessionary Ireland. He appeared pleasant and competent and to be a loving husband and father. However, just as he had shown a different side in his childhood and student years, sometimes another side of the adult Dwyer emerged. All kinds of stories emerged after his arrest. His short fuse. His status obsession. His uncontrolled envy. He lost one of his early jobs because of the fallout from an argument with a colleague in the pub after work one Friday. The following Monday morning the person with whom he had clashed found his desk trashed. The company sacked Dwyer following a disciplinary investigation. Apparently his employers were so concerned about his behaviour that they changed the locks on the doors after he left. Another former colleague told a story about Dwyer's fixation with colleagues' earnings. He hacked into the computer system at the firm where they worked to look at the payroll figures and went 'berserk' when he discovered that some people were being paid more than him.

However, nothing about Dwyer's less attractive traits could have prepared anyone who knew him for what was starting to emerge and being talked about in shocked conversations in Dublin's professional circles. There were rumours about some BDSM element to the crime of which he was accused, though initially nobody could really imagine that, horrific as it was, the situation was anything more than Dwyer having hidden kinky sexual interests and something having gone badly wrong with the woman who had died. The Gardaí, on the other hand, knew that they were dealing with a very dangerous man who fitted the same kind of profile as some of the worst killers in history.

When Brid Wallace had investigated Elaine O'Hara's Apple MacBook, one of the documents recovered was a PDF copy of a book about serial killers that included a chapter on the Ripper murders in Victorian London and discussed their distinctive signature: piquerism. The more the Gardaí found out about this particular perversion – the desire to pierce or stab someone for sexual gratification – the more the label seemed to fit Dwyer.

In an analysis of the modus operandi and signature of the Ripper murders in the *Journal of Investigative Psychology and Offender Profiling*, US academics Robert D. Keppel, Joseph G. Weis, K. M. Brown and Kristen Welch described how the killer displayed the characteristics of piquerism: he achieved sexual gratification through the 'eroticized power of violence, the domination of the victim, and the mutilation and bleeding of the victim rather than sexual intercourse'.

Several other serial killers around the world have had piquerist traits. The Russian mass murderer Andrei Chikatilo, the 'Butcher of Rostov', was known to be impotent but derived sexual satisfaction from stabbing and cutting his many victims. American serial killer Albert Fish, also known as the 'Brooklyn Vampire' and the 'Moon Maniac', engaged in piquerist behaviour with many of his victims.

Just as Dwyer's trial was commencing, an article in *Psychology Today* included a further description of piquerism that again seemed to fit Dwyer's particular appetites. Dr Mark Griffiths of Nottingham Trent University defined it as 'paraphilic sexual arousal which hinges on the sadistic piercing and stabbing of another person, especially in the breast, buttocks and groin, which may cause enough bleeding to be fatal'. A paraphilic disorder is a sexual desire to cause an unwilling victim psychological distress, injury or death.

Knowing what they did about Dwyer's make-up, the Gardaí were determined that he would remain locked up until his trial. At a hearing in the High Court in November 2013, Chief Superintendent Diarmuid O'Sullivan strenuously objected to Dwyer's application for bail on grounds not heard before in an Irish court. To back up the State's argument that Dwyer was too dangerous to release, he revealed some of the explicit text messages and the stories exhumed from Dwyer's computer. O'Sullivan told the High Court: 'The accused has an ongoing insatiable desire to stab women to death for the purpose of achieving sexual gratification.' He also said it was his belief that Dwyer would interfere with witnesses in the case, including Emer McShea, who was terrified of her former partner. The evidence at the bail hearing was so explicit that the court imposed a reporting ban. When bail was refused, Dwyer instructed his lawyers to appeal to the Supreme Court. It also refused the application.

In January 2014, Dwyer finally got an opportunity to read the content of the case against him when he received the book of evidence. He noticed that the Gardaí had placed a big emphasis on the fact that he had ordered a Buck

Special hunting knife that was delivered to his office on 21 August, the day before Elaine disappeared. Printouts of the weapon had been found in her apartment when she first went missing. Dwyer, it seems, concluded that he had a surprise for the cops, something that would take the wind out of their sails.

On 17 February, Detective Sergeant Peter Woods received a phone call from Dwyer's solicitor, Jonathan Dunphy, and an accompanying fax message with a sketch map of the basement at the office of A&D Wejchert. The fax was sent at Dwyer's behest. The map, which was drawn by Dwyer, was accompanied by a list headed 'items of interest'. Woods and two other detectives immediately went to the Wejchert premises and using Dwyer's map he found the Buck Special knife, which had a cocobolo handle and a six-inch stainless-steel blade. He also found a smaller flick knife hidden in a corner where old files were stored. The discovery of what was believed to have been the murder weapon boosted Dwyer's confidence that he was going to beat the rap.

But his unexpected cooperation did nothing for his chances of getting bail. On 10 March 2014 the Central Criminal Court refused his third attempt to get out of prison. Dwyer would remain in custody until his trial. Meanwhile, at just about the time Dwyer sent the investigation team his helpful map, they had identified the woman referred to in his 'Killing Darci' story. He might have believed he had wrong-footed the Gardaí but in fact they were building an ever stronger case against him.

*

On Sunday, 9 March 2014, a death notice was published on the website RIP.ie:

> *The death has occurred of Elaine O'HARA*
> *Killiney, Dublin*
>
> *O'HARA (Killiney, Co Dublin) (left home August 2012) Elaine, beloved daughter of the late Eileen. Very sadly missed by her heart-broken father Frank, sister Ann, brothers Frank and John, brother-in-law Mark, sister-in-law Aisling, her adored goddaughter and Sheila, extended family and many friends.*
>
> *Elaine's funeral has taken place privately. Her family would like to thank everyone for their understanding, kindness and continued support.*
>
> *May she rest in peace*

Since the previous September, Elaine's remains had been held by the State for ongoing forensic tests. The family buried her beside her mother, Eileen, in Shanganagh Cemetery.

Later that year Frank O'Hara accepted his daughter's BA degree in Montessori Education from St Nicholas Montessori College. It was a bitter-sweet moment. It would have been the proudest day of Elaine's life: she had overcome all the obstacles to earn the qualification that meant so much to her.

13. The Trial Begins

Paul Carney, the most experienced trial judge of the Central Criminal Court, was not a man to pull his punches. 'In this case it will be difficult for anybody who is particularly squeamish,' he warned before the jury had been selected for the trial of Graham Dwyer. He also cautioned that anyone who knew Elaine O'Hara or had any connection to the Alt.com website could not serve. He told potential jurors that the trial would last between six and eight weeks. People were excused from jury duty for different reasons, including concerns over personal commitments, medical issues or their jobs. One woman said her brother had been murdered and another said she was very squeamish. After the defence and prosecution teams had rejected seven potential jurors each, it took twenty-five minutes to empanel the seven men and five women who would decide the guilt or innocence of Graham Dwyer. The jury was appointed on Monday, 19 January 2015. The trial would commence later that week.

The Central Criminal Court is the criminal division of the High Court and has responsibility for the prosecution of all rape, manslaughter and murder trials. As its presiding judge, Paul Carney would most likely have heard the case if it hadn't been for his imminent retirement from the bench. Instead, this trial was to be presided over by Mr Justice Tony Hunt, who had been promoted to the High Court the previous October. It would be his first murder trial.

Normally in a trial as lengthy as this one looked set to be, two seniors would be appointed on either side. However, this time just one senior counsel would represent each side. The men who would battle it out to persuade the jury one way or the other were Seán Guerin for the prosecution and Remy Farrell for the defence. Guerin and Farrell were two of the most in-demand lawyers in the country and considered to be among the brightest stars in the new generation of seniors emerging from the Law Library. The two had been classmates in UCD's School of Law and were both called to the bar in 1997. They were also relative newcomers to the Inner Bar: Farrell became an SC in 2011 while Guerin took silk in 2013.

In summer 2014 the two men had faced each other in similar roles – Guerin on the prosecution team, Farrell for the defence – in the high-profile trial of Limerick gangsters Wayne Dundon and Nathan Killeen for the murder of businessman Roy Collins. On that occasion the prosecution was successful. Guerin had also inadvertently become a household name after his investigations into allegations of Garda malpractice and incompetence, and the handling of the whistle-blower who raised concerns about these, led to the resignation of the Minister for Justice Alan Shatter in 2014. However, the battle the two senior counsel were about to enter would be like nothing either of them had ever experienced before. Seán Guerin was to be assisted by junior counsel, Anne Marie Lawlor and Sinead McGrath. Farrell was joined by juniors Ronan Kennedy and Kate McCormack. Jonathan Dunphy was Dwyer's solicitor.

The time allocated for the trial reflected the huge amount of evidence gathered by the investigation team in the previous fifteen months. The level of thoroughness, teamwork and attention to detail was truly impressive. The Gardaí had pursued 619 individual lines of enquiry, interviewed 488 people and taken 788 statements. They had retrieved and examined 2,612 text messages and 5,300 hours – over seven months – of CCTV footage. A total of 408 witnesses, including members of the public and Gardaí, had been subpoenaed by the State while the book of evidence ran into seven volumes, containing 540 individual statements. In addition to the CCTV footage, there were five terabytes of data in computer evidence and 925 exhibits. In order to prove their case the State intended to throw everything they had at it.

In the absence of evidence determining the cause of death, the prosecution's strategy would be to prove beyond all reasonable doubt that when taken together the text traffic, cell site analysis, CCTV footage, Dwyer's admissions and the material exhumed from his and Elaine O'Hara's phones and computers added up to an absolutely clear picture that Graham Dwyer was not just the man Elaine called 'sir' but that he had planned to kill her and carried out his plan.

On the other side the defence case would be that Dwyer had no case to answer because there was no evidence of cause of death. They would argue that the volumes of evidence collected by the Gardaí were purely circumstantial and were incapable of explaining how Elaine O'Hara met her death. While the prosecution's job was to prove its allegations, the defence had to sow seeds of doubt in the mind of the jury. This would necessitate focusing on Elaine O'Hara's sexual interests, to suggest that she was a willing participant in any BDSM activity that the prosecution presented, and on her mental health history, to introduce the possibility that she had taken her own life.

Graham Dwyer was very hands-on in his own defence, arguing strategy with his experienced legal team and telling them what he wanted done. But in reality he didn't have much of a defence to offer. He had been advised at one stage that his best option was to offer a guilty plea to manslaughter if the DPP was amenable, but he rejected that out of hand. He remained confident that he would be acquitted. When the trial was set to be heard in April 2015, Dwyer instructed his lawyers to seek to have it brought forward by three months.

In the course of research for this book, a source close to Dwyer revealed that in the run-up to the trial he had bragged about having an ace up his sleeve that would blow the State's case out of the water. The root of his optimism was a bizarre notion of his to subpoena a number of women with whom he had been involved in BDSM activity through the years, including at least one of the women who featured in the videos found on his computer hard drive. Dwyer also claimed he was considering calling a number of well-known professional men he knew had been involved in BDSM from what the women had told him previously. He was determined to call one woman in particular because of her professional background. Dwyer told prison officers that he could use information he had gleaned from the woman in pillow talk to embarrass the State, the Gardaí and possibly undermine the prosecution's case. He said he was happy to, in his own words, 'name names'. He was equally bullish about taking the stand and giving evidence in his defence, though as a defendant he was not required to testify because in murder cases it is up to the State to prove its case.

It is likely that Dwyer's defence team convinced him that the subpoena idea was certain to backfire and have the opposite effect to the one he anticipated, and might persuade the jury of his guilt rather than his innocence. As for taking the stand in his own defence, Dwyer would have found it impossible to explain the huge amount of evidence against him in cross-examination. It appears that he was dissuaded from calling the witnesses and that he took his counsels' advice and decided to keep his mouth shut.

The trial was adjourned until Thursday 22 January. It would take place in Court 13 on the fourth floor of the impressive Courts of Criminal Justice building beside the Phoenix Park. From early that morning, members of the public queued alongside a large contingent of journalists at the courtroom door to get a seat inside. Such was the demand for media access that the Courts Service had to allocate the limited number of seats in the press gallery so that each media organization was represented. Pensioners and retirees, some of whom had travelled by train from as far as Limerick, had come to spectate like it was some kind of free entertainment.

Between Gardaí, witnesses, the legal teams and curious onlookers, Court 13 was quickly jammed to the door, with standing room only. Just before 11 a.m. Graham Dwyer emerged through a side door flanked by prison officers. He seemed upbeat and confident. Necks craned to get a glimpse of Dwyer, who with his clean-shaven boyish face, smart dark blue suit, white shirt and red tie looked more like one of the legal team than the man accused of what were rumoured to be monstrous deeds. If he hadn't been in the bench reserved for the accused he would have remained unrecognizable to those in the public gallery. Dwyer seemed oblivious to the eyes focused on him as he stood smiling and chatting to his legal team, a hand stuck casually into a trouser pocket. Spectators could be heard muttering things like 'That couldn't be him' and 'You wouldn't think he could be accused of this.' He was the image of the suave, entitled, unflappable chap, who would soon brush off this terrible injustice. He would wear this mask for the duration of his trial.

Then all eyes turned to Frank O'Hara and his family. A momentary hush descended on the courtroom as they were escorted along a path the Gardaí had cleared through the throng of spectators. A bench had been reserved for them and they sat without speaking, shoulder to shoulder, a few yards away from the man accused of killing Elaine. They had all been called to testify. The Gardaí had already explained the content of the harrowing evidence that they would hear over the coming weeks. They were not required in court other than to give their direct evidence. Despite this, Frank O'Hara was determined that he would see this through to the end, when the man accused of killing his daughter would either walk away a free man or spend the rest of his life behind bars. He said that it was the least he could do for his beloved daughter. Frank O'Hara sat with his hands in his lap, looking straight ahead, flanked by a Garda liaison officer and a Victim Support volunteer.

Further over to the side of the courtroom, on a smaller, two-person bench, sat Dwyer's parents, Seán and Susan. They had moved to Dublin for the duration of the trial. They shared the same stoic expression as Frank O'Hara as they sat behind a glass panel that separated them from their son. From time to time he glanced over at them and smiled.

Like the O'Hara family, the Dwyers were dignified and composed.

At 11.11 a.m. the jury trooped in to take their seats and Mr Justice Tony Hunt told them: 'Mr Dwyer is now in your charge.' He outlined their responsibilities, saying they had only one question to answer at the end of the trial: 'Have the prosecution proved the allegations that they make?' He asked them to bear in mind that Dwyer was presumed innocent, meaning that the burden of proof was on the prosecution. 'The advantage a jury has is twelve heads are better than one,' he said. Judge Hunt advised them to use common sense and be rational, saying it promised to be a lengthy case and that a considerable body of material would be presented to them. He then asked them to listen closely to the opening remarks of the prosecutor, Seán Guerin.

The tall, thin and bespectacled lawyer rose to his feet and turned towards the jury. There was no hint of the pomposity that is synonymous with the Law Library. Guerin spoke in a gentle monotone, his soft delivery acting as a counterweight to the violent, obscene content of much of what he was saying. There was no need for theatrics because the material contained its own horrific drama. As part of his preparation for the trial the lawyer had spent a day with the investigation team, visiting each scene associated with the murder he was about to prosecute. The lawyer had walked in the footsteps of Elaine O'Hara through the wooded plantation in Killakee where her remains were discovered, and stood on Sally's Bridge at Vartry Reservoir where Dwyer had stopped to dump the phones, the keys and the BDSM gear. He wanted to be familiar with every detail of the case before the trial.

Guerin began by painting a picture of the circumstances

of how the murder had been discovered in September 2013, outlining in detail the sequence of discoveries at Vartry Reservoir and Killakee. The prosecutor admitted that the State had no cause of death. He said there was no medical or forensic evidence and no witnesses linking Dwyer to the scene where the remains were found in the Dublin Mountains. But he said the series of 'remarkable coincidences' supported the prosecution's case that this was 'a simple, straightforward case for murder'.

Getting down to the core of the State's case, Guerin then turned to the text messages retrieved from Elaine's two phones and the two mobile phones recovered from the reservoir. He said the State's case would be that the messages were between Graham Dwyer and Elaine O'Hara. The texts would show they had a sexual relationship.

'That relationship was an unusual one because it featured, as a central part, acts of stabbing committed by Graham Dwyer on Elaine O'Hara. That was a feature of the sexual relationship that existed between them, and that reflected a deep-seated and passionately held, irrepressible desire on the part of Graham Dwyer to get sexual gratification by stabbing a woman. You will see that Graham Dwyer arranged to meet Elaine O'Hara at Shanganagh Cemetery to take her up to the mountain to kill her in satisfaction of that desire.'

He told the jury the messages would show how, over the course of time, Graham Dwyer 'elaborated carefully and thoughtfully about a range of ideas of how he could kill a woman and get away with it'.

Seán Guerin said Dwyer had bought a phone using the number of his personal work phone with one digit changed and the variation of the address of a family member in County

Tipperary. These were all 'slight corruptions of details known to Mr Dwyer', which he used as a 'slightly disguised effort to purchase what was an untraceable phone'. That might not amount to an awful lot, he said, but the content of the texts between Elaine O'Hara and the person using the 083 (Goroon) phone would put beyond all doubt that it was Dwyer.

He then read a selection of key texts, those that included the detailed and specific information that pointed to their source being Graham Dwyer: coming fifth in a model plane flying competition; complaining about pay cuts; becoming a father for a second time and sharing the name of his baby girl; expressing a strong dislike of smoking. Guerin said of these, and other unusual details contained in text messages on the two phones, 'when you put them together [they] point to only one conclusion – that Graham Dwyer was the other person on the end of the phone.' He said a lot of the prosecution's evidence would be presented to the jury for the purpose of proving that connection. The phones used were effectively untraceable and were for the 'specific purpose of communicating between them'.

The prosecutor pointed out the fact that CCTV footage from Belarmine Plaza showed the accused man on 15 August 2012 leaving with a rucksack that 'looks just like the rucksack found in Vartry reservoir'. Dwyer's DNA matched that of a semen stain found on the mattress in Elaine O'Hara's apartment. 'This tends to confirm that he was the party engaged in the sexual relationship described in those text messages.' The messages, he said, 'told the story of their relationship'.

Guerin contended that the texts showed Dwyer had

renewed contact with Elaine O'Hara in March 2011 and the relationship involved 'what is called BDSM – bondage, domination, sadism and masochism'. He said: 'Ms O'Hara was someone whose sexual preference was submissive, involving restraint, being tied up, being controlled by another person and allowing herself to be punished by another person.'

Guerin continued reading the texts aloud.

'I want to stick my knife in flesh while I am sexually aroused. Blood turns me on and I would like to stab a girl to death sometime.'

Guerin's voice was amplified against the deathly silence that had descended on the courtroom when he first rose to his feet, the sound of his words punctuated only by the odd gasp from the public gallery. A female member of the jury recoiled at some of the obscene language. Dwyer distracted himself by looking through documents and scribbling notes with his left hand.

The lawyer told the jury that it was clear that Elaine O'Hara did not want to indulge in Dwyer's stabbing fetish. He quoted her text from March 2011: 'I am not into blood any more.'

The relationship was complicated by Elaine O'Hara's psychiatric difficulties, 'of which Graham Dwyer knew full well'. It also appeared from the messages that there had been a discussion years earlier about her being suicidal and there had been incidents of self-harm. 'The discussion was that if she were suicidal, Elaine O'Hara might allow herself to be stabbed to death by Graham Dwyer,' said Guerin. He illustrated this with a text from Dwyer: 'If you ever wanted to die, promise me I can do it.'

Guerin said the communications showed Dwyer was

abusive and manipulating. 'He took advantage of her mental health and groomed her to the idea of blood loss by getting her used to what he wanted as being normal.'

The prosecutor went on to read dozens more texts, explaining how each one supported the State's case that Dwyer was driven by a visceral desire to stab and kill for sexual gratification. Mr Guerin said the messages turned to threats, warning that if Elaine O'Hara didn't help Dwyer find a victim she would suffer the consequence of being stabbed to death. He asked her to identify targets and do research for him. The prosecutor said Dwyer also claimed she put the idea of killing in his head, texting at one stage: 'It's your fault I want to kill and you won't let me stab you.'

Guerin said it appeared the sexual practice between them, where Elaine O'Hara was stabbed by Dwyer, was causing difficulty for her and for her mental health. She had resisted his constant badgering about being stabbed. When she said she wanted a child, Dwyer volunteered to be the father as long as she helped him to find a victim to murder. She later rejected the offer, telling him it would be better to have a child in a relationship, though it was hard to meet someone when she was 'marked with so many stab wounds'. Dwyer reacted by insulting and belittling her, saying that 'she was old, fat, a smoker and disobedient'.

The prosecutor said it was clear by October 2011 that Elaine no longer wanted to 'play with him', and while the relationship had not quite ended, it was certainly not as intense and was perhaps more sporadic than before. 'What I suggest to you from the text messages is that from that point on, the person who wanted to renew the relationship was Graham Dwyer and the person resisting that was Elaine

O'Hara,' he said. 'The prosecution's case is that he starts putting in place a plan he had formed to use Elaine O'Hara to get his sexual gratification by stabbing a woman to death . . . Graham Dwyer committed very nearly the perfect murder and Elaine O'Hara was almost the perfect victim. He killed her exactly as he said he would [in the texts].'

After the murder Dwyer dropped the two phones, Elaine's keys and a bag into Vartry Reservoir, close to the flying club where he spent Wednesday afternoons. Elaine O'Hara had a history of psychiatric illness and was last seen walking towards the sea after visiting her mother's grave. 'There would be every reason to think it was the suicide that it looked like. When you look at all the elements and put them together, the prosecution's case will be that it was very nearly the perfect murder, but for the fact that 2013 was such a warm summer,' he said.

It took Seán Guerin almost two hours to deliver his opening speech. As he spoke, Dwyer seemed sometimes to grin as he glanced around the courtroom. He had the demeanour of a disinterested bystander, simply there to watch the show, just like the members of the public who were crammed into every crevice. However, his face turned bright red and he sniffed and shifted awkwardly in his seat as Guerin described his crime. And he had an occasional nervous tic where he opened and closed his mouth like a goldfish.

Guerin sat down at 12.55 p.m. Despite his understated approach, his opening address was one of the most dramatic ever witnessed at the start of a murder trial. Inevitably it received saturation media coverage. Word of the horrific acts Dwyer had been accused of carrying out quickly reached the ears of fellow inmates in Cloverhill. In the criminal world, crimes such as these are considered a class apart, and those suspected of carrying out such depraved acts are reviled by other criminals. Inmates' responses to what they heard about Dwyer gave the prison authorities concern for his safety. When he returned from court that first evening, he was moved to a new landing for his own protection.

On the second day of the hearing, Dwyer arrived in a furious state and demanded that his counsel complain about his move to Judge Hunt. So, before the jury was called in, Remy Farrell told the court that as a result of the media attention the trial had attracted the previous day, his client had been placed on a landing reserved for punishment and medical issues. There was neither bedding nor pillows in his cell and, as part of a suicide watch regime, inmates were woken every twenty minutes. Dwyer had no access to his books or notes. 'It is entirely intolerable that anyone be expected to go through a trial when they have been woken up every twenty minutes,' Mr Farrell said. Judge Hunt said the concern was that if this persisted it was going to make it 'impossible for [Dwyer] to participate'. What had been done was 'probably for safety considerations more than anything else'. He said he did not have a direct input into the operation of the prison, but added: 'that kind of thing is going to impinge on proceedings'. As Dwyer's sleeping arrangements were not raised again for the remainder of the trial it must be assumed that the prison authorities made suitable arrangements for his comfort and security.

With the subject of Graham Dwyer's discomfort dealt with, the jury was brought in. Elaine's father, Frank O'Hara, was the first major witness called to testify. He was led through his evidence by Seán Guerin. Mr O'Hara said he spoke with

Elaine by phone every day, sometimes twice a day, and would see her three to four times a week. He recalled the last day he saw her alive, 22 August 2012, and their visit, with his granddaughter, Elaine's godchild, to his late wife's grave.

'Elaine was in the car texting, I don't know who she was contacting. I remember saying: "Could you put the phone away for a while?"' Frank O'Hara said that at the grave Elaine had been upset, which would not have been unusual, and had kissed her mother's gravestone. Afterwards they returned to the house and Elaine took her godchild for a walk. She left his house shortly after 4 p.m. She was excited about the Tall Ships Festival the following day. 'She was in extremely good form,' he said in a voice that was heavy with sadness.

Frank O'Hara described the last time he saw Elaine alive, as he stood in the doorway waving goodbye. 'She said she needed to go home to get some rest because she needed to get up early the following morning. She was a bit nervous of it but she'd gone through the training, she was happy to do it, but Elaine was always a little nervous going in to a new situation,' he said, smiling gently.

Pain was etched on his face as he told the story of her troubled life and early mental health difficulties. 'She became very withdrawn, very into herself.'

He described how much his daughter loved working with children in school and wanted to be a Montessori teacher. Frank O'Hara said his daughter suffered from a number of physical ailments, including diabetes and polycystic ovaries but these posed no obstacle to her studies that he was aware of. 'She had an incredible work ethic,' he said. She was dyslexic and 'quite intelligent', but she found it 'very hard to get it down on paper'. Elaine tended to get agitated and this happened more after her mother died in 2002. She had not required the same level of care in the years before Eileen O'Hara's death as she had when she was younger and her psychiatrist had been trying to reduce her medication gradually. He felt that she had stabilized over the years and her mental health was improving. 'I thought she was doing pretty good,' he said.

In July 2012 Elaine told her father she was going to ask her doctor in St Edmundsbury Hospital to admit her. Mr O'Hara told the court that he had considered that she was doing very well and had told her he did not think she needed to be admitted. 'She said: "You don't know what I have tried to do" and mentioned something about a noose on a bookcase in her apartment,' he said.

Frank O'Hara said there had been incidents of self-harm – one involving cutting her wrists when she was a teenager in 1992. He recalled the two incidents in 2005 and 2007 when Elaine had taken overdoses. On the latter occasion he had rushed to her flat after she said she had taken something during a phone conversation. Mr O'Hara described finding her collapsed on the couch with 'pills all over the floor'. He rushed her to hospital, where she was in a coma for twenty-four hours.

Mr O'Hara was then asked to revisit the 2008 argument that had deeply affected him. 'She said: "I am seeing somebody" and I said: "Who?" She said: "A professional." I tried to enquire but she was very reticent to give me any information. I said: "Is he married?" She said: "Yes." She said: "He ties me up and masturbates over me but we haven't had sex." Then she told me he was an architect from Foxrock. I was shocked.'

Seán Guerin said: 'I don't think you pursued the matter?'

'No, she told me it was over and we never discussed it again.'

Over the years, Mr O'Hara said, Elaine told him that there was a 'play in her mind' but she never discussed what it was. He said he thought it 'might be unsavoury'. He suggested she write it down and show it to her psychiatrist. 'She was always worried about this play, it upset her.'

In cross-examination by Dwyer's defence counsel, Remy Farrell, Mr O'Hara was questioned about his relationship with his murdered daughter. He said her mental health problems 'absolutely' affected their relationship as she could be difficult to deal with sometimes. Elaine also had problems with money and paying for her mortgage, which he helped her out with from time to time.

Throughout Seán Guerin's questioning of Frank O'Hara, Graham Dwyer looked around the courtroom as if completely disinterested. But when his own counsel asked if there was a history of psychiatric problems in the family, Dwyer's gaze settled on Elaine's father. Mr O'Hara replied that there was none.

Farrell also asked him about something he had said in his Garda statement regarding the married man she had spoken about. 'I think I remember her saying also that she had asked him to kill her but he wouldn't. I was shattered after hearing the news.' Farrell asked Frank O'Hara if he was concerned that his daughter had taken her own life when she first went missing. 'I was confused . . . It obviously had crossed my mind. I had an open mind at that stage.'

Mr O'Hara told the court he had not noticed any unusual wounds or marks on Elaine before she disappeared. 'You have to understand Elaine wore long sleeves and long trousers to cover the self-harm, so I would not have seen it.'

14. The Evidence Mounts

As the trial progressed, the story of Elaine O'Hara's destruction began to emerge from the testimony of a procession of witnesses. Each person who took the stand had a role to play in the unfolding drama. Every line of testimony, no matter how small, contributed another piece to the story – gradually fortifying the wall of evidence being constructed around Graham Dwyer. The jury heard how the crime had been discovered through the eyes of the people who were there. Scores of Gardaí gave evidence of preserving and searching scenes associated with the crime. Forensic and medical experts outlined how the remains had been identified and how mobile phones that had lain under water for over a year had been brought back to life.

Every detail of the murdered woman's life was dissected and examined. Elaine's friends and work colleagues described what she had been like as a person and recalled the significant details she had shared about a mystery man who tied her up and stabbed her. The dead woman's ghost hung over the courtroom as her mental health issues were scrutinized in minute detail when her doctors, counsellors and nurses in St Edmundsbury were called to the stand. The picture that emerged was of a vulnerable, troubled and confused woman who was easily manipulated. However, on the day of her disappearance everyone had believed that Elaine was doing much better and had a bright future.

Elaine's interest in BDSM was also laid out and there were gasps in the crowded public gallery when the chains and other restraints found in her apartment were shown to the jury. The clank of heavy metal and clinking chains echoed around the panelled walls of the Central Criminal Court as the items were heaved from big evidence bags. Several men who had come into contact with Elaine through Alt.com and other websites came to court voluntarily to tell their part of the story.

Various protagonists, and some with only walk-on parts in the drama, spoke of the bad feelings and coincidences that brought them to Court 13. William Fegan recalled the bad feeling he got about the handcuffs, blindfold, ball gag and other items they had found under Sally's Bridge. 'I had a good think about what I found, I was driving at night and had good time to think,' he told the court. 'It was niggling me and I went back the following morning, put them in a bag and brought them to Roundwood Garda Station.' Garda James O'Donoghue described going back to the arched bridge again for the third time on 16 September 2013. 'Conditions were far more favourable. I remember it was sunny actually, no wind,' he said. 'On this occasion I could see a shiny object in the water which I could identify visually by looking at it.' He described climbing down the embankment to find the handcuff, but his boot sank in the mud, turning the water brown and black. 'I couldn't see it but knew it was there,' he said about his search.

In the witness box Garda O'Donoghue demonstrated how he found the keys that had proved so crucial, stretching out his arm to show how he searched underwater by touch. 'I felt something perhaps an inch or two under the mud. It was buried under the mud. I identified these as a set of keys.' He had then fished out a leather mask that had a zip closing over the mouth and each of the eyes, and air holes for the nostrils. He also described finding a large black-handled kitchen knife and a rusty chain with a heavy metal ring. There was more muttering as the items were unpacked from evidence bags and a photograph of the keys was shown on a large screen.

Psychologist Sheila Hawkins, Frank O'Hara's partner, recalled the events leading up to Elaine being reported missing. She described Elaine as a very conflicted girl who, in her professional opinion, had the emotional maturity of a fifteen-year-old. Ms Hawkins said she was aware of Elaine self-harming and described an incident when they were shopping for clothes in Dundrum town centre. When Elaine called her into the changing room for her opinion on a dress, she noticed two marks on her leg, like 'bramble scratches' but symmetrical, and three to four inches long. 'I knew they weren't accidental and she said she had cut herself again.' Elaine, she said, had a habit of 'embellishing stories' but was 'not creative enough' to make up elaborate lies and so they would always fit in with information that the family already had.

Elaine's sister, Ann Charles, said Elaine had phoned her in November 2011 to say she had suffered a miscarriage in the previous May but that she had 'fudged' things when Ann had tried to find out more. 'She said it was a result of a one-night stand and wouldn't talk about it any further.' Ann Charles described her sister as a naive person who would 'tell a man on the street her life story'. They had been close as children but were not particularly close as adults. Elaine's psychological difficulties meant that she 'acted quite young . . . She never really grew up as much as the rest of us. She was very naive, very trusting of people.'

Elaine's brother John said she had never talked about her private life and he was completely unaware of anything about her sexual relationships until he discovered the address for a fetish website on her laptop after she went missing. He told Dwyer's counsel that he was shocked to find his sister was interested in S&M. 'Elaine treated me very much like a baby brother,' he said, adding that they got on well and would talk a lot about college as they were both studying. He said that when her car was discovered at Shanganagh Cemetery, the family were concerned that she might have come to some harm or 'been grabbed' while she was at her mother's grave.

A Gordon Chisholm, an architect, told the court that he had first met Graham Dwyer when on a study trip to DIT Bolton Street from an architecture school in Glasgow and that they had reconnected when he moved to Ireland in 1994. Indeed, he had invited Dwyer to his wedding in Kilkenny and when he could not attend Dwyer had visited him to wish him well and give him a present. He was shown the order for the Goroon phone purchased from the Three Store on Grafton Street and said he had never bought a phone in the shop, and would probably have been at work in Waterford IT on the date of the transaction. He also had no knowledge of the address on the receipt, nor of three email addresses read out in court.

A large proportion of the evidence dealt with the cyber technology used to dredge secrets from the deepest recesses of computers and phones. It seemed fitting that in this case against a man who had so malevolently used and destroyed a vulnerable woman, two women had played such a vital role in constructing the case against him. Between them, Detective Garda Brid Wallace and police analyst Sarah Skedd had worked like Trojans to put together the technological picture that was so central to the case. Now they had to translate these huge swathes of highly technical evidence into something accessible for the jury. Of the 194 witnesses that were eventually called, these two women became the most familiar faces in the prosecution case, spending many days each in the witness box and conducting themselves with impressive understated professionalism.

Brid Wallace was frequently on hand to explain the process involved in retrieving material from the various phones and computers and describing its content. Over the course of the trial she was called to the witness stand on ten separate occasions. At the beginning of her testimony, Sarah Skedd explained how she had been given mobile phone records for five numbers of interest, downloads from handsets, data retrieved from computers owned by Dwyer and his victim, CCTV images, toll road data and documents seized from Dwyer's home and workplace. She then created a thirty-page document, including colour-coded graphics, to demonstrate the frequency with which the different phones used different phone masts. Her analysis showed how the Goroon and 'master' phones shadowed Graham Dwyer and tended to be in the same areas when he was picked up on CCTV footage. The prosecution took Ms Skedd through the entire 2,612 text messages that the Gardaí had managed to retrieve.

Four weeks into the trial, in the absence of the jury, the defence tried to have the Garda interviews with Dwyer excluded from evidence. In the legal argument that unfolded, those in the court were surprised to learn that the officer in overall charge of the investigation, Chief Superintendent Diarmuid O'Sullivan, had identified Graham Dwyer as a suspect a full week before the investigation team identified him, but had not shared this information with them. Remy Farrell revealed to the court that O'Sullivan and a detective had conducted what he described as a 'covert operation' in the dead of night to retrieve a DNA sample from Dwyer's bins. He argued that the interviews conducted by Peter Woods were fatally tainted by his superior's 'dumpster diving' activity.

O'Sullivan explained that on 20 September 2013 – three days after Elaine O'Hara's remains were identified – he had received confidential information suggesting that a person by the name 'Dwyer' or 'O'Dwyer' might have been in contact with the murdered woman. The only other information was that this person was an architect who worked on Baggot Street.

Keeping secrets came naturally to Diarmuid O'Sullivan. He was a veteran anti-terrorist investigator, a former head of operations with the Special Detective Unit (SDU), and he had an impressive track record and vast policing experience at home and in liaison with the FBI, MI5 and security services across Europe. He had also been responsible for the country's first witness protection programme following the murder of journalist Veronica Guerin. His instinct was to keep the sensitive information under wraps and away from the main investigation team until it could be developed. He was anxious not to distract the main enquiry in case the tip-off proved to be untrue. Instead he shared the intelligence with a former SDU colleague, Detective Sergeant Tom Doran. The two former 'spooks' had conducted countless covert intelligence operations in the past and this one was no different. Doran quickly identified who this Dwyer or O'Dwyer was likely to be – an architect who worked for A&D Wejchert and lived in Foxrock – and he conducted discreet enquiries and used open sources to build a detailed profile of the man.

On the same day that O'Sullivan had been tipped off, 20 September, forensic experts developed a DNA sample from a semen stain found on the mattress in Elaine O'Hara's apartment. Once they had identified their man, O'Sullivan and Doran decided to surreptitiously obtain a sample of Graham Dwyer's DNA and have it tested to establish if he was a legitimate suspect. At 5 a.m. on 27 September the two men took a number of items, including a Turtle Wax container, from Dwyer's bins, which had been left out on the street for collection. Such a search, for intelligence purposes, was legal and supported by case law.

Less than twelve hours later the main investigation team, having followed the technology trail, officially identified Graham Dwyer.

On 3 October the DNA sample taken from the Turtle Wax container was found to be a match with the one taken from the mattress. However, O'Sullivan did not divulge the findings of his enquiry because the main investigation was focusing on the right man and proceeding in a productive direction. In any event the sample was for intelligence purposes only and was never intended to be used as evidence. It had merely established that the DNA of someone living in Dwyer's house matched the DNA found on the mattress. When Dwyer was arrested, a DNA sample would be taken from the man himself. O'Sullivan did not want to muddy the waters for a future prosecution case.

The main investigation discovered that this DNA test had taken place when a report by the Forensic Science Laboratory weeks after Dwyer's arrest referred to two positive

DNA tests. This was the first that Detective Sergeant Peter Woods and his colleagues knew of any DNA test other than the one they had requested on the day of the arrest.

There was nothing either procedurally or legally wrong with O'Sullivan's secret operation. But Dwyer's defence counsel challenged his decision to search the suspect's bins, accusing him of conducting an 'off the books' enquiry.

'It was an operation to confirm intelligence that I had received from a confidential source,' O'Sullivan replied. 'I thought that it was important to develop that intelligence for the purpose of assisting the investigation but it had to be firewalled from the rest of the investigation.' He added that he was also concerned to protect the source of the original information.

O'Sullivan also told the court that he was mindful of the fact that while Dwyer might be a suspect at that early stage, 'the consequences of getting that wrong were problematical'.

Seán Guerin said that the DNA collected from the bin was not revealed to the main investigation and was not being used in evidence, so it had no impact on the Garda interviews. The so-called 'dumpster diving' was also within the law.

Having heard all the arguments, Mr Justice Tony Hunt ruled that the intelligence-gathering operation had not tainted the investigation and that there was sufficient evidence for Detective Sergeant Woods to make a lawful arrest. He was therefore allowing the interviews to be admitted in evidence.

At a later stage in the trial, in the presence of the jury, Remy Farrell returned to the subject of the clandestine operation while cross-examining Peter Woods. He referred to it as 'funny business'.

'I wouldn't describe it as funny business,' Woods said.

Farrell put it to him: 'You became aware weeks after all of this that in fact Chief Superintendent O'Sullivan had arranged to go rummaging through Mr Dwyer's bins some weeks before and taken a can of Turtle Wax?'

'A number of items were taken, but that's one of them,' he said.

Farrell asked if he had ever come across a Garda chief superintendent out in the early hours of the morning with a detective.

'No,' he said.

'It's hard work to get a chief superintendent out of his office,' Farrell said.

'Not in this particular case. He's very hands-on.'

15. Emer McShea and Gemma Dwyer Take the Stand

In the midst of the huge volume of evidence pitted against Dwyer, three women proved to be among the most compelling witnesses for the prosecution: his former girlfriend Emer McShea, his wife, Gemma, and Darci Day, the troubled and frail young American he had found while prowling through websites seeking a victim who would allow him to fulfil his fantasy of stabbing a woman to death.

After lunch on the afternoon of Friday 20 February, the twenty-second day of the trial, Seán Guerin turned and glanced to the back of Court 13. 'Would Emer McShea please make her way up to the witness box,' he said in his customary quiet monotone. McShea, a slim, attractive, brown-haired woman, got up and made her way through the crowd. She kept her head bowed as she passed Graham Dwyer to her left, ensuring not to make any kind of eye contact. Her appearance would not have been a surprise to him. Her allegations had been raised during his interrogation in October 2013 and he knew from the book of evidence that she would be called by the prosecution. Dwyer remained expressionless and if he felt any anxiety he hid it by searching busily through his documents while she took the stand.

Though Ms McShea had a much bigger story to tell about Graham Dwyer, for the purpose of the trial her contribution was confined to his bizarre sexual interests. If she or any witness dared venture outside the strict parameters of what was relevant to the crime with which Dwyer was charged, there was a risk that the trial would collapse and the entire punishing process would have to start again.

Once she had taken the oath and settled into her seat, Seán Guerin began leading her through the relevant sections of her original statement.

'Ms McShea, I think you were in a relationship with the accused man, Graham Dwyer, in the early 1990s, isn't that right?'

'Yes, that's right,' she said, in a soft Donegal accent.

'I think you were in college at the time, isn't that right?'

'Yes, that's right.'

'I think in 1992 you gave birth to your and his son, Sennan McShea, isn't that right?'

'Yes, that's right.'

'I think you recall one night during the course of your relationship when you had a discussion with him about fantasies, is that correct?'

'Yes, that's correct.'

'And Graham Dwyer told you his fantasy was stabbing a woman while having sex with her?'

'Yes, that's right.'

'And I think after that he began to bring a kitchen knife into your shared bedroom, isn't that right?'

'Yes, he did.'

'And I think he would pretend to stab you during sex, is that right?'

'Yes, that's right.'

'But I don't think he actually did, is that correct?'

'That's correct.'

Ms McShea went on to agree that she had identified Dwyer in stills taken from CCTV footage that Gardaí had shown her on the day of Dwyer's arrest. 'I was shown stills initially, and then I was shown video clips,' she told Seán Guerin. The footage was that taken at Elaine O'Hara's apartment complex on various dates in 2012.

It also emerged that Dwyer had sent a birthday card to Sennan McShea on his twenty-second birthday in the previous November. In it Dwyer wrote to his son: 'Everything going well here, all forensics clear and we are sure of an acquittal now we have a mountain of evidence that it was suicide.'

'With Sennan's consent, you handed that card and the envelope to Detective Sergeant Peter Woods. Is that correct?' Guerin asked.

'Yes, I did.'

It may have lasted for a mere five minutes, and the number of words spoken may have been sparse, but Emer McShea's evidence was devastating for Dwyer's defence. It clearly pointed to his early interest in piquerism and the practice described in the thousands of text messages. Dwyer's counsel chose not to cross-examine her, which reinforced the impact of her evidence.

Seán Guerin then called Sennan McShea, whom he also led through his original Garda statement. The young man agreed that he had spent time with his grandparents in Cork in the summer of 2006. He was fourteen at the time and had been smoking in secret; his grandmother found out and told his father.

'You had planned telling him yourself?' Guerin said.

'But I hadn't actually got around to it.'

Guerin asked if his father got very upset over this and 'hit the roof', giving him a lecture on the dangers of smoking.

'That's right.'

Sennan McShea said that he was living in Ballyshannon, County Donegal, in July 2012 when his father texted. Dwyer was working on a hospital project in Letterkenny. A faint smile broke out on Dwyer's face when Sennan McShea told Guerin: 'I was actually in my home address in Ballyshannon and he collected me and we went to Bundoran together.'

This evidence was crucial because it confirmed the cell site analysis showing the 'master' phone pinging off masts in Ballyshannon and Bundoran at the same time as Dwyer's work phone on that date. (To further prove the point, the Gardaí called a witness from Dorrian's Imperial Hotel in Ballyshannon who also confirmed Dwyer had spent the night there.) Sennan McShea confirmed that he had identified his father in a booklet of CCTV images. His evidence lasted a few minutes and Dwyer's counsel chose not to cross-examine the young man. He left without making eye contact with his father.

Gemma Dwyer's world had fallen asunder when Detective Sergeant Peter Woods knocked on her front door in October 2013. Sixteen months later she came to court to give evidence against her husband. In law, spouses can exempt themselves from giving evidence against each other, but Gemma Dwyer was determined to take the stand. During the sixth week of the trial she was the prosecution's 167th witness.

Gemma Dwyer was ushered into the court by members of the investigation team just after lunch on Wednesday

25 February. She waited to be called, sitting huddled on a bench beside Peter Woods as other officers stood shielding her. Slightly built and wearing a sober navy dress she shivered and wrapped her arms around herself, as if trying to get warm. Anxiety and pain were etched on her pale face, which was partially veiled by her short blonde hair. It seemed like she was battling, not entirely successfully, to keep the tears at bay.

Silence descended when the judge and then the jury resumed their seats. Seán Guerin looked to the back of the court and asked quietly if Gemma Dwyer would please come to the witness stand. All at once the heaving room went still and became focused on this small, broken woman. Uniformed Gardaí and detectives silently opened a path through the throng, walking in front of Gemma Dwyer as she followed nervously, her head bowed and her shoulders hunched. Peter Woods stayed reassuringly close behind her as she made her way along the wall of the courtroom and behind the dock where her husband sat, thereby avoiding any risk that she might see him. The Graham Dwyer she had known and loved had died the morning the Gardaí came calling.

Everyone waited patiently as she took her seat, angling her back to her husband and facing Judge Hunt. The judge smiled gently as if to reassure her that she was safe, and his tipstaff placed a glass of water on the desk in front of her. Dwyer turned his gaze elsewhere, folding his hands in his lap. Though trembling, Gemma Dwyer maintained her composure as Seán Guerin began by asking if it was correct that she was the wife of 'the accused man, Graham Dwyer'. 'I am,' she said, her voice frayed. He asked her when they had first met.

'We were both students of architecture in Bolton Street.'

Asked if it was the mid 1990s, or 'that sort of time', she said: 'Correct.'

She agreed that they had begun dating around 1997 and had subsequently married. She confirmed the details of their lives through the years – the cottage in Rathmines, the move to Foxrock, Dwyer's job with A&D Wejchert, their two children. She had to steady her hand as she wrote the children's names and dates of birth on a piece of paper. It was handed to Judge Hunt, who ordered that to protect them the children's names should not be reported. She also confirmed that she knew about Dwyer's son, Sennan McShea.

'Were there issues with Sennan's smoking when he was younger?' Guerin asked.

'Yes, it was something that upset Graham greatly,' she said, her voice growing a little stronger, and added that there was a similar issue with their childminder. 'My childminder smoked but we agreed where and when she smoked, but he was never . . . he was always quite against that.'

Guerin asked her about Dwyer's level of interest in model aeroplane flying.

'It was huge, it was every day he would work on his planes and every weekend he would practise or participate in competitions. He would research planes on the Internet a lot of the time, it was a huge interest.'

Gemma Dwyer's voice again trembled as she described the Graham Dwyer she once knew: the quintessential modern man. Her husband's working hours were generally between 8.30 a.m. and 4.45 p.m. When they first moved house, she was initially working in the city centre and their child was in a crèche. She went through redundancy and got another job. He would leave first in the morning and she would wait for the childminder to arrive, and then leave for her office. He would be home before her in the evening and the childminder would have left by the time she got back, except on days when Dwyer was working late. He would have dinner prepared and the children organized.

In terms of free time he went to his model aeroplane club on Wednesday afternoons, and she would sometimes go sailing in Dun Laoghaire on Thursdays. He would go flying directly after work and she would expect him home around 8.30 p.m.

Her voice began to tremble again and she fought back tears when asked about the birth of their second child in March 2011. She had stayed in Holles Street one night and had a lot of family visiting over the following days. 'It was a wonderful time, the birth of a child,' she whispered. By the time she was testifying against him, Gemma Dwyer was well aware that while she had been nursing their new baby, her husband had been rekindling his relationship with Elaine O'Hara. Her baby was born six days after the master first renewed his contact with Elaine on the Goroon phone.

Seán Guerin asked her how many computers were in the home.

'Graham's own laptop, I had a laptop. There would have been computers used from Graham's office he would have had permission to bring home,' she said. Gemma said he had been 'fantastic' and 'could do anything' with a computer.

Gemma Dwyer was also asked about his cars and replied: 'There were a lot of cars. He would buy and sell cars quite frequently.' She said he had been particularly fond of a Porsche 911 and 'he called it his baby'.

Graham Dwyer broke into a smile when he heard this and looked towards his wife's back as if wanting to share that cherished memory. As she spoke of his abilities with computers and planes and cars, he seemed chuffed by the compliment. In contrast, when Gemma Dwyer spoke of life with her husband, it was in the manner of a woman who had been widowed suddenly and violently and whose shock and grief were still raw.

Seán Guerin asked about the day when Elaine O'Hara's remains were found, 13 September 2013, and if Gemma Dwyer was aware they had been found that day.

'I am aware of that, yes.'

Guerin asked if the date was significant.

'My birthday is the 13th of September and Graham's birthday is the 13th of September. We went out to dinner. We went out to a Mexican restaurant on South Great George's Street and celebrated our birthday together.' Her voice trailed off, as if her mind had returned to that night of innocent enjoyment.

Guerin asked if she recalled any kind of unusual reaction in her husband when news of the finding of a body in Killakee was reported.

'No,' she said.

She was then shown pictures of several exhibits, including the rucksack found in the reservoir – of which she had no recollection – and two knives, which she said had not come from her kitchen.

Guerin asked if her husband had any identifying marks.

'He has a tattoo on his shoulder,' she said, describing it as a symbol from the Book of Kells, around the size of her palm, on his left shoulder. She said he had got it in his student years, 'before I met him'.

When asked how he normally dressed for work, she

replied: 'Most frequently in a black polo neck and jacket.' She was then shown an exhibit photo of a jacket and replied: 'Yep, Graham had a North Face jacket.'

She agreed that her husband was also interested in cycling and mountain biking and said she thought he used to meet others at the Hellfire Club in the Dublin Mountains.

Seán Guerin produced a photograph of a spade and asked Gemma Dwyer if she recognized it. The spade had been found close to the spot where Elaine O'Hara's remains were found.

'I do. The spade from our garden,' she said, her voice growing stronger again. Its absence 'was something that came to mind after the arrest', she said. 'In relation to this spade, I recalled that the spade had been missing from our garden for the whole summer of 2013. I spent a lot of time in the garden with the children with the swing set, the trampoline and the sandpit.'

She explained that this was clear in her memory because the dog from next door would foul in her garden, and she used the spade to clean the dirt from the grass. 'I mentioned it to Graham a number of times and in the end I used a spade from the sandpit,' she added. She said she recognized the spade as the stickers on the handle were familiar and there was a splatter 'of orangey red paint on it'.

Dwyer smiled again as his wife described what a sloppy painter he was: 'The fencing and the garden shed had been painted in a fence-like paint that had gotten everywhere. It was on the ground and over his clothes.'

Gemma Dwyer was shown a second spade, which she found in the garden when she returned to her home after Gardaí had searched it. 'Things had been put back in place for the most,' she said, however compost had been turned out on to the back lawn. 'There was a spade among it. I said that the Garda Siochána must have left that spade behind.'

She sipped water as she was shown a photograph of a swing set in her back garden. The photograph was taken on 5 March 2011, she believed. 'Before my daughter was born we bought this swing set for my son and my dad and Graham built it. I believe the picture was taken when it was built,' she said. Seán Guerin asked her to look to the left of the slide in the image.

'That's our spade. That is the one that had gone missing.'

Seán Guerin asked her about various dates, and she said she remembered her husband visiting Ballyshannon in July 2012. She also confirmed spending a few weeks with the children at her parents' home in Sligo in June 2011 when their baby daughter was three months old. While away, she was aware her husband was having 'a lads' night' with old friends from the Hammies. 'I knew he was planning to have something. Him and his old school friends – every year or two one of them would have something.' She confirmed Dwyer also went camping with his father and brothers to Blind Stand in Cork. He had been away with them on 18 August 2012, because she met him the following day at a family day at Roundwood Flying Club.

All of these answers were important to the prosecution's case. The 'lads' night', the holiday in Sligo and the camping trip all featured in the texts from 'sir' and the 'master'.

Seán Guerin asked if she could also clarify the date of her husband's fortieth birthday party in Cork – 15 September 2012?

'That's right, yeah. I arranged it and it was in a restaurant in Bandon.'

She also agreed that her husband had attended an An Bord Pleanála hearing near Cathal Brugha Street, which she said was quite unusual. Gemma also recalled repairs to a silver Audi that she said 'was expensive to be fixed' and 'caused a lot of upset'. The significance of the planning hearing was that Sarah Skedd's analysis showed that one of the phones was active in that part of Dublin at the same time and also that call credit had been purchased from a shop close to where the meeting was taking place. 'Sir' had complained about the cost of fixing the car in texts to Elaine O'Hara, who, in a reply, referred to the car as 'Ah your baby sir'.

Gemma Dwyer also agreed that she sent Christmas and birthday cards to her sister-in-law, Mandy Wroblewski, and that for a time the address she had been using was slightly wrong. When Mandy Wroblewski gave her the correct address Gemma Dwyer had amended it in her address book, crossing out the incorrect address, which had been 'Oaklawn, Clerihan, Co. Tipperary' – the address given when the Goroon phone was registered.

'I don't think you've any specific recollection of the week 20 August 2012, you just recall being busy in work?' Seán Guerin said.

'Yeah,' she said.

At one point Guerin asked her to look at a video still of her husband from their days in the cottage in Rathmines. There was sadness in Gemma Dwyer's face when she turned towards the smiling face on the screen. As she gazed at it she wept quietly, as though remembering someone she had once loved and no longer knew.

Seán Guerin asked about a letter Graham Dwyer had sent to his wife from prison on 28 February 2014. She had recognized the handwriting on the letter as his and afterwards handed it over to the Gardaí as evidence. Guerin then read out some of the letter's content, avoiding anything of a more personal nature. Gemma Dwyer sat in silence as he read:

> Do not believe the gardaí. They actually have no evidence apart from my name and someone else's phone number in that awful girl's diary. I did know her, yes, I was helping her and I wasn't totally honest with you. There is another man, someone who likes Real Madrid and wears pink underwear who is involved in this. I believe this girl committed suicide and this man disposed of some embarrassing items on her behalf.
>
> Why do you think none of her family are pushing this? She tried to kill herself several times. I saved her life once. She was released from a mental hospital that day and was on eight prescriptions. I should have gone to the police when she went missing, I could have known where she might be but I did not.

In a brief, terse exchange about her identification of the spade, defence counsel Remy Farrell put it to Gemma Dwyer that she had been shown a spade by the Gardaí and said it was 'the same type of spade as ours'. She had told Gardaí she had noticed paint on the spade and that this reminded her of her husband painting the fence and shed in their garden towards the end of 2007 or 2008. She had said spatters of the paint had gone everywhere.

Remy Farrell put it to her that the basis of her identification of the spade was the paint. 'And other characteristics,' she said, adding that it was the same type of spade and had the same stickers. Remy Farrell challenged her: 'Oh, come now, Mrs Dwyer, when I asked you about this a few minutes ago you were quite emphatic that it was just the paint that made you identify it. To coin a phrase, a spade is a spade.'

'Yes . . . Oscar Wilde,' she said, referring to Wilde's use of the phrase in his work.

Gemma Dwyer concluded her evidence after fifty minutes. Leaving the witness box she took the same circuitous route around her husband's back and was escorted from the court among a phalanx of Gardaí.

The following day an expert from the Forensic State Laboratory said she found that the paint on the spade was not compatible with the paint on the sheds in the Dwyers' garden. However, the splatters of paint were similar in colour and composition to the paint used on a fence in the garden. There had been minor differences in the components of the paints tested. But it could not be proved beyond all reasonable doubt that the paint was the same. Graham Dwyer smiled.

16. Darci's Story

A defendant is rarely surprised during a criminal trial. Long before the judge takes his seat and a jury is sworn in, the accused will have full knowledge of every witness and piece of evidence that the State intends to present against him. In the pre-trial process the accused is entitled to full and unfettered disclosure of all the information in the hands of the DPP – except, that is, for material considered to be security sensitive such as the identity of confidential intelligence sources. And during the trial there are also strict parameters laid down beyond which the prosecution dare not step because to do so would prejudice the jury and result in either the trial collapsing or an acquittal.

So, when he studied the seven volumes in the book of evidence it appeared that Graham Dwyer realized that the women in his life had the potential to do a huge amount of damage to his defence. This was likely his motivation for sending his son a strangely worded birthday card and a letter proclaiming his innocence to his wife: if he could somehow convince his former girlfriend and his wife that he was likely to walk, then they might be dissuaded from going to court. But the ploy failed and by late 2014 Dwyer knew that they were going to appear for the prosecution. The women could not endure the prospect of him being free to torment them in the future.

There was one final witness that Dwyer believed he could

manipulate: Darci Day. When he read Day's statement, his mistake in discussing Elaine O'Hara's suicidal ideation would have been clear to Dwyer. Her evidence would clearly be of huge benefit to the prosecution. She could confirm his connection with Elaine and his intention to kill her. She could also corroborate his predilection for rape and murder. Most important, the prosecution could present the real-life 'Cassie' who was the central character in his 'Killing Darci' story. 'Cassie' was the pseudonym Day had used when she first met Dwyer online.

In December 2014, Mr Justice Paul Carney had refused an application by the State to have Darci Day's evidence received via video link from the United States. His ruling meant that if the 23-year-old was to be a witness for the prosecution she would be required to travel to the courtroom in Ireland and face the man who had fantasized about her death. Darci Day had never been on a plane and did not have a passport. She suffered from psychiatric difficulties that were much more acute than those of Elaine O'Hara. She had been the victim of child sexual abuse and she suffered from a variety of conditions, including attention deficit disorder (ADD), post-traumatic stress disorder (PTSD) and learning difficulties. Like Elaine, she had been self-harming from the age of twelve. She had met Dwyer as she sought out someone to help her take her own life.

Day's witness statement was a reminder of her vulnerability, much of which she had shared with Dwyer in the past. He had plenty of experience in pulling the psychological strings of a fragile woman. So he decided to get in touch.

On 22 December 2014, Darci Day contacted Detective Ryan Brockway from the Major Crimes Unit of the Maine

State Police, who had been liaising with her on behalf of the Gardaí. She was in a panic and seemed terrified. That morning, out of the blue, she had received a Christmas card from Graham Dwyer. The message inside was short and to the point. Dwyer told her that he was being wrongly blamed for a murder that had really been a suicide. He said there was no forensic evidence linking him to the death and that there was no evidence to suggest that Elaine O'Hara had been murdered. The lack of evidence meant that he was confident of an acquittal – and freedom. Dwyer wanted Darci Day to know that he knew where she lived if he ever fancied a visit once he had regained his freedom. He signed off by wishing her and her dog Bruno a merry Christmas.

The card subtly conveyed the message that Day's evidence would make no difference to the outcome of the trial, which was a foregone conclusion. And it was obvious that he knew where she lived and could come to visit her.

Day was frantic. Her only contact with Dwyer, which had ended over three years earlier, had been via email. He should not have known her home address.

Dwyer's ploy proved to be a massive miscalculation. The Maine police contacted the Gardaí in Blackrock and the police on both sides of the Atlantic agreed that this was a classic example of attempting to intimidate a witness. Peter Woods and his colleagues in Maine rushed to reassure the frightened young woman that Dwyer would never harm her. She agreed to make a further statement describing how his Christmas card had put her in fear of her life.

Armed with this new statement, Seán Guerin made a fresh application to have Darci Day's evidence received from Maine by video link. On the fifth day of the trial, in the absence of the jury, Guerin drew Judge Hunt's attention to the threatening communication that had been sent to Day since the initial video-link application had been turned down by Judge Carney. Detective Sergeant Woods told the court that Ms Day had serious concerns about being required to travel to Ireland for the trial. He referred to the 'Killing Darci' document found on Dwyer's computer: 'There is the first name of the witness and you can see the nature of the document,' he said.

Woods said that in her statement about the Christmas card, Day 'was feeling very much in fear of the defendant'. He added that receiving the Christmas card had 'solidified' her reason for wanting to testify via video link. 'She doesn't want to be in the same room or the same country as Mr Dwyer,' Woods said, as Judge Hunt read the card. The detective sergeant said that Darci Day's biggest concern was how Dwyer had got hold of her address in the first place.

When cross-examined by Dwyer's counsel, Remy Farrell, Woods agreed that the witness was someone with 'substantial psychiatric difficulties' and was on psychotropic medication. She had been in contact by email with the accused but had deleted the messages. The investigator said attempts had been made to recover the emails but it had not been possible. He said that Ms Day did not wish to disclose her medical and psychiatric records.

Remy Farrell pointed out that Ms Day's address had been at the top of the statement furnished by the prosecution. Detective Sergeant Woods said it should have been redacted and he did not know 'where he [Dwyer] got the address'.

Farrell said that in her first statement Day had said that she did not want her name to be made public 'in case he gets out'. Farrell said this concern was 'wholly irrational' as Dwyer had been in custody since his arrest. Peter Woods disagreed and said Ms Day's fear was 'definitely not irrational'.

Farrell then argued that the original video-link application had lasted three minutes and the only issue raised was that the witness did not have a passport. He claimed the new application was 'an abuse of process' and it was hard to see the additional statement as 'anything other than a ready-up'. Judge Hunt reserved his judgement and later granted the State's application. In his arrogance Graham Dwyer had scored an incredible own goal.

After lunch on day twenty-nine of the trial, Tuesday 3 March, Darci Day's anxious pale face filled the overhead screens in Court 13. With her heavy black eyeliner and long grungy hair, dyed platinum blonde on top and jet black underneath, she looked like a goth. She was wearing a white T-shirt and fingerless black gloves. She sat in one of a number of green leather chairs that were lined up behind a large oval mahogany table. Behind her was a bookcase packed with books. The setting appeared to be a room in a courthouse or official building. When she stood up to take the oath, which was administered by a Maine court official, the slogan 'God's Got Me' could be read on her T-shirt. Detective Brockway was also sworn in. He put his hand on the Bible and pledged not to speak to the witness or allow anyone else to speak to her while she gave her evidence. He was dressed in a three-piece suit and sat in another green leather chair to one side of the screen.

Darci Day appeared to be an emotional wreck. Her hands fidgeted constantly on the table in front of her and her laboured breathing was audible in her microphone. Several times she broke down and sobbed as her evidence was tested. She was hesitant and nervous as she found herself in the surreal situation of giving evidence to strangers, across the Atlantic Ocean, in a country nearly 4,500 kilometres away, against a man she had never met.

Seán Guerin brought her through a summary of her early life. Her parents had divorced when she was young. Her father had 'relationship and alcohol problems', and her mother's boyfriend also had 'issues'. She was sexually abused as a child. 'I struggled a lot with depression. My grandmother was the one woman I really looked up to and I lost her to bone cancer when I was in seventh grade [age twelve] and when I became suicidal my mom was going through a court battle with my dad. I basically felt like I was worthless to my family and I just didn't want to live any more and my presence in their life was hindering them so I struggled a lot with suicide and self-harm. Very, very depressed.' As she spoke she rubbed her hands across the table.

She started going online to find people who had similar thoughts and fantasies. One of two sites she accessed regularly was called Darkfettishnet.com and on it she used the name 'Cassie' and shared her fantasies about 'myself dying'. 'I didn't have the courage to actually kill myself,' she said.

She recalled that she was struggling at the time, in 2011 and 2012, when 'there was just a bunch of different stuff going on' including the loss of both her dog and a job on the same day.

Seán Guerin then asked her if the name Graham Dwyer meant anything to her.

'It does . . . I can't remember what website I found him on or anything but we talked a lot through gmail.'

They had mainly been in contact through her email address, suicide.silence923@gmail.com, and via some texts, but they never met.

'A lot of our discussion was about similar fantasies and I unloaded all this stuff on him about things I was going through and feeling like a failure to my family and we discussed him basically ending my life,' she said. 'I told him a lot of stuff going on in my life. I needed someone to talk to. He was there and he listened to me and offered me a solution.'

Darci Day said a lot of the fantasies that they exchanged were about rape and murder. While they texted through her regular mobile number, 'he had talked about getting a separate cell phone for communication, like a track phone,' she said, later explaining that this was a term for an unregistered phone.

'We sent links to videos – YouTube videos – of throat-cutting or strangulation videos. There were some pictures, I don't remember them all. I do remember diagrams being sent,' adding that the diagrams were of arteries 'so you couldn't miss'.

Day said she knew Dwyer had a wife, but she didn't know too much about him, except that he liked planes.

Seán Guerin asked if he had mentioned any other person.

'Yes, he did mention Elaine O'Hara. I knew they had an intimate relationship and he told me she was similar to me and was suicidal.'

When Seán Guerin asked if she knew anything else about their relationship she began to sob again, and put her head down in her hands. Then she recovered her composure and continued. 'He said that he used to cut her . . . on the stomach area and stuff.'

When asked about the circumstances she said 'that it was mutual and sexual' and also that it involved 'bondage-type stuff'.

'I believe she had asked him to kill her in the past.'

'What did Graham Dwyer say about that?'

'I honestly don't remember too much about it. His fantasy was basically wanting to stab a woman to death during sex.'

Mr Guerin asked if Dwyer had expressed any fantasies that featured Elaine O'Hara.

'Yes he did . . . that he basically wanted to go after her and if she wanted to, he wanted to kill her and come after me.'

Seán Guerin asked if there had been any discussion of the possibility of her meeting Dwyer.

'He didn't talk too much about Elaine but in reference to me, he was looking at places in Maine that were likely disposal sites.'

The lawyer asked if there had been any discussion about the method that he had planned to use in killing her. Darci Day hesitated and then agreed that there was. Seán Guerin asked what that was.

'That he would have me meet him somewhere and then from there I would leave my car and get in the car with him and he would drive me to the location and then basically from there . . . he wanted to have sex and then cut my throat until I lost consciousness during intercourse,' she said slowly, her voice wavering.

In cross-examination Remy Farrell quizzed Ms Day about her medical and mental health history. She confirmed that she suffered from ADD, PTSD and had a learning disability, but said she was not currently on any medication. She did not want to discuss her medical history, but agreed she'd seen a counsellor for 'memory' issues among other things. Asked what those memory issues were, she said: 'I don't remember . . . all the molestation.'

Farrell asked if the circumstances of her life had changed since 2011 when she first encountered Dwyer.

'They have changed amazingly. During that period, I ended up giving my life to Christ and turning my life around.' Darci Day said she had never felt peace like when she turned to God. She had been to counselling but did not stay with it for long.

The defence lawyer asked if the counselling was to discuss 'the issues that we are discussing here'.

'No, I didn't discuss anything about that part of my life with my counsellor . . . I only discussed the family stuff.'

Farrell reminded her that she had first met Detective Ryan Brockway on 29 April 2014 when he called to her home and interviewed her. Detective Brockway had recorded that interview and Ms Day had said in it: 'I actually went to a doctor about some of this and they sent me to a counsellor.'

Day insisted that she did not discuss it with the doctor, who she said gave her a series of tests aimed at assessing her learning disability and 'memory issues' before diagnosing her.

Asked if self-harm was still a problem for her, she shook her head and said: 'Absolutely not.'

Farrell wanted to know if she had provided any of the emails that passed between her and Dwyer.

'I don't have any of that old stuff. I got rid of everything when I turned my life around. I didn't want to be reminded of the pain of this stuff. They [the emails] are all gone, there is no record. It's all gone.'

She confirmed the name she had used in her gmail address – suicide.silence – which was the name of a deathcore band. (Deathcore is a genre of extreme heavy metal music.)

Farrell said that in 2011 she had described being interested in murder fantasy, and asked her if that was something she had wanted to follow through.

'I just really needed someone to talk to at the time. Part of me wanted to follow through on it and part of me didn't.'

He asked if she had been under the impression that Dwyer would not act on the fantasies.

'Yeah, I didn't think he was actually serious about it. If I had any idea that he was actually serious, I would have done something. I would have reported it.'

Farrell then put it to Darci Day that she met other men and there was one person – not Graham Dwyer – that she thought was serious and he scared her.

'That is correct,' she agreed, adding that ultimately it had been her who ceased contact with Dwyer and he didn't contact her again.

'He was very respectful about leaving me alone. He never tried to contact me.'

When Detective Brockway first visited Darci Day and asked her about Dwyer's email, she had recognized his name.

'So he used his own name with you at all times?' Farrell asked.

'That is correct.'

Farrell then put it to her that in her original statement to Detective Brockway she said she thought Dwyer would come to her home and she would get in his car and go with him and he would 'do it' for her. The defence lawyer pointed out that this was different from the account of the fantasy she had just given in court. He suggested that what she was saying now bore a closer resemblance to 'the facts of this case'.

She said she did not want to explain this.

Farrell suggested that Detective Brockway told her Dwyer had some of her Facebook material on his computer and 'keeps it to go over and over again'.

'I don't think so,' she replied.

'He said: "Knowing these people, they keep these things till they die." Did he say that?' Farrell said.

'I don't remember exactly what was said. I have been in shock since day one and I am still reeling.'

She said she did not remember the content of all the videos they had exchanged but agreed that they 'contained scenes of murder and so on'. She also accepted that she 'might have' sent him pictures of her knife collection, and that she still had it. 'I guess I haven't gotten rid of those.'

Remy Farrell asked if she had sent Dwyer maps of locations of where she lived and worked.

'No, I don't think so.'

'Would you accept that part of the fantasy you were exchanging was that he [Dwyer] might turn up at any time?' Farrell asked, and she agreed.

Asked if they swapped written stories, Darci Day said she may have sent Dwyer 'some stuff' but did not remember the details.

She collapsed and sobbed uncontrollably when Remy Farrell quizzed her about a picture of herself that she had sent to Dwyer which he had photoshopped to depict her with horrific stab wounds. The image had been recovered from Dwyer's hard drive by Detective Garda Brid Wallace. Darci Day slumped across the table, sobbing and slapping her hands on the polished mahogany. 'I don't want to answer this question. I don't wanna do this,' she wailed. Her cries from the wall speakers filled the courtroom in Dublin. The screens went blank and Judge Hunt sent the jury out briefly to allow the witness some time to collect herself back in Maine. Ms Day was still visibly upset when the large screens flashed into life again.

Mr Farrell assured her that he was 'nearly finished' and then asked about a video on her Facebook page, in which a woman was having sex with a corpse. She agreed she had been tagged by a friend and commented how she found it 'hard to look away' as it was 'horrifying'. The senior counsel also questioned her about a short video comment she had made about the case which she posted on YouTube and which he said had been a 'somewhat unusual thing to do'.

'I didn't mention any details in it,' she replied as the tears continued to flow down her cheeks. 'I made that video to give the people out there hope and courage if they are going through a hard time, because no matter how hard things are, people are still loved,' she said. 'I want to say a huge prayer for the family of Elaine . . . I am so heartbroken, I feel so terrible . . . I am so sorry. I'm just praying for all of you guys. I'm praying for Graham and his family. I wanted to reach out, I just wanted to tell people from the bottom of my heart that I'm so sorry.'

She smiled weakly and then the screens went blank.

17. Five Minutes That Stunned the Courtroom

Two days after Darci Day's appearance, the trial took another dramatic turn when Mr Justice Tony Hunt invoked a rarely used section of the Criminal Justice Act of 1951 permitting a judge to exclude the public from a court on the grounds that the material was indecent and obscene. The judge's decision came as the prosecution prepared to introduce the most harrowing evidence yet to be heard or seen: Graham Dwyer's fantasy stories and home movies.

Dwyer's father, Seán, a quiet, courteous man who had not missed a day of the trial, left with the public as they filed out. The O'Hara family had been made aware of the nature of the disturbing material to come and had chosen not to attend while it was being dealt with. The large media contingent, most of whom were female journalists who covered the entire trial, were allowed to remain.

Explaining why the court had empty seats for the first time in seven weeks, Judge Hunt warned the jury that what they were about to hear would be difficult. Detective Garda Brid Wallace then explained how she had discovered the 'Killing Darci' document on the Seagate hard drive found in Dwyer's home. It had been created on 2 March 2011 and edited for eighty-nine minutes before it was saved. The author name and last modified name was 'A&D Wejchert'.

Seán Guerin then read the document aloud and as he did so Graham Dwyer's face flushed bright red and his nervous tic – opening and closing his mouth – was in overdrive. As Guerin delivered the sickening fantasy in his usual monotone, Dwyer began to stoop down in the dock, as if he wanted to hide. Eventually he sat with his head in his hands.

The following morning Judge Hunt again invoked his powers and cleared the public from the court, this time for the whole day. He repeated his warning to the jury that they were about to hear and see more material of a 'difficult nature'.

The first exhibit was the doctored photograph of Darci Day. In it she was lying on her back, with her hands around her head and naked from the waist up. She looked lifeless. It appeared that her throat had been cut, that there were multiple stab wounds on her body and her intestines were protruding from a stomach wound. Dwyer had done such a good job that the picture looked authentic.

Brid Wallace then told the court how and where she had discovered the story 'Jenny's First Rape' and other stories. Again, Seán Guerin read the graphic material slowly and without emotion. As he continued, Graham Dwyer could barely be seen in the dock.

While Dwyer's stories were damaging, the secret home movies of him having sex and stabbing women would be a complete disaster for his case and he knew it. He instructed his defence team to have them kept from the jury. The subject came up for discussion, in the absence of the jury, the day after Darci Day's appearance. The media cannot report proceedings when the jury is absent. The prosecution made an application to play a selection of the videos, which included Elaine O'Hara tied up and being stabbed during sexual activity.

Seán Guerin read a statement from Detective Sergeant Peter Woods in which he described a total of eleven short clips the prosecution proposed to show, including the one in which Dwyer used chloroform and the one in which he pretended to stab himself. The other nine clips were of Dwyer having sex with women. Elaine was in six of these. Two other women were in the other three and their faces would be pixilated to protect their identities.

Remy Farrell argued for the defence that while 'one can understand the relevance' of the videos, and why the jury might be entitled to know of them, the question was how they should be put to the jury. 'It would be extraordinarily difficult for any jury to approach material like this without a strong visceral reaction,' Remy Farrell said. 'How can any presumption of innocence survive the jury seeing material of this sort?' He said it was a question of weighing up the prejudicial effect of the videos and their probative value (i.e. their value to the prosecution in backing up its argument about Dwyer's predilections). He asked why they could not be entered into evidence simply by means of a 'narrative' description, taken from Detective Sergeant Woods' statement.

Seán Guerin argued that Woods could only be a witness and that the evidence itself should be assessed by the jury. He accepted the jury 'may have a reaction' but said it was their function to decide what was true and untrue; he said the video evidence 'gives the lie to' what the accused had told the Gardaí. In relation to the argument that an 'enormous amount' of clips could 'turn the jury against the accused', he said the prosecution wanted to play only a small number of what had been retrieved. He said the nature of the relationship of the accused and the deceased was 'absolutely central to this case'.

Guerin went on to say that throughout the trial the defence had tried to suggest there were sexual activities that Elaine O'Hara had a particular interest in, an interest that was not shared by Graham Dwyer. 'In interview, he repeatedly and at length sought to maintain that these were things that he had no real interest in and that he was doing it for the benefit of Ms O'Hara,' Guerin said. Dwyer had tried to portray himself as a 'chancer' who was 'getting sexual intercourse' but had no real interest in the other aspects of the activity. 'It is difficult to convey how false that suggestion is without viewing the material,' said Guerin.

Judge Hunt interjected: 'It seems to me the suggestion [by the defence] is this lady met her end by her own hand.'

Seán Guerin said this was true, but it was also a part of the defence case that Dwyer had no interest in particular sexual practices he and Elaine O'Hara engaged in and did not derive any sexual satisfaction from them. He had engaged in this activity only to satisfy her. 'Central to the prosecution's case is that he had a strong urge to stab women, this was not merely some fantasy,' Guerin said.

Judge Hunt said he had had a quick flick through Peter Woods' statement and said that 'one can only imagine' the video material. He said the defence's argument seemed to be 'that this is just going to put them [the jury] over the edge into a place where pre-judgement will happen. They will be so horrified by this they will not be able to be impartial.'

Seán Guerin said the defence's case depended in part on an attack on the character of the deceased and the prosecution had been put on formal notice of that. He said the defence could not impugn the character of the victim and then seek to 'hide' relevant material from the jury. He referred to what Dwyer had told Gardaí when he had been interviewed: 'I'm not a big part of the [BDSM] scene . . . She was deeper into it than me.' When shown the items found in the reservoir, Dwyer had said: 'This is her stuff.' On knife play, he had told Gardaí: 'That is something she is interested in. I am curious about it, sure, but I wouldn't ever hurt anybody, I wouldn't cut anybody, I wouldn't bloodlet.'

Guerin continued: 'The prosecution's case is these are lies by the accused man and are of enormous significance. It's only by looking at the material and the look on the face of the accused that one can see how far from the truth all that is. Sergeant Woods cannot get that across. The jury can only judge that by seeing the way the accused behaves with the deceased. He denies that he wanted to hurt anybody. The jury needs to see quite how much he enjoyed hurting her. What Sergeant Woods can never get across is quite how visceral an experience that was for the accused man. This is something that the accused got an enormous, visceral, deep satisfaction out of. This is something the accused wanted to do and enjoyed doing and nothing Sergeant Woods can say in the witness box can convey the force of that to the jury.'

Judge Hunt said he accepted that a narrative was different from seeing and hearing the material itself, but it was a trial.

Seán Guerin said it was a trial by jury, not by Sergeant Woods. 'I am entitled to have the evidence seen and assessed by the jury and by nobody else,' he argued.

'So is it captured in the common or garden phrase "You should have seen your man"?' Judge Hunt said.

Guerin said the State was not going to deal with it in any

sort of gratuitous or unnecessary way. They had selected nine clips, six of which were activity with the deceased. He said they were relevant and probative 'because they show the accused man stabbing the deceased and because they appear to show that is something he is doing – I won't say necessarily contrary to her wishes – but certainly the videos give that impression. That doesn't come across clearly on the printed page, that there is some considerable reluctance on her part and some considerable enjoyment on his part in relation to what's happening.' There were also two videos he proposed to show of the accused on his own.

Judge Hunt asked if it was necessary to show so much material. Mr Guerin said he was open to the quantity being reduced further, conceding: 'This is undoubtedly unpleasant material.'

'Even the description is unpleasant. I can only imagine what the real material is like,' the judge responded. He said that viewing the material himself was 'the last frontier' and he did not want to look at it unless he had to. The prosecuting lawyer said he did not think the judge could rule without seeing it.

'The facts of the case are unpleasant,' he said. 'This material is what that case is about. It is fundamentally about the case which the prosecution makes, which is that the accused man lured Ms O'Hara up to the Dublin Mountains for the purpose of murdering her for his sexual satisfaction.'

He said the prosecution's evidence was not just circumstantial: there was direct evidence of an expressed intention to kill in the text messages. The cross-examination of witnesses had suggested it was open to interpretation that this was 'some sort of fantasy world'.

Judge Hunt responded that the previous day Ms Day had said in her evidence that she did not think it went beyond that.

Guerin said the videos made it very clear that this was a fantasy the accused was willing to act on. 'There can be no doubt after viewing the videos that he was acting on it, in pursuance of a deep sexual urge,' he said, adding that Ms O'Hara was 'not obviously a very willing participant'.

Judge Hunt summed up the defence argument as being 'that this material is simply so horrendous that the jury would be diverted from its true path and they wouldn't consider the case on its merits and would simply say: "Look, this is desperate."'

Seán Guerin responded: 'The point is, however horrendous, it is absolutely core to the issues in the trial. Mr Farrell has been making the case that this is some sort of fantasy and it's not real. His client lied to the Gardaí and said he was not interested in these things.'

The judge pointed out that mortuary photographs were not shown to juries.

While noting that they had been shown occasionally, Guerin agreed that they were not generally shown because usually they were not probative. He also pointed to the example of cases of child pornography where juries were not exempted from viewing the material.

Judge Hunt again pressed him on the necessity of screening the videos. Guerin replied: 'The prosecution's case is that the accused man lured Ms O'Hara up to the Dublin Mountains for the purpose of stabbing her, in the course of sexual activity, to death because he had a sexual urge to do so.' He said the case he had to meet was that that was a fantasy.

'It is a highly unusual scenario, like so many things we have discussed in the course of this trial,' the judge said, sighing.

Guerin said: 'This was not evidence of bad character, but of the accused engaging in precisely the type of activity the prosecution alleges he engaged in.'

The judge asked if it was evidence of 'propensity'. Guerin said it was not propensity because the text messages had established that. He pointed out that Mr Justice Paul Carney had given the jury a squeamishness warning at the start of the case.

'Now I'm beginning to understand why,' Judge Hunt said.

Guerin reminded the judge that when the warning had been given, one potential juror had declined to serve on the jury because she was squeamish. 'It was always something that was going to be an issue in this case,' he added.

In his submission Remy Farrell said that when discussing the videos his colleague had made a number of comments, including that they showed Ms O'Hara as 'not obviously a very willing participant'.

'These matters are couched very circuitously in the negative,' Farrell said, adding that the prosecution's purpose in showing the videos was to demonstrate that the activity depicted was non-consensual. This, he argued, was effectively straying into some sort of character reference issues. The defence lawyer said the prosecution was seeking to show that certain things had been done that showed a willingness to do certain things and 'if this is not propensity, I don't see the distinction'.

He said Mr Guerin spoke of notice having been served of an intention to impugn the character of Elaine O'Hara, but

Mr Guerin couldn't show this attack on the deceased being carried out.

'The dead are inevitably spoken ill of, that is the way it is,' Judge Hunt said, adding that the defence's cross-examination had been 'very economically and skilfully directed'.

The judge continued that in child pornography cases, the jury were not generally shown material if the issue was possession. 'Would it be considered appropriate for the jury to sit through one hundred hours of child pornography, or even one hour?' he asked.

Farrell said the videos were not videos of murder or stabbing with intent to do particular harm. 'They are videos of fantasy role play,' he said.

'These depict occasions where a weapon is actually applied to a body,' Judge Hunt responded. 'That is not fantasy. They may be an overlaid fantasy in the person's mind, but it's an actual assault.' He then corrected himself to say it was not assault if it was consented to, but if not consented to, it was a very serious assault.

Judge Hunt sat back in his chair and remarked: 'It's a pretty abnormal aspect of a normal activity. A middle-aged man who dresses up as Batman and jumps from the top of the wardrobe into the marital bed to ravish his good lady wife, when he takes off the mask, he is not Bruce Wayne all of a sudden.'

He said the prosecution's point was that the 'alternative means of conveying the same fact' (describing the videos' content) was not an alternative because it did not convey 'the feeling of satisfaction'. The judge added: 'Sergeant Woods is a good talker but I don't think he is equal to that task. It is the difference between reading something and seeing it – I don't think any of us are arguing with that.'

Seán Guerin said the jury had to decide between two versions of the facts, in other words on the truth of the matter: the first version was that this was relatively harmless fantasy role play; the second was 'something much more sinister and manipulative'.

Judge Hunt agreed to review the video clips before making his decision. 'I can't make a rational decision if I'm comparing apples with oranges,' he said. But he warned that if he decided that the videos should be shown, it would not be done in the presence of the public, apart from the media and people directly involved in the trial. 'I am not turning this into some sort of movie theatre,' he warned. 'If it's being done in the presence of the jury, it is not being done with casual spectators present.'

Judge Hunt viewed the material overnight and the following day ruled that they could be shown to the jury. The eleven selected clips would be shown once and there would be no commentary with them.

The following Monday, 9 March, the trial went into its thirty-third day and eighth week. That morning the large contingent of onlookers, including those who had travelled from outside Dublin, queued for a seat in Court 13. They had been excluded on the previous Thursday and Friday and hoped that the exclusion had been lifted. However, they were soon disappointed. When Judge Hunt took his seat on the bench he again invoked the 1951 Criminal Justice Act and for a third day he turned away the public. Members of the media and those involved in the case remained. Frank O'Hara and his family, who were exempt from the order, also decided to leave.

When the jury had taken their seats, Judge Hunt warned that they were about to see short video clips. 'What you are about to see is not, I think, going to be easy,' he said in a reassuring voice. 'I have to say now it is going to be difficult material.' He urged them to leave aside any emotions or feelings that the material might evoke. He reminded them that they had to 'rise above the material to a certain extent'. He said: 'Remember, you are required to be objective, you are required to look at it as evidence to be weighed. Please bear in mind that you are required to put feelings and emotions to one side and look at this information as pertaining to a decision that you have to make.'

Detective Garda Brid Wallace again took the stand and explained where on the hard drive she had found the clips. These were then each played on small screens in front of the judge, each juror and the legal teams. Some journalists had a view of the material from where they were sitting. They were not displayed on the large wall-mounted screens, or on the screen in front of Dwyer in the dock. Against the stunned silence in the courtroom, the muffled sounds of Elaine O'Hara crying and screaming in the various clips seemed amplified. On the screens she could be seen naked and bent over, bound and gagged, with her arms behind her back and her feet chained. As Dwyer had sex with her from behind, he stabbed her in the sides with a retractable knife. The stabs became more frequent and violent until he reached his climax and ejaculated over her.

A different clip featured Dwyer, again naked, having sex with Elaine O'Hara as she lay tied up on her back with duct tape across her face. Again she was screaming in pain. Her head thrashed violently from side to side as he poked her in the stomach with a knife. Her thrashing and screaming stopped when he ejaculated. 'Ssh . . . ssh . . . now that wasn't bad, was it?' Dwyer's voice echoed around the courtroom. He could then be seen getting up and his naked pot belly filled the screen as he reached to switch off his camera phone.

The clips included the one showing Dwyer cutting Elaine's breast with a knife and squeezing blood from the wound. Again, in the background, there was more muffled screeching.

In another clip Dwyer sat behind a woman as they both faced the camera and he stabbed her in the upper body with the retractable blade. His face was contorted, transformed by what Seán Guerin had described as 'enormous, visceral, deep satisfaction'. When Dwyer finished, the woman seemed angry that he had gone too far and she could be heard exclaiming in a strong English accent: 'Fuck's sake . . . what the fuck . . .'

Apart from his comment to Elaine O'Hara, the only time Dwyer's voice could be heard in the clips was during his bizarre chloroform experiment. It was the only time in the trial that anyone heard him speak.

The eleven video clips took just over five minutes to play. Female jurors could be seen recoiling in horror and looking away from the screens in front of them. Women in the legal teams also looked away from the screens. The material caused both male and female journalists to wince, gasp and start in their seats. Dwyer's face flushed ever deeper shades of purple and he tried to detach himself from what was going on by reading through his documents. He fidgeted in his seat, sometimes sitting on his hands, keeping his head bent down. Every now and then he would peek at the jury to gauge their reactions.

When the screening was over, Brid Wallace continued to describe the contents of other stories and videos located on Dwyer's computers.

Two days later, in the absence of the jury, Dwyer's lawyer had an angry spat with Mr Justice Tony Hunt when he made an application to have the jury discharged because of how the judge had looked at the accused man during evidence. Remy Farrell said his client insisted that the judge had looked over at him, 'glared' and shaken his head when a map of cell site analysis was being examined.

Refusing the application Judge Hunt said while he may have looked at the accused, he could not sit through the trial with a 'poker face'. Clearly annoyed by the accusation, he said there were legitimate ways he could influence the jury if he wanted to without using 'nods and winks'.

'It's not something I saw myself, but it's something that I am told happened,' Mr Farrell said.

'I look at people, I look at the jury, I look at you, I look at people at the back of the court and very occasionally I look at the accused,' Judge Hunt said.

'It was put to me that you were glaring and shaking your head,' Mr Farrell continued.

'I imagine that the jury are paying attention to things other than me,' the judge replied.

'It has been a source of some concern that during some of the more difficult parts of the evidence, the [judge] has made certain facial expressions . . . I have no option but to apply for the court to discharge the jury,' Remy Farrell said.

Judge Hunt conceded that he had looked over at the defendant. The defence lawyer said the jury would have seen him because they had the best view in the entire court. He added: 'I have no option but to apply for the court to discharge the jury. My client is to be tried not by a judge but by the jury and if the perception arises in the course of the trial that the judge regards a particular piece of evidence as damning . . .'

Judge Hunt interrupted to say that he was entitled to 'go quite far' in his charge to the jury so he was not sure 'what's behind all this apart from being a scrum down'.

The comment sparked an angry exchange as Remy Farrell asked the judge to withdraw the remark, saying he was not in the habit of making silly applications and was raising a matter regarding his client getting a fair trial. He was not doing so for any 'tactical' purpose.

Seán Guerin intervened to say he saw the judge looking at the accused but hadn't noticed 'any untoward expression'. He only saw what he did because he was handing in a document. 'Whatever impression may have been in the mind of whoever raised the issue with Mr Farrell, it will be dispelled in the clearest possible way when the judge charges the jury,' Guerin stressed.

'I can't sit here for thirty-six days with a poker face. That is not the way it is. I am entitled to shake my head and have an expression and I'm entitled to go much, much further than that in charging the jury . . . I am going to give the jury my usual directions. There are very serious things to be considered by the jury in this case and they don't include anything to do with my opinions,' Judge Hunt said. 'I shall be telling them it's their decision, not mine. Although I am entitled to make strong comment, it is not my practice to do so.'

The judge said he regretted any offence caused to Mr Farrell by his remark about 'a scrum down' and that it was not intended.

The trial was punctuated by several other days of legal argument in the jury's absence as the defence made a number of applications to have the case thrown out. One challenge concerned the reliability of the methods used by the computer experts to extract and interpret the text messages central to the prosecution case. Another related to a European Court of Justice ruling concerning the retention of call record data held by service providers. Mr Farrell argued that the directive meant the phone records were inadmissible. After deliberating, Mr Justice Hunt turned down both applications.

Towards the end of the trial the defence asked the judge to direct the jury to return a verdict of not guilty on the grounds that there was no medical evidence relating to cause of death. However, the judge refused, saying that it would be an affront to common sense to suggest there was no basis for causation to be inferred.

18. Verdict

On Friday, 13 March 2015, Seán Guerin announced to the court: 'That is the evidence for the prosecution.' After thirty-seven days, spread over eight weeks, the State had finished presenting its evidence. The following Wednesday the defence called just three witnesses, none of whom had anything of significance to say, a reflection of the weakness of Dwyer's defence. The next morning, Thursday 19 March, Seán Guerin rose to address the jury. It was the beginning of the end of the gruelling trial – the closing scene in a remarkable drama that had gripped and shocked a nation.

The courtroom was packed as usual, the public craning to hear and see everything. The round glasses perched on his boyish face and his long black robe made Guerin resemble a slightly older version of Harry Potter. Standing with a hand in his pocket, he began by thanking the jury for the time they had given and patience they had shown over the length of the marathon trial, particularly as the evidence was lengthy, complex and at times difficult.

'The prosecution's case against the accused man for the murder of Elaine O'Hara, as indicated at the outset, is that he murdered Elaine O'Hara by stabbing her for his sexual gratification, having arranged to lure or bring her up the mountains to Killakee on 22 August 2012.' He said Dwyer had a deep-seated desire to stab a woman to death, and Elaine O'Hara was 'amenable to being used as part of that plan'. He continued: 'She had been for some time in an abusive and manipulative relationship with Graham Dwyer which enabled him to isolate her and exploit her for the sexual purpose he had in mind.' Dwyer was sure in the knowledge, more or less, that the murder might be seen as suicide. 'That very nearly worked out for him.'

Guerin said there were four broad strands to the prosecution's case. The first was the evidence connecting Dwyer to Elaine's disappearance and the second was to show that he had not only the sexual fantasy but also the intent of murdering her by stabbing. The third strand was to demonstrate the circumstances of her disappearance, including the detailed plan he had elaborated over a period of time. The fourth was to address any other theories and disprove any other possibilities, for example that there was someone else involved or that her death occurred by suicide.

He reminded the jury that the prosecution had to prove that Dwyer killed Elaine O'Hara, or intended to cause her serious injury. 'The onus of proof is on the prosecution. I remind you as well the accused man was and still is presumed innocent of the offence as charged.'

Guerin then set out his stall in forensic detail, examining each piece of the huge puzzle the Gardaí had put together. In relation to the Goroon and 'master' phones, he admitted that there was no direct evidence from anybody to say Dwyer bought the phones or used them, but he maintained there was enough circumstantial evidence – and enough weight behind that evidence – to show that there was 'no other possible conclusion' other than they were his phones. The owner of the phones had a firm, very clear and determined intention to do something, not merely a desire or fantasy.

He said that fantasy is the opposite of reality, with 'fantastical novels and movies about orcs and elves fighting unicorns and leprechauns and all sorts of fantasy' that are not true. But he questioned the fantasy used in relation to the documents, stories and text messages the jury had been shown. 'Fantasy has another name, it means desire. Sexual fantasy isn't something not real. I suggest to you if fantasy is the expression of a desire, it may not be real. It may be something the person who has that fantasy wishes was real. What this case is about is that this person, who has extraordinary and quite frankly disgusting fantasies, goes about making them reality.'

He brought the jury back to the testimony of Emer McShea, who described how Dwyer's fantasy to stab a woman in bed went back to the mid 1990s. The defence had not challenged her evidence. In order to make his fantasy a reality Dwyer had to find victims, people who would willingly – if not reluctantly – submit to what he had in mind. 'These are real people,' he said, asking the jury to remember Dwyer used 'real people' in the fantasies in his 'disgusting mind'.

He said at least three were identifiable people in three documents. 'Darci Day, Elaine O'Hara herself and Ms Quinn, the auctioneer who had the misfortune of working in an office across the street from A&D Wejchert. When I say documents, I include text messages and two documents, Darci Day and the woman named Jenny documents, imagining vivid and graphic details of the most vile and sickening torture and murder of women. When you look at the documents, bear in mind the significance of the real people Mr Dwyer knows in one form or other.'

Seán Guerin spoke about the relationship between the

slave and the master. 'I suggest to you Mr Dwyer had, from the very outset, the limited purpose of starting a relationship with Ms O'Hara to use her for a sexual fantasy he had. You know that he said he's a sadist who enjoys other people's pain,' he said, reading a text message about wanting 'to stick my knife in flesh when sexually aroused'.

'The warning lights those messages cause to flash don't seem to be sufficient to warn off Elaine O'Hara.' He told the jury that there had been 'a good deal of evidence about difficulties in her life', including an admission statement when she attended St Edmundsbury mental health facility in July 2012. Under the heading 'Social Support Network', which included a network of friends, relatives, etc., were four words: 'Supportive dad. No friends.'

'That's a tragic, sad and unfortunate situation that Elaine O'Hara appears to have known and a reality Graham Dwyer was only too happy to take advantage of.' He said information retrieved from a laptop that Elaine O'Hara sold in 2010 showed she had viewed the profile 'architect77' on the website Alt.com in October and November 2007. 'That appears, from evidence you have, the likely beginning of a relationship that ended on the side of Killakee Mountain on 22 August 2012.'

Seán Guerin referred to Elaine's medical records and state of mind. 'She was a very sad person; she was undoubtedly a very troubled person, troubled by thoughts of low self-worth,' he said, adding that she didn't value her worth for her work, family or community. He quoted an old Irish adage, '*Is fearr an troid ná an t-uaigneas*' – 'Fighting is better than loneliness', adding: 'Being lonely is worse than an awful lot else and people do settle in relationships they are unhappy with rather than be alone, that is what I suggested happened to Elaine O'Hara in her relationship with Graham Dwyer.'

Seán Guerin reminded the jury of an email in 2008 which he said came from Dwyer and in which he offered to help her end her life in the guise of being a friend. 'This wickedness hiding behind a mask of pity, offering a troubled and sometimes suicidal woman help in the form of a way out.'

Guerin also reminded jurors about the videos they had been shown. 'What you see is a vicious and brutal act of violence perpetrated on Elaine O'Hara by Graham Dwyer. When it concluded you can hear Graham Dwyer say: "Now that wasn't bad, was it?" It shows Elaine O'Hara didn't want to do that or be the victim of this attack and afterwards he told her: "Now that wasn't too bad" or "as bad as it feels". He was able to overcome her unwillingness to do these things.'

He said Dwyer thought he had the perfect plan. 'For all of the planning and plotting he had no idea how fully the record of their conversations would be extracted from her iPhone and computer.' The key to the case and what happened was on the other two phones, which he would shortly throw away in the reservoir. The lawyer argued that on 22 August 2012, Elaine O'Hara was in fear of the punishment she was going to face. He again read some of the last messages between the phones, up to the final one, 'Go down to shore and wait.'

'All the elements of the plan – isolation; carefully selected location checked before; the phones; it being made to look like suicide . . . telling her she'd be back and to think it was real, pretend it was real; and disposal of the evidence – everything points to this careful, elaborate and thoughtful plan being implemented on the day.' He asked how Elaine

O'Hara could have committed suicide and left Shankill when her car was still there. Dwyer expected them to believe that she had driven to Vartry, thrown in personal items and the clothes she was wearing, and made her way semi-naked to Killakee.

'So instead she had the assistance of someone. Graham Dwyer suggested someone helped her and disposed of her belongings. Who was that person? You can't get away from the fact that that person was Graham Dwyer as he made the arrangement to meet her through the phones and checked out the location the previous evening. If Elaine O'Hara had been suicidal he would have been more than happy to help her.'

Mr Guerin conceded that not everything pulled out of the reservoir was connected to either of them – like the Real Madrid dressing gown, pink underpants and a mattress – but he said it was too much of a coincidence that the bag Dwyer was seen carrying out of her apartment on 15 August was in the reservoir with her clothing, glasses, keys, the phone she used and items of a sexual nature that came from her apartment. He added that the man she was meeting had no interest in football or Real Madrid, his only interest was model aeroplane flying – and stabbing.

He went into great detail about Elaine's mental health over the years, noting that the day before she disappeared her therapist had noticed she was cheerful, spontaneous, smiling, happy, and excited about the Tall Ships. 'It's a matter for yourself and bring to bear the experience you all have of life,' he told the jurors. 'The tragedy of suicide may have touched some of your lives or someone you know. We can't say one thing or a number of things point to suicide, but probably the most defining feature is a loss of hope and a loss of sense of future and anything to look forward to or contribute in future.' He said that all the evidence was that the murdered woman was not suicidal when she vanished.

The stabbing fantasy had been on Dwyer's mind for twenty years and he had got to the stage where he was so agitated by it that he was going to do something that would get him into trouble. Mr Guerin said that in the 'Killing Darci' document Dwyer spoke about sending money to facilitate that woman tying up loose ends. 'But look at what Elaine O'Hara was doing,' he said, telling the jury that she was talking about seeing relatives and had 'not lost hope for the future'. It was a 'completely different situation. She is thinking of the future.'

When she had texted: 'I know what's coming', Dwyer had replied: 'What do you mean?' Guerin said: 'He appears to be worried that he's been rumbled.'

Guerin asked if the 'mountain of evidence' from the reservoir could be 'blown away by the fact that a random pair of underpants and a dressing gown were found in the reservoir.'

A picture of the black and red bag found in the reservoir was shown again to the jury. He said the accused had been seen on CCTV leaving Ms O'Hara's apartment complex with it. He said the bag allowed the jury to say Dwyer was connected to the 'beginning, the middle and end' of Ms O'Hara's disappearance. 'It's an important part of the evidence and when Mr Dwyer told the Gardaí that he didn't know anything about it he was telling a lie and it was another lie in a series of lies that he had thought long and hard about telling the Gardaí.'

He said that there was no contradiction between the content of the texts, the movement of the phones or the nature of the relationship, except for the lies that were told by Mr Dwyer to the Gardaí.

Seán Guerin took a day and a half to outline all the evidence that had been laid before the court over the previous eight weeks and concluded his address: 'I ask you to take at face value the unguarded and open expression of an intention to kill given by the accused man himself in the documents he wrote. Those are the words of the accused man, if you are satisfied that it was Graham Dwyer who had these phones; the videos that he recorded were videos of his actions made by him, recorded by him, archived by him; the documents were the creation of his imagination, his desire, his fantasy. The text messages repeat those fantasies and desires and set out a plan. All I am asking you to do, ladies and gentlemen, is believe that when he showed himself in those documents and texts to be a sadistic and brutal pervert with nothing on his mind other than murder, he was telling the truth.'

Seán Guerin finished quietly and sat down to allow his former classmate to make his closing remarks.

Defence counsel Remy Farrell was equally eloquent when he tried to convince the jury of his client's innocence. He surprised everyone in the packed courtroom by beginning with the opening lines of the 'Killing Darci' story. 'I had always fantasized about killing ever since I was a teenager and I got hard every time I had a knife in my hand, wielding the power, knowing that I could decide who lived and died, just like my hero God.' Remy Farrell sighed as he put the document down and looked towards the jury. 'These are indisputably the words of Graham Dwyer,' he said. 'When you heard those words in evidence, indisputably they represent a most unpromising start to any speech in a murder trial.'

The senior counsel said that he had never before had to refer to material like that when closing a case. 'This is one of the unique features in this case,' he said. It had been necessary for a judge to issue a warning to potential jurors who might be squeamish at the start of the case, and that 'all of that makes a lot more sense now'. He said what they'd seen could be described as difficult and distasteful, even repellent in some aspects. 'It's hard to disagree with Seán Guerin's description of it being fairly disgusting. There are a lot of things at this stage of the case that may make you regard him [Dwyer] as repellent. It's not possible for me to suggest from evidence you have seen or heard [that he] can be characterized as even close to normal. I'm not going to try and do that. I'm not here to try to convince you that Dwyer is a nice guy,' Remy Farrell said with disarming candour.

He said members of the jury might have already made up their minds, but he asked them: 'What's all this evidence mean when you take it at its very height?' There was a huge gap in the prosecution's case and their evidence could only go so far. He maintained that every time the prosecution tried to make the distinction between reality and fantasy they attempted to jump this gap. 'But when they tell the jurors what happened on Killakee Mountain on 22 August 2012, they come up short. That's putting before you an elaborate theory not on the basis of any evidence. They are attempting to fill the gap, they are somersaulting over it. Seán Guerin said this was a murder with a knife, not asphyxiation, not a gunshot. That's it.'

Farrell accused the prosecution of getting Deputy State Pathologist Michael Curtis and other witnesses to give evidence early in the trial because it didn't fit with the prosecution's case. 'The prosecution suggests various documents in the case represent not just a desire of Mr Dwyer, but his plans. You can draw an inference,' he said. He also accused them of 'pushing buttons' and trying to shock the jurors early in the trial by reading the guide to the Gorean lifestyle that outlined how women were slaves.

His son Sennan McShea was also presented as a witness – giving evidence about his dad's anti-smoking stance and the CCTV images – to show the jury 'even his own son is prepared to swear against him', he said. 'You might want to balance the importance of his evidence with the emotional impact of a man's son going against him . . . think who's pushing buttons and why. More significant, and very deliberately, evidence problematic on the cause of death was called at the start. Does anyone really remember it? It's a very, very long time ago, like trying to remember something that happened before a traumatic event in your life. Does anyone remember anything you saw before those videos? Yet at the time you heard that Dr Curtis gave evidence it was relevant and there really was a serious issue.'

Remy Farrell said the evidence did not stack up with the prosecution's claim that Dwyer acted out a stabbing like the one outlined in 'Killing Darci' as there was no nicking on any of the bones. He said it was largely a case of circumstantial evidence and so they would have to look at all the possibilities, even if unattractive. 'Cast a cold and rational eye over the evidence. You need to do it in a way that the Gardaí in this case didn't. This is about who owns a particular telephone and immense resources were put into that,' he said. 'You have to ask yourself whether you accept Mr Dwyer is the owner of the phone . . . a lot hinges on that. If you do not, what happens then? The prosecution's case then becomes wobbly.'

Farrell said that anything that the Garda investigation threw up as suicide, and anything that conflicted with the idea that Graham Dwyer killed Elaine O'Hara, was brushed under the carpet. He said the prosecution did not claim Dwyer 'delicately cut Ms O'Hara's throat', but that he had an insatiable desire to 'stab and rape and stab some more' and that 'Killing Darci' was a template for what occurred. He questioned how this 'orgy of violence' and fantasy to stab a belly, cheek, shoulder and neck as part of a moment of passion and depravity 'fits the evidence'.

Farrell reminded the jury that Detective Sergeant Woods described the case as attracting unprecedented media attention and said that they could not have anything but sympathy for Elaine O'Hara's family. Farrell then called into question the credibility of the evidence given by the O'Hara family, explaining that it was his job to comment on the evidence in the most sensitive manner he could. He said Elaine's sister Ann had described Elaine as 'very trusting' and he said this was a very deliberate expression. 'It is a very stark contrast in evidence when one looks in places, particularly in texts – it is clear Elaine O'Hara was able to deceive others and engage in fantasies of killing and [was] consistently described by doctors as having difficulty trusting other people,' he said.

He said that family members had said the murder victim was 'not at all suicidal and happy on the day, yet in cross-examination evidence emerged she was upset at a graveside' and that she had lain on her mother's headstone.

'More telling was, perhaps, when she went missing their reaction was to go to Shanganagh Cemetery to see if she was there, and her car was found. A telling reaction and one you can draw your own conclusions from.'

Farrell claimed there were also inconsistencies in statements by her father, Frank, and his partner, Sheila Hawkins. He recalled Ms Hawkins' discovery of the fetish suit in Elaine's apartment after she first went missing. 'Frank O'Hara, when he gave evidence, had no memory of a latex bodysuit or a rope, but those are things that must have stuck out like sore thumbs.' He said undoubtedly he understood the reasons for 'fudging' issues like this, 'but you must glance a more critical eye over the evidence'.

The defence lawyer said as distasteful as the 'Killing Darci' document was, he queried it being a template for murder. He said the defence had tried to use the fantasy documents like a 'huge tub of Polyfilla – any time there was a gap in the case, you could take bits of the fantasy and stick those into the evidence'. He then asked about fantasy and if it 'crossed the line' when it involved real people, asking if it was OK to fantasize about a cartoon like Jessica Rabbit from *Who Framed Roger Rabbit*, or Angelina Jolie, but not the 'girl next door'. He claimed the view being put forward by the prosecution was 'psychobabble'.

The State was suggesting that if there was evidence in the case that looked like it was suicide, then that was evidence that it was not suicide. 'The prosecution are looking to co-opt all the evidence of suicide and say that it's actually evidence of non-suicide. I say that is nonsense.'

Farrell then asked the jury to use their own common sense in relation to suicide and asked if it was their experience that only those who had nothing to live for committed suicide. 'Is it only those who have cleared their diary, cancelled their milk delivery and perhaps fed the cat who commit suicide? I suggest that it's not. People who have everything to live for do so [commit suicide] for wholly inexplicable reasons, out of the blue.' He said this was not the situation with Elaine O'Hara, where there were 'strong indicators' for suicide.

He asked the jury to consider the idea of reasonable doubt and what they might think about their decision in the future. He said they had to decide whether murder had been committed in the first place. 'The gap I referred to at the start, it's a gaping chasm and one you have been asked to jump over,' he added. They were being asked to do this on the basis of 'fantasy documents' and that the forensic evidence contradicted the prosecution's thesis.

Farrell told the jury that after they came to their verdict, whatever it was, they would go their separate ways and be left to wonder if they had made the right decision. With such immense public interest in the case, he said, 'books will be written and movies made'. He said that Benedict Cumberbatch would play Mr Guerin and he would be played by George Clooney. His quip was greeted with chuckles of relieved laughter. He said the case had everything – 'sex and lots of it, kinky sex, middle-class professional, woman with dark secrets' – and that its technical and forensic aspects would be perfect for an episode of *CSI*.

'Mr Dwyer, Elaine O'Hara and others were put under the spotlight. People tend not to survive that level of scrutiny,' he said. 'The lives of others were also considered with considerable scrutiny. The men who came forward after their numbers were found in Ms O'Hara's phone did their civic duty and gave evidence, and their reward was to have their faces plastered on the front of every newspaper, and their names trumpeted to all and sundry because they had an extraordinary sexual taste.'

Farrell asked the jurors to look beyond the evidence that was emotive and 'undoubtedly turns your stomach and makes you look away'. He said much of the material found on computers and phones owned by Dwyer was 'deeply misogynistic at least'. The lawyer told the jury: 'You have seen him engage in explicit sexual acts and, however abhorrent, wrong, unusual or disgusting, you think you have seen him in a particular way.

'There's an expectation in the media and among bar-stool jurors in pubs around the city, and that expectation is you should really convict Mr Dwyer, irrespective of doubts, because he has peculiar sexual tastes. You're expected to plaster over the cracks in the prosecution's case. You are expected to convict Mr Dwyer without the evidence – that is what the public expectation is and that is what the media expectation is. That's the conclusion to the story. That's how it's wrapped up, and if you acquit Mr Dwyer you will be doing the unpopular thing. Make no mistake about that. Many of the people haven't heard all the evidence and haven't seen all the exhibits in the jury room. A lot of the evidence is emotive. A lot of buttons were pushed.'

He asked why the prosecution was insisting on intuitive

leaps and flights of fancy. 'When you ask yourself that, you come to a very clear conclusion.'

It was Friday evening when Remy Farrell finished his closing speech. The following Monday, 23 March, Judge Hunt began his charge to the jury. He swivelled his chair to face the seven men and five women and leaned towards them to begin his summing-up of the dreadful case.

'We've all heard bad things about Mr Dwyer and if you still feel that, get it out there at the start of your deliberations and blow it away. It's irrelevant. It will only obscure the road you have to travel and take. Put any lack of sympathy you may have to one side, as Mr Dwyer's activities are irrelevant in the context of any opinion you form. Feelings arising from the evidence have no part to play in your verdict. I want to triple underline that. I want you to get it out of the way at the start.'

The jurors had been asked to absorb 'coming up to five years' worth' of information about both the defendant and the victim, their relationships, tastes and behaviour, and 'you are being asked to use all that to come to a conclusion about what happened after six o'clock that evening'.

An accused person normally had certain aspects of their character shielded from the jury, enabling the jury to take an objective and cold view of the case. This included knowledge of any previous convictions or 'bad behaviour'. But prior criminal convictions did not apply in this case as the defendant did not have any. However, he told the jury: 'You saw a side of him in a very harsh and unforgiving light.' He said the purpose of this evidence was not to make Mr Dwyer look bad, adding: 'Nobody looks good in those circumstances.'

He referred to the documents found on Dwyer's computer that had potential relevance and pointed out that it was up to the jurors to decide what was actually relevant. 'You are the arbiters of what is relevant and what is not,' he said. The documents got 'zero marks for content and prose style . . . They were put forward because the prosecution wants you to consider them in the context of a picture they paint.' They were not there to make Dwyer look bad or make it easier for them to convict him. The video clips were shown because the prosecution asserted that what was depicted in them was part and parcel of its case against Dwyer.

The clips had a 'visceral impact' and he said that while he did not think the jury had been watching him, they might have seen that he was not viewing the videos as they were played. This was not because he was particularly squeamish, but because he had already viewed them several times before they did and 'simply didn't have a desire to see them a fourth time'. He said the jury members were all adults and should not have been shocked by seeing people having sex. The prosecution did not need to show the videos to prove the accused and Elaine O'Hara had had a sexual relationship – there was other evidence for that, including Dwyer's own admissions.

The activities shown were accompanied by the unusual feature of stabbing, but he stressed: 'The people in those clips were agreeing to do it. I suggest to you that when the immediate impact of that type of thing has died down you can let the shock drift away. The fact of the matter is that what the people were doing was on the basis of agreement.' He said clearly it had been painful and 'though someone might have a desire to let someone stick a knife in them, that desire did not make the consequences any less painful'.

He explained that the reason they had been shown the videos was because of assertions made by Dwyer in Garda interviews about the nature of his relationship with the murdered woman and to allow them to assess the content of the relationship, the motivations and 'who enjoyed what'. He said: 'Any feelings it engenders in you, any dislike or lack of sympathy, you have to put to one side.'

He told the jury foreman he would have a sheet with one charge on it: whether Graham Dwyer was guilty or not guilty of murder. Any other misconduct on his part did not constitute a criminal offence.

Over two days, in his role as invigilator, the judge brought the jury through the evidence again, cautioning them repeatedly that they must assess it rationally and impartially. He told them that whether they were adjudicating a trial at the lower end of the scale, or the higher end like this one, they had to remain vigilant and meticulous in their application of the safeguards to ensure there was no slippage. 'Has the prosecution proved the case?'

In reference to the unprecedented amount of media attention the trial had attracted, he said there had been a lot of 'hoopla and fuss' about the case, and he took it that none of the jurors live in a cave. 'You've been out and about on business outside the jury. It's probably very hard to avoid the hoopla,' he said, adding that while it was important that the case was reported in newspapers and on TV, 'you can safely leave all that to one side'.

Graham Dwyer followed Judge Hunt's remarks closely, sometimes shaking his head slightly, as if in disagreement.

Other times he hunched over and looked at the floor or threw his eyes up to the ceiling.

In his conclusion Judge Hunt told the jury that although the State's case involved circumstantial evidence, one thing was clear: 'This is that two people met that evening; one came home, one didn't. The question is why did one person not come home? Is the person who came home responsible?'

Judge Hunt finished his charge at 3.29 p.m. on Tuesday afternoon and sent the jury out to begin their difficult task. But as they were about to leave, the jury foreman asked: 'What do we have to find the defendant guilty of?' The question sent a ripple of nervous laughter through the court. Even Dwyer smiled broadly. It was a bad sign that the jury was still confused, despite a comprehensive charge from the judge. But it was also understandable in the context of a complex and lengthy trial.

'You don't have to find him guilty of anything,' the judge replied. 'You have to find him guilty or not guilty of murder.'

The jury filed out to begin their deliberations. However, Seán Guerin raised issues about the charge, so Judge Hunt recalled the jury the following morning and re-charged them.

The jury's deliberations continued through Thursday and Friday as the investigation team, the media and the large audience of onlookers loitered around the gleaming courts building, sipping coffee and gossiping. The non-story coming from the courts continued to be the main item on the news bulletins as the whole country seemed gripped, as if waiting for the final whistle in a crucial match or the unmasking of a villain in the climax of a soap opera plot.

There was a ripple of excitement when the jury returned shortly after 3.10 p.m. on Friday 27 March. They were asked if they had reached a verdict. The foreman replied with an emphatic shake of his head. Instead he asked: 'What are the ingredients of murder?'

Mr Justice Hunt explained that they would have to be satisfied that the accused had the intention of killing or causing serious injury to the deceased. The jury promptly left again, leaving the court deflated as everyone prepared for the deliberations to run into another week.

Despite all the evidence that had laid bare his sordid secrets, Dwyer had remained outwardly cocky and confident, even bragging to the prison warders that he planned to celebrate his acquittal with a steak meal and a bottle of wine in Bandon. But the jury foreman's question had rattled him and he got no comfort from his legal team, who also looked concerned. It seemed that the jury had decided where it was going and just wanted to be clear before revealing its decision. Dwyer stood awkwardly for a few moments after the judge left, hands in his pockets and was led back to the holding cell.

Less than half an hour later the jury minder whispered to the court registrar that there was a verdict. The tension was almost palpable as the legal teams resumed their seats and Chief Superintendent Diarmuid O'Sullivan and the rest of his investigation team came rushing back into Court 13. Anxiety was etched on Frank O'Hara's face as he led his family, their arms linked in solidarity, to the seats where they had sat for the past nine nightmarish weeks. They seemed braced for whatever the result would be. Only a handful of onlookers were still in the court. Graham Dwyer was led in and mouthed: 'Verdict?' to Remy Farrell. As his father and sister returned, they looked towards him quizzically and Dwyer mouthed to them: 'It is, yeah.' He smiled briefly and clasped his hands in his lap and watched the jury-room door.

When Judge Hunt resumed his seat, he warned: 'Whatever the verdict is, I want silence in court. I want Gardaí to keep an eye on that.' The jury trooped quietly back to their seats as the registrar recorded the time of their return as 15.39. They had been deliberating for seven hours and thirty-three minutes in total.

The court registrar asked the foreman if they had a verdict on which they were all agreed. He said they did and handed her the issue paper, on which the verdict was written.

'You say the accused Graham Dwyer is guilty – is that the verdict of you all?' she asked.

'Yes.'

The silence was broken only by a gasp from the bench where Elaine's family were seated.

Dwyer took a sharp intake of breath when the verdict was delivered, cocking his head slightly to one side as if he had misheard. Leaning forward, he shook his head in slow motion and puffed out his cheeks, as if unable to comprehend the decision. He looked to where his father and sister were sitting and shook his head again, more emphatically this time, as if in disbelief.

Then a spontaneous gasp of relief rippled through the courtroom. Frank O'Hara smiled and embraced his partner and children, maintaining the dignity and composure that the family had shown throughout the trial. Seán Dwyer stared into space as tears welled in his eyes. His daughter also wept. The entire investigation team, who were crammed into a corner of the room, all smiled and some of them seemed to be stifling an urge to cheer. Judge Hunt thanked the jurors for their service and said even he, as a professional with the best part of thirty years' experience, hadn't found it easy to absorb some of the 'pretty horrendous' material presented during the trial.

'You're private citizens. You've done your duty and you've done your duty in an exemplary manner,' he said. 'There is no doubt you are human like myself: when you are cut you bleed. These things are not easy. If it's any consolation to you, I 110 per cent agree with your verdict based on the evidence. On the basis of the facts, the question of suicide simply wasn't there and I agree with you. I wholeheartedly endorse that conclusion, speaking as someone who heard and saw everything that you did. I don't mind expressing my view at this time.'

Though the mandatory sentence for murder was life in prison, Seán Guerin asked the judge to adjourn sentencing in order to allow for the preparation of a victim impact statement. When the judge and jury had left, the investigation team hugged and shook hands and the prosecutor, Seán Guerin, smiled broadly. The two legal teams began packing away their volumes of evidence. The journalists had rushed off to file their stories and attend a hastily arranged Garda press conference. Every newspaper in the country had reserved most of their news pages for the story in the event that a verdict came through, and news packages were being pulled together for TV and radio. It was rare that a murder trial received such a level of coverage.

As he was about to leave with his prison escorts, Dwyer's mask slipped for a brief moment. A kindly prison officer asked his weeping sister: 'Do you want to talk to him?' before he was taken away. She nodded, but as she moved towards her sibling he brushed past her and marched out. 'Graham . . .' she was heard calling as he disappeared through the door.

Within fifteen minutes of the verdict Court 13, the venue for one of the longest, most disturbing murder dramas in Irish criminal justice history, had fallen silent. The media and court officials had moved on and the last of the die-hard onlookers had gone home. The investigation team and the State's legal representatives headed to the pub.

Within an hour, in a breathtaking demonstration of arrogance and detachment from reality, Graham Dwyer took the unprecedented step of issuing a press statement through his lawyers. Never before could anyone recall a convicted murderer doing such a thing. It read:

> I wish to take this opportunity to formally thank my legal team, my solicitor Jonathan Dunphy, senior counsel Remy Farrell, barristers Ronan Kennedy and Kate McCormack, for their work and dedication since 2013. I also wish to thank my family, friends and colleagues for their continued unwavering support throughout this period. To the members of the media, I am grateful for the privacy you have afforded both my family and people close to me during the trial. I now respectfully ask that you continue to respect their privacy and I confirm that there will be no further comment by my family or myself concerning this case whatsoever. Thank you.
>
> Graham Dwyer.

In a completely unconnected move his estranged wife, Gemma, one of those to suffer the most collateral damage from her husband's dark obsessions, also issued a statement:

> Gemma Dwyer and her immediate family have noted the proceedings of the court and its guilty verdict today. Their thoughts and condolences are with the O'Hara family for the grief and pain they are suffering. In the interests of maintaining privacy, and in particular to protect the interests of her children, Gemma Dwyer and members of her immediate family – parents, siblings and children – will not be making any further comment now, or in the future, on the case. The family would request that the media and members of the public respect their privacy in any further reporting or commentary, particularly with regard to the need to protect their children from any intrusion into their lives.

Later, Chief Superintendent Diarmuid O'Sullivan chaired a press conference flanked by Detective Superintendent Kevin Dolan, the officer in command of all serious crime investigations in the Eastern Division, and Superintendent John Hand, the officer in charge of the Blackrock District, where the enquiry had been based.

'This was a crime that had profound and devastating consequences for a number of people and will affect families for many years to come,' Diarmuid O'Sullivan said. 'But today my thoughts, and the thoughts of the entire investigation team, are with the O'Hara family. Personally I can only hope that no other family will have to endure what Frank O'Hara and his family have endured.'

O'Sullivan said that the investigation had 'proved to be both varied and complex, involving all the Garda disciplines . . . It ranged from the diligent work of Garda [James] O'Donoghue at Roundwood Garda Station to the excellent and meticulous work carried out by the investigation team in Blackrock. This investigation was grounded in the era of information technology that married the detailed and often minute information derived from fundamental policing. This resulted in the piecing together of the complex picture of events.'

O'Sullivan could rightly be proud of the Elaine O'Hara investigation. It had shown the Gardaí at their best and provided a massive public-relations boost for the force after a prolonged period of controversy and perceived scandal.

19. Elaine's Epitaph

The public began queuing early on the morning of Monday 20 April. That afternoon Graham Dwyer would be sentenced in Court 13. It was obvious that the courtroom could not accommodate the crowd. From its opening day three months earlier, this trial had attracted unprecedented crowds, and interest in it only increased over the weeks. People came for many reasons, ranging from a deep concern to see justice done for Elaine O'Hara to unabashed curiosity: a devious murder plot, a privileged, middle-class defendant, extreme sexual practices and an extraordinary police investigation all made for compelling drama.

For one last time Frank O'Hara, his partner, Sheila, and his children, Ann and John, were escorted to the bench that had been reserved for them throughout the trial. Seán Dwyer, the loyal father who had stood by his son, sat alone in the seat he had occupied every day for the nine difficult weeks of the trial. Throughout that horrendous ordeal he had shown the same dignity and composure as Frank O'Hara – two fathers broken by losses of different sorts. Graham Dwyer was expressionless as he was led to the dock by the prison warders. He looked as smart as ever: clearly, his conviction had not diminished his attention to sartorial detail.

Eleven members of the jury had returned, at Mr Justice Tony Hunt's invitation, for the epilogue to the drama that had taken over their lives since 19 January. These ordinary citizens had spent nine gruelling weeks journeying through the life of Elaine O'Hara and the mind of the man who had taken her life. When Judge Hunt arrived on the bench he smiled at the jurors as if welcoming old friends, and thanked them for taking up his invitation.

Prosecutor Seán Guerin led Detective Sergeant Peter Woods through a brief synopsis of the evidence. Woods' handling of the case had won universal praise and admiration, so it was fitting that he played a role on the day that Dwyer would receive his sentence. As Woods spoke, Dwyer gazed around the courtroom, focusing on nothing in particular. He seemed detached and aloof.

When Peter Woods finished, Seán Guerin told Judge Hunt that Frank O'Hara had prepared a victim impact statement on behalf of his family but did not wish to deliver it himself, so he would be reading it. Dwyer stared straight ahead, occasionally folding his arms, as Seán Guerin began to read.

Frank O'Hara had put great thought into the poignant and heartfelt document. This was Elaine's epitaph, and his opportunity to remind the court and the public that his daughter's life amounted to so much more than the one-dimensional picture that had emerged in the course of the trial. As his words filled the silence of the packed courtroom, there were tears in Frank O'Hara's eyes as he held the hands of his loved ones beside him. Sheila Hawkins and Elaine's sister, Ann, wept quietly as Seán Guerin read. This is the full statement:

> We know that we are not the only victims of this crime. We recognize that other families are suffering too and we feel for every other person affected. Words cannot adequately

describe how we are feeling and we would never want any other family to go through what we have endured over the past two and a half years.

We have lost a daughter, a sister and a friend in the most brutal, traumatic and horrifying manner. We also have many unanswered questions which we will have to carry with us for the rest of our lives.

Elaine was a very intelligent girl, who never fully realized her potential due to her psychological difficulties. She was prescribed a lot of medication and this did have an impact on her ability to be a regular teenager, particularly socially.

She was emotionally immature and very trusting of anyone who showed her kindness. In later years her medication was reduced, hospital stays became less common and she functioned more effectively. However, she had missed out on those important, formative teenage years.

She had a strong work ethic and loved working with children, as she could relate to them better than to adults. She was always there to help and assist others, giving lifts, covering shifts at work or collecting many of the items for the Christmas Fair at school.

Elaine adored her niece, who was also her goddaughter, and loved reading, painting and playing with her. For months after she went missing, her goddaughter would point out cars that were like Elaine's, saying: 'There's Elaine's car.'

We smiled and nodded – how can you explain something to a young child that we couldn't understand ourselves? Since she left us, Elaine has two more nieces, but they will never know their aunt.

Elaine's ambition was to be a teacher and she was studying Montessori. In 2014, we collected a BA in Montessori

Education which was awarded to her in St Nicholas Montessori School. She would have been so happy and proud to stand up in her gown and hat to accept that degree herself after overcoming many obstacles to finally get the qualification she longed for. But unfortunately this was not to be.

When Elaine went missing in August 2012 we were devastated. At that time she appeared to us to be progressing well in life. She had a new apartment, was studying and working in two jobs.

She had a setback in July 2012, and was voluntarily admitted to hospital. However, on weekend release, she was in very good form and was looking forward to the future.

The assumed suicide in August 2012 was a surprise to all the family but lack of evidence pointing to any other cause for her disappearance meant we reluctantly needed to accept that she had most likely taken her own life around Shanganagh.

We spent many hours walking the shore from Blackrock to Bray searching for any sign of her. A year after her disappearance we laid flowers in the sea at Shanganagh in her memory and in an effort to find some closure for us as a family.

Our attempt at closure was premature as when in September 2013 Elaine's remains were discovered, the Garda investigation changed from that of a missing person to murder. This led to further anguish for the family as we now faced the unimaginable horror of Elaine having been murdered.

The trial has been an incredibly difficult experience. It was distressing to see Elaine's private life laid bare before the nation, despite the fact that she was the victim. Some of the reporting in the print media was insulting to Elaine and deeply upsetting for the family. At times, Elaine's life was relegated to a lurid headline in a newspaper.

It was heartbreaking for us to listen to the texts Elaine received from a depraved and diseased mind. The manipulation of her vulnerability was apparent and when she tried to resist, she was reined back in.

We can hear her voice in those texts, just wanting to be loved. Hearing the contents of the videos will haunt us for ever. We were upset that the credibility of our evidence was questioned, as throughout the two and a half years all we wanted was the truth and justice for Elaine.

We will probably never know what happened in Killakee on Wednesday the 22nd of August 2012, but there are questions that trouble us:

When did Elaine realize it was not a game any more?

When did she realize that the intention was to kill her for real?

Did she try to run?

Was she restrained?

Did she suffer much?

Could she and did she cry out?

Was she left on the mountain to die alone?

This is OUR life sentence. For us there is no parole.

Before passing sentence Judge Hunt again thanked the jurors for accepting his invitation, telling them their presence demonstrated that they were responsible people who were anxious to see the very end of the process, and that his invitation was not a usual feature of it. 'But then, so little about this case can be described as usual,' he said.

It had been a very harrowing trial involving a number of families, including Dwyer's family, whom he described as blameless. The judge said that he could now comment on the case, something he couldn't do during the trial, with 'even a momentary frown over forty days pounced upon by the defence', which was a reference to Dwyer's claim that the judge had glared at him. It was clear that he wanted to express his contempt for Graham Dwyer and his deepest sympathies to Elaine O'Hara's family.

'On behalf of the O'Hara family I would like to say now and in the strongest possible terms what I could not say during the trial. I thought each and every one of them were spectacularly courageous and brave in giving their evidence in the circumstances in which they did. They were subjected to the nightmarish scenario of having to sit through Elaine's most intimate details in court at the behest of Mr Dwyer,' he said. He went on to say that the family had given evidence with great dignity, compassion and in a measured way, contrary to the attack the accused made on their credibility in the defence's closing speech. The judge described this as 'an attack by a person whose own credibility and truthfulness is at the level of the floor, if not below'.

He said that it was clear that Elaine had been well loved and well cared for by her family. 'They did the very best they could to look after her,' he said. 'The statement just read captures the essence of Elaine more accurately. She had her difficulties but the evidence from the statement shows that Elaine was not all about her illness, which was a small part of her make-up.

'I do hope they have some answers and some insight into how their daughter and their sibling was taken from them and in some corners of this very dark story, some light has been shone. There is only one person who knows the answer to these questions but that person has told nothing but manifest untruths to date and unfortunately the answers to those questions will probably never be known. It is my view that during her life, Elaine was cynically misused and abused by Mr Dwyer to the extent that he was responsible for ending her life as part of that prolonged campaign of misuse and abuse. And it's actually worse than that because her suicidality continued to be cynically misused and abused by Mr Dwyer after her death in an attempt to slither out from under his responsibility.

'Because the obvious was never conceded or could not be conceded without bringing the whole roof tumbling in on him, he had to persist with this ludicrous delusion. Shame and embarrassment were something in very short supply over in that corner of the court,' he said, nodding curtly in Dwyer's direction. 'He carefully preserved evidence of his debauchery in documentary and video form, presumably to be revisited on private occasions to look on his great works. We can be thankful that a very dangerous man is out of the way. I am satisfied that that is what he is.'

The judge noted that no reports had ever been carried out on Dwyer. 'I don't know what's up with him. He is in his place of denial. He is in his place of arrogance and delusion and there he will stay for the life sentence that I am going to commit him to in a moment. It's now time to face his responsibilities. He is committed to a sentence of life imprisonment dating from 17 September 2013. It is a sentence he richly deserves.

'I point out the fact that no remorse of any kind has been

expressed; instead we have the bizarre spectacle of a convicted murderer issuing a press statement, another first. The statement moreover makes no reference to the principal injured parties – the deceased, her family and his own wife. That perhaps again is a penetrating shaft of light into the mind of Mr Dwyer.'

As the judge expressed his contempt, Dwyer glanced up at the bench. For a fleeting moment it seemed like he was going to say something but then thought better of it.

Judge Hunt continued by saying that three family units had been profoundly affected by Dwyer's actions, including his wife, Gemma, who, he said, was 'most cruelly deceived by his actions'. The judge said that when Gemma Dwyer had appeared to give evidence it had been 'dreadfully upsetting to see the pitiful condition she had been left in by her husband'. 'It beggars belief and hardly bears thinking about,' he said, noting that Dwyer had purchased the Goroon phone days away from his wife giving birth to their second child. 'That, perhaps, tells you everything you need to know about Graham Dwyer.' He described her statement, expressing condolences with the O'Hara family, as a 'Christian and charitable' act.

The judge complimented the Gardaí on their 'hard and diligent work and analysis'. He singled out Roundwood Garda James O'Donoghue for particular praise for his 'dogged devotion to duty'. He also praised the men who brought the unusual objects in the almost-dry Vartry Reservoir to Garda O'Donoghue's attention in September 2013. He said that Dwyer had been a very fortunate man for some time but had been unfortunate when good weather, a diligent Garda and his own computer hard drives conspired to undo him.

Dwyer's lack of prior convictions could not be offered as any kind of mitigation. 'It is difficult to look beyond the chilling and premeditated murder – execution almost – carried out after a protracted campaign of the most vile manipulation and abuse of a woman too weak to resist, and who made a fatal mistake by trusting Mr Dwyer that he wasn't going to go any further than he indicated. When you read that booklet of texts you want to cry out to her to stop and turn back, but of course it's much too late.'

Judge Hunt looked down into his courtroom and concluded: 'So that is it. Life it is.'

As the judge rose from the bench, prison officers escorted Graham Dwyer through the door leading to the cells and the rest of his life in prison. It is likely that if he ever tastes freedom again it will be as a very old man.

As the prison van drove out from the Courts of Criminal Justice, Frank O'Hara was walking down the steps of the court, having politely refused to make any comment to the media. It had been 969 days since the day he walked into Stepaside Garda Station to report his daughter missing. It probably felt like a lifetime had passed in the meantime. Justice had been done. Now, maybe, Elaine could rest in peace.

Appendix: Investigating Team

Chief Superintendent Diarmuid O'Sullivan
Superintendent John Hand
Detective Superintendent J. J. Keane
Detective Superintendent Kevin Dolan

Incident Room

Detective Inspector Brian Duffy
Detective Sergeant Peter Woods
Sergeant Grace O'Boyle
Garda Lisa McHugh
Garda Aoife Cronin
Garda David L'Estrange
Garda Paul Kane
Detective Garda James Mulligan
Detective Garda Colm Gregan
Garda Timothy McAuliffe
Garda Michael McCarthy
Detective Garda William Kavanagh
Sergeant Kevin Duggan and CCTV team
Sergeant Brian O'Keeffe and search teams
Detective Garda Paul Corcoran, family liaison
Detective Garda Padraig Cleary
Detective Sergeant John Colgan

Computer Crime Investigation Unit

Detective Garda Brid Wallace
Detective Sergeant Alan Browne

Analyst

Sarah Skedd

Also

Forensic Laboratory Staff
Garda Ballistics Unit
Garda Telecoms Unit
Garda Traffic Central Tasking Unit
Garda Water Unit
Interpol
Criminal Assets Bureau
Gardaí who assisted in searches and enquiries
Maine State Police

Acknowledgements

I would like to express my deepest gratitude to the people who agreed to share their information and insights despite the fact that it was sometimes uncomfortable to do so. People who knew Graham Dwyer at the various stages of his life spoke on the understanding that they remain anonymous and, where necessary, certain details have been obscured to protect their identities. Their insights were invaluable. Thank you for your trust and honesty.

This is an opportunity to remember with respect not only Elaine O'Hara, but also the people whose lives have been thrown into unimaginable turmoil by her killer. Elaine O'Hara's family and Gemma Dwyer have suffered most and have been left to pick up the pieces of their lives. Dwyer's parents and siblings are also blameless and deserve every sympathy.

It is also right to acknowledge the meticulous and painstaking work of the Garda investigation team. The murder enquiry reflected the highest standards of professionalism and dedication and served to win back the confidence of the Irish public in their police force after a prolonged period of criticism.

I would like to thank Patricia Deevy, my editor at Penguin, for her hard work, penetrating insights and relentless motivation. She has given new meaning to my understanding of a taskmaster. My thanks also to Michael McLoughlin, MD of Penguin Ireland, for his boundless enthusiasm, and libel expert Kieran Kelly – 'the Consiglieri' of Fanning Kelly and Company.

I want to express my thanks and admiration to court reporters Andrew Phelan and Sarah Stack, my colleagues in the *Irish Independent* stable, for their invaluable assistance and advice. Andrew and Sarah are both consummate professionals who sat through every day of the marathon trial, recording every harrowing detail.

My sincere thanks to the Independent News & Media editor-in-chief, Stephen Rae, group head of content, Ian Mallon, *Irish Independent* editor, Fionnan Sheahan, and its news editor, Kevin Doyle, for giving me the space to complete the book.

Thanks also to Dr Matt Bowden and Dr Nicola Hughes, lecturers in the Dublin Institute of Technology's MA in criminology, for their understanding while I was working on the book. I would like to acknowledge the very helpful staff and superb facilities at Ballyroan Library in Rathfarnham, where I became a semi-permanent resident over the past year.

And, as always, my love to the people who had to endure the months of book-writing gloom in our home – Anne, Jake and Irena.